White Identities

White Identities

A Critical Sociological Approach

SIMON CLARKE and STEVE GARNER

PlutoPress
www.plutobooks.com

First published 2010 by Pluto Press
345 Archway Road, London N6 5AA and
175 Fifth Avenue, New York, NY 10010

www.plutobooks.com

Distributed in the United States of America exclusively by
Palgrave Macmillan, a division of St. Martin's Press LLC,
175 Fifth Avenue, New York, NY 10010

British Library Cataloguing in Publication Data
A catalogue record for this book is available from the British Library

ISBN   978 0 7453 2749 5   Hardback
ISBN   978 0 7453 2748 8   Paperback

Library of Congress Cataloging in Publication Data applied for

10   9   8   7   6   5   4   3   2   1

Designed and produced for Pluto Press by
Chase Publishing Services Ltd, 33 Livonia Road, Sidmouth, EX10 9JB England
Typeset from disk by Stanford DTP Services, Northampton
Printed and bound in the European Union by
CPI Antony Rowe, Chippenham and Eastbourne

CONTENTS

ACKNOWLEDGEMENTS

We would like to thank and acknowledge the Economic and Social Research Council (ESRC) for its support in funding the empirical research that this book is based on (Project: RES-148-25-003). We would also like to thank Professor Margie Wetherell, director of the ESRC 'Identities and Social Action' programme and the project administrator, Kerry Carter, at the Open University. Thanks to all the colleagues on that programme who encouraged us and shared insights, and to the people who have given us constructive feedback on the various presentations of our findings that we have made.

Invaluable support was given by colleagues at the Centre for Psycho-Social Studies at the University of the West of England and in particular by Julia Long, and then Glynis Morrish, who kept us organised throughout the project. We would also like to thank everyone at Pluto Books for their time and patience. Rosie Gilmour played a huge role as research associate in this project, organising interviews and painstakingly transcribing them. Steve would also like to acknowledge the support his family has given throughout the project, and especially during the last few months of writing.

Finally we would like to thank the most important set of people – the people who we interviewed, who shared their life stories with us and welcomed us into their homes. Throughout the book, the names of all our interviewees quoted or referred to have been changed.

1

RESEARCHING 'WHITENESS': AN INTRODUCTION

This book is an exploration of sociological and psycho-social theories of the construction of whiteness vis-à-vis perceptions and imaginings of otherness. It has three main aims. First, to introduce the reader to the history and theoretical unfolding of contemporary studies of whiteness in North America and Europe. Second, to explore the structural facilitating factors of these constructions, through such institutions as the state and the media. Finally, the book synthesises a psycho-social perspective to look at the underlying mechanisms which fuel social exclusion and inclusion in society. Theory is never separated from practice and the book makes full use of empirical examples from the authors' own research and secondary examples. We also discuss the theoretical problems and methodological dilemmas in this field of research in a journey that takes the reader from the social construction of whiteness to the psychological othering of marginalised groups in society.

This book aims to provide the reader with an in-depth analysis of the construction of white identity, or 'whiteness', in the British context through the exploration of sociological and psycho-social ideas which the authors synthesise to provide a fuller picture of the social and psychological construction of identity. Whiteness, as a form of ethnicity, is rarely acknowledged by its bearers, yet it has significant ramifications in terms of the construction of 'other' identities; in the creation of community; in processes of exclusion and inclusion; and discourses around 'race' and nation. We start from the perspective that what we are researching is specific to a time and a place. The paradigm developed from

American sources but that does not exhaust its potential for application or illumination of social relationships (Garner, 2006). We show that in provincial England in the first decade of the twenty-first century, some threads of the discursive construction of Englishness link people in different class positions to each other through mechanisms of exclusion, entitlement and belonging that function to racialise the speakers as white and entitled, and their Others as not white and un-entitled.

What is the Whiteness Problematic?

Whiteness is as much an analytical perspective as a describable social phenomenon. Indeed, in the introduction to his cultural analysis of white people, John Hartigan's concise definition of whiteness is qualified, 'as a concept honed by academics and activists' (Hartigan, 2005: 1). 'Whiteness', he argues, 'asserts the obvious and overlooked fact that whites are racially interested and motivated. Whiteness both names and critiques hegemonic beliefs and practices that designate white people as "normal" and racially "unmarked"'.

This is a good starting point because it exemplifies the inextricability of epistemology and objectification in this project. The debate among American labour historians and partially pertinent critiques such as those of Kolchin (2002) and Kaufman (2006) testify to some of the circular arguments that potentially ensue from this 'catch-all' use of whiteness.[1] This debate appears irresolvable: the positivist empirical tradition dominant in the discipline of history seeks a different type of evidence from the interpretive tradition. If the proof of the pertinence of whiteness consists of people referring habitually and explicitly to themselves being white, then British fieldwork will not generate much data that satisfies this criterion. However, there are also potential drawbacks to using the whiteness problematic: when we look through this prism, we risk seeing everything as whiteness and not accounting for specifics, where other concepts might be equally effective (racialisation comes immediately to mind). The emphasis of the whiteness problematic, as we see it, should be on how white British subjects identify themselves through an often contradictory system of codes, involving evasion of direct references to 'race' with discourses involving culture, nation, class and gender, and combinations of them. These 'discursive repertoires' (Frankenberg, 1994: 2) are exemplified by some of Bridget Byrne's (2006) London mothers, who talk about getting 'the right mix' (of racialised groups, in which whites remain in the majority) in local schools. Indeed, Reay et al. (2007) observe that the right mix is vital to some middle-class families' projects of accumulating what they term 'multicultural capital' for their secondary school-age children. This is accomplished as a process of making themselves better people by learning how to interact with their Others: both ethnic minorities and working class.

Implicit in the enterprise of analysing whiteness is a recognition that its field of application and epistemological grounding are not concerned with what can be covered by the term 'race' alone, but also with class and gender, nationality and status. While this type of perspective might draw the critique that racialisation is here over-emphasised vis-à-vis the other elements, it might be worth considering that work that postulates a white class-based identity as normative – without referring at all to the effects of racialisation – is equally a conceptual error.

So the paradox of this enterprise is evident: although the actual objective is to deconstruct whiteness, objectifying it as 'white identity' risks reification. 'Whiteness' as a problematic is merely an instrument to be deployed within the sociology of racism. It should not become a separate field of 'whiteness studies', which, in the British context, we consider an intellectual and political dérive. Rather, probing whiteness has two main objectives:

1. the problematisation of white identity as a raced, privilege-holding location that is part of the social relationship in which structural racism flourishes;
2. to force recognition of the limits and the parallels drawn between less privileged white actors and racialised minorities by confronting the complexities of the intersections of class, 'race', ethnicity and gender.

In conclusion, using the whiteness problematic in terms of the UK is a project aimed at highlighting the fluidity, contingency and power relations bound up in white identities rather than shoring up their homogeneity.

The Context and Empirical Research

The context of this book sits within a three year Economic and Social Research Council-funded research project entitled 'Mobility and Unsettlement: New Identity Construction in Contemporary Britain', which formed part of the larger Identities and Social Action programme. This project explored the links between the themes of mobility, home and settlement (through ideas about community) in the way 'white' British identities are constructed vis-à-vis those of Others. It was therefore located at the confluence of literature on nationalism, ethnicity, racism and whiteness. Our assumptions were that identities are multiple and contingent, and that racialisation in twenty-first century Europe is not fixed by a black–white binary (Garner, 2003), with culture as important as skin colour in racialising discourse. The timeliness of this exploration of English people's conceptualisation of belonging and identity is underscored by the post-7/7 climate of questioning multiculturalism; early experiences of European labour migration as a result of EU enlargement; and the impact of devolution on attitudes towards Britishness.

The nature of immigration and asylum has changed over the past two decades, and different forms of hostility have arisen. Hostility now seems to have shifted to access to welfare, rather than simply employment. Processes of racialisation are more locally contingent and have become more dependent on the perceived presence of asylum seekers and the intense projective identifications between individuals and groups. This runs hand-in-hand with a growing suspicion of the state. In this project and book we explore the implications of this for contemporary identity construction, in particular the way in which 'white' Europeans 'other' other Europeans, and the way in which new stereotypical discourses of racialisation are emerging which abound with projective identifications. When people were asked what picture the word 'immigrant' conjured up for them, many commented that in the past it could have been a black or Asian person, but now it could quite easily be an Eastern European. Indeed, in Bristol and Plymouth people were well aware of such migrants filling local economic niches in the period during which that stream of migration was expanding.[2]

So several strands of thought and questioning emerge in this research project. The first, and this is the bigger research question, concerns the way in which white identities are constructed, and are changing in subtle ways in the UK. Second, the nature of immigration into the UK has also changed: there is now more of a focus on white, with refugees seeking asylum from East European countries (although the biggest popul___ ___ e still from Iraq, Zimbabwe, Afghanista___ ___ ___hird, the construction or ___ ___ ___gely based i___ ___ ___asy.

T___ ___he
te___ ___rs
an___ ___or
refu___ ___
one___ ___
non-___ ___
seeks___ ___
and a ___ ___
on the___ ___
to notic___ ___
poignan___ ___
the Britis___ ___
asylum se___ ___
by contin___ ___ational Party
(BNP) and ___ ___), which leads to our final
point. It ap___ ___ in the general discourse, particularly in the media, that arguments around entitlement, in other words who gets what, have shifted from access to employment to encompass

the question of who is entitled to welfare benefits – who gets housed, who receives a home and why.

The research project focuses on two major cities in the south west of England. Both have very long histories of immigration, transition and trading, both are sea ports with a seafaring tradition that is as old as British history. The big difference is that one city has a long history of multiculturalism and a relatively high population of minority ethnic groups, the other is largely white. The first city is Bristol, once at the heart of the Atlantic slave trade, famous for its imports and exports of tobacco and sherry. Once home of the Merchant Venturers and John Cabot, it is now a modern business centre within easy reach of London. The second is Plymouth, again with a very long seafaring tradition, synonymous with the name of Sir Walter Raleigh and Sir Francis Drake, the famous pirate, circumnavigator of the world (1579) and mayor of Plymouth, as well as John Hawkins, the first licensed English slave trader (1564). Plymouth is the home of the senior service, the Royal Navy, and has been so since the defeat of the Spanish Armada in 1588. Devonport – HMS Drake is the largest naval port in Western Europe. Plymouth is very much white and we sense because of the long history of seafaring has a very strong identification with 'home' for its inhabitants.

We have therefore chosen two sites with different welfare and labour markets and also with different histories of minority settlement: Bristol, which has a tradition of limited but real multiculturalism (8.2 per cent of Bristol's population being ethnic minorities) and Plymouth, which remains overwhelmingly monocultural (just under 2 per cent ethnic minorities, according to the 2001 Census). Both cities are ports and have a long tradition of transition. Bristol also has a long history of immigration and emigration, whereas in Plymouth this has been limited. The development of the university and Derriford Hospital has been responsible for most of the city's ongoing diversity. The *Observer* newspaper (Bright, 2003) reported that Plymouth had become a 'city of hate' with on average 22–30 racist attacks per month, many of which involve asylum seekers. Refugee groups claim that as many as six times this number may go unreported.

We hypothesise that processes of racialisation are locally contingent, in other words, who gets 'othered' in Burnley may be significantly different from Reading or Barking. Indeed Bristol and Plymouth demonstrate this phenomenon to a certain extent, with Bristol contrasted by a number of Plymouthians with their city as a place of (black and Asian) diversity. Yet they also demonstrate the virtual character of much of the discourse. A lot of what people spoke about (asylum, areas of self-segregating minority concentration, etc.) seemed to be happening 'elsewhere'. The arrival of new migrants may paradoxically facilitate the inclusion of longstanding 'black' minorities into the indigenous ('white') 'us'. It appears that a central locus to these processes is still very much centred on entitlement, but entitlement to welfare rather than employment.

The research had as its focus in-depth interviews using psycho-social methodologies in the two locations. Two sets of people were interviewed: those resident on large former or current council estates, and in middle-class residential areas (the indicators were to do with socio-economic groups, levels of higher education and home ownership) that were roughly comparable. This represents a sample which is slightly based in social class but predominantly based on access to social housing and home ownership. The specific research questions were as follows:

1. How do people construct their identities in relation to Others (groups and individuals), and why?
2. What are the most important sites of identity construction (nation, welfare, employment, Europe, class)?
3. Are there local factors that differ between Bristol and Plymouth and which structure the way people construct their identities?

The interviews were conducted in a way that we could elicit material that was open to a psycho-social or sociological reading, and were constructed along these lines:

1. A biographical interview exploring the respondent's work, housing and life history with particular reference to social

location, identity, community and belonging, whether real or imagined.
2. A second interview that explores key themes such as nation, belonging, the changing nature of Europe, welfare entitlement, identity and geographies of exclusion.
3. Emphasis in both interviews on both socio-structural determinants, and imagined and phantasied attachments.

We provide a detailed overview of these aims and methods in chapter 9, which changed over the course of the three-year project as we listened to the 'lived' lives of the people we interviewed.

Before going on in the main part of this book to discuss constructions of whiteness, we want to note that historically and more recently there have been some key myths and distorted perceptions of immigration in the UK. Immigration to the UK is not a modern twentieth or twenty-first century phenomenon. The history, or at least the early history, of the British Isles is one of colonisation, first Celtic and Pict tribes and then the Romans. Later in 250 AD Rome sent a contingent of Black Legionnaires drawn from the African part of the Roman Empire to stand guard on Hadrian's Wall against the marauding Celts (Scots) (Fryer, 1984: 1). When the Romans left in the fifth century, the Germanic tribes – Jutes, Angles and Saxons – colonised Britain. One of the largest waves of immigration, which changed the face of law and culture in Britain, was that of the Norman invasion of 1066. This also saw the largest influx of Jewish people whom William the Conqueror invited to England to take up positions in commerce and banking. In the 1770s, largely as a result of the slave trade, around 14,000 black people lived in Britain. The abolition of the slave trade in 1833 all but stopped black immigration to Britain. Between the two great wars many black people fighting on behalf of Britain (and empire) settled and the culmination of this was the docking of the *Empire Windrush* in 1948 at Tilbury docks where hundreds of men came from the West Indies to join the RAF and take up jobs in the post-war days of labour shortage. They were followed by thousands of often skilled migrants of both sexes, many of whom were directly recruited into factories, the health service and the transport sector (Peach, 1968).[3]

This is just a brief outline of the history of immigration and colonisation in the UK, but as you can see, with that sense of history, it would be very difficult either to define, or point to, a monolithic ethnic British identity. It is also difficult to imagine that sense of home and nation that is often portrayed by right-wing politicians (and not just those from the right any more) and racists. Britain has always been a multicultural community but, as MacDougall (1982) indicates, this identification is not simply with the Anglo-Saxon, stiff upper lip, village greens, fish and chips or warm beer, but there is also an identification for people which goes way back to the Celtic roots of the country, in the language, folklore and culture of the Welsh, Cornish, Scottish and Irish who became the oppressed minorities of Britain, as they were colonised by the kings and queens of Britain (England).

There is something contradictory about British identity and it is based in thousands of years of hatred of the Other. Exactly who that Other is at a given moment changes. Linda Colley's classic study (1992), for example, argues that Britain became a Protestant union by focusing its identity on not being Catholic (mainly French or Spanish) in the eighteenth century. Whether contemporary racism is based in archaic phantasies around Britain's original occupations, a sense of what Freud (1961 [1919]) would call the 'Uncanny', is another matter, but 'we' the British are forever living in fear of being swamped by aliens, who may be simply 'white' classed Others (Young, 1997), despite strong evidence to the contrary. It seems that now, as opposed to the 1940s and 1950s when people came over to 'steal our jobs', jobs that we didn't want to do in the first place, the new Other is here to steal our welfare, our benefits, money and houses, and, in the terms of Žižek (1993), our 'enjoyment'. Again, this is despite evidence to the contrary. Fact: asylum seekers are not entitled to council housing, they are housed in the private sector; fact: only those who are granted asylum are allowed to work; fact: asylum seekers are not entitled to welfare benefits – income support or housing benefit. They have a parallel system of 'benefits' in which amounts are capped or benefits given in-kind on a case-by-case basis. Until recently asylum seekers received food vouchers for essential living needs only.

So, perceptions of otherness, ideas around difference, nation and identity are based not so much in any fact but in the human imagination, and asylum seekers are but one area of construction. In a paper (Garner, 2006) in the journal *Sociology*, we provided an outline of the concept of whiteness and how it has been used in North American sociological analysis. We argued that whiteness emerges as a fluid, contingent and contested identity that is fragmented into degrees of belonging (to 'home', class, gender, ethnicity, nation, etc.). It should thus be viewed as a set of contingent hierarchies, with co-existing external boundaries (whites/non-whites) and internal ones (separating various racialised sub-groups from each other). The concept of 'whiteness' tells us something about acute types of struggle for social, cultural and economic capital. Deploying the concept as a working tool focuses us on the more productive view of migration as a long process (of white Europeans moving across borders), rather than concentrating only on the last 50 years or so. It should also be noted that the majority of migrants to some nations in Europe are still white Europeans. We have also to be aware of the contingent nature of the relationship between whiteness and non-whiteness and pose the question as to why some minority ethnic groups adopt the strategies and values of white groups, particularly when examining racist attacks and resentment to third parties. In particular, we are thinking of Paul Hoggett's (1992) study of the Bangladeshi community in Tower Hamlets where the local community increasingly adopted the values of the white working class.

So, if we start to think about the construction of whiteness, and of British identity, then certain themes start to become clear. First, that Britain is made up of multiple ethnicities, and hierarchies, so whiteness is a specific stream of this that, due to its historically dominant position, is not just an ethnicity like any other. Second, immigration to the country, in a significant minority, has been white European, and this has been a very long process. Third, white identity is contingent vis-à-vis the specific structural context, for example East European asylum seekers, and Eastern European migrants working as tradesmen, agricultural workers, shop assistants, bus drivers, etc. On the other hand, our fieldwork was carried out either side of the London bombings, and it is clear that Muslims are the first group in the collective white imaginary that are cited as being disturbingly and often annoyingly different from the mainstream. We feel that is very much a product of the historical context in which we are working. Finally, the adoption of values taken on by some minority groups in some sense reproduces the discourses of racialised exclusion used by dominant white groups.

Chapter Outline and Key Themes

The book is organised in a set of distinctive chapters that examine various aspects of the construction of whiteness. The chapters, although building on each other, are designed to be stand alone so that they can be used for teaching purposes or as a set text for part or the whole a course. The book can be broadly divided into two sections. The first looks at sociological aspects of the construction of whiteness while the second half of the book addresses psychosocial interpretation of otherness. All chapters use a review of the literature in the area as well as empirical examples from the authors' own research to guide the reader. Examples are used from both UK and North American literature. Chapter 2 provides an overview of whiteness studies in the North American context suggesting different ways that 'whiteness' has been conceptualised there in multidisciplinary work, for example, as a form of terror, as a type of invisibility, a form of values and norms, and as a set of contingent hierarchies. Following on from this, in chapter 3 we examine studies of white identities in the context of British social science research, comparing them to US research and then noting the distinction between the two traditions. The main distinctions, we argue, are to do with themes around nation and empire, and these themes form the basis of chapters 4 and 5. In chapter 4 we examine discourses around belonging to communities and nations. We look at how Britishness is now the subject of a very ambivalent discourse in which people are actively abandoning Britishness to occupy Englishness, seen as smaller, purer and more exclusive. This is juxtaposed with the devolution of powers to the constituent countries of the UK, and the perception that Britishness is becoming increasingly diverse.

In chapter 5 we look at whiteness and post-imperial Britain. By examining data from our fieldwork we advance a tentative argument about the presence of empire in people's construction of identity in post-imperial Britain. This has to be understood against the discussions of segregation and integration that our interviewees engaged in, without prompting (we never used the terms 'integration', 'segregation' or 'multiculturalism' in our questions). The associations made when people talk about these topics link nation, class and whiteness principally through narratives of unfairness that place British culture as unreasonably imposed upon, and white English people as being culturally and politically disenfranchised.

The second half of the book develops a psycho-social analysis of the construction of the 'not white' Other. Chapter 6 examines psycho-social interpretations of identity construction. The social construction of white identity, or indeed identities in general, can offer us a real insight into how we perceive the self and others. In this chapter we argue that a psycho-social dimension goes beyond traditional analysis and allows us to understand the emotional, affective and visceral content of identity construction. Drawing on psychoanalytic ideas and concepts, we unravel the psychological dynamics involved in the construction of the white 'we' in relation to the otherness of the Other. Cultural identities are marked by a number of factors – 'race', ethnicity, gender and class to name but a few – yet the real locus of these factors is the notion of difference. The question of difference is emotive; we start to hear ideas about 'us' and 'them', friend and foe, belonging and not belonging, in-groups and out-groups, which define 'us' in relation to others, or the Other. To further complicate this matter we could also ask whether identity is a social construction or part of a psychodynamic process. We argue that it is a complex amalgam of both. We draw on literature from both North America and Europe from the psychoanalytic field as well as our own research to develop a psycho-social perspective on white identity construction. In the following chapter, we examine the issue of asylum and immigration in contemporary Britain in the context of media representations. In it we argue that there is a worrying trend towards the conflation of asylum issues with terrorism. Using examples from the media and politics we argue that there is a new politics of fear emerging which more than ever concentrates on difference and the demonisation of the Other. In particular, this othering process constructs 'not white' in an atmosphere of global insecurity (Bhattacharyya, 2008). This politics uses emotional and psychological methods to play on our social fears and anxieties around community. This goes hand-in-hand with the mainstreaming of anti-immigration policy as a political value: a process that has drawn Left and Right into the battle to appear toughest on defending the nation against external threats. Finally we ask why these policies are becoming acceptable, and indeed ask in the following chapter why the notion of 'community' has become so important.

The idea of community has always been central to the construction of group and individual identity. It has been the site of moral panics about the disintegration of traditional community and values as well concerns around racism and segregation and their public policy ramifications (Phillips, 2005). The notion of community is of central importance in contemporary policy and political thinking (Putnam, 2000; Commission on Integration and Cohesion, 2007). In chapter 8 we set out to explore how people today construct their identities in relation to community and whether traditional forms of identity construction – such as class and ethnicity – still hold. We start by examining sociological notions of community, before going on to look at the lived lives and ideas that came from the people we interviewed. As most of us are essentially sociable creatures, much, although not all, of this identity construction takes place against the background of the communities that people live in. We therefore look at what people mean when they talk of a 'community' and the factors that increase or decrease community cohesion between groups in provincial Britain. Based on the authors' empirical research, this chapter examines the construction of 'white' community within the context of an increasing political interest in the notion of community. In chapter 9 we ask what does a psycho-social method look like? How do we put it into practice? How useful is it for the study of 'race', ethnicity and in particular whiteness, when subjects are often not even aware of their ethnicity? Indeed, many would suggest that this lack of awareness (of the salience of a white identity in terms of what it procures for the bearer) is constitutive of white identities (Frankenberg, 1994; Mills, 1997; Yancy, 2008).

These are some the questions that we pose, in proposing a psycho-social research methodology that 'gets to grips' with the unconscious and unspoken dynamics of ethnicity and identity. Drawing on recent literature in this new and cutting edge field of sociology, the authors outline a psycho-social method for the social sciences and once again draw on their own empirical research to guide the reader with examples of the methodological application of theory through the use of a case study of the 'lived' life of one of the people we interviewed. Finally, we conclude by looking at some of the ramifications for public and social policy that this research highlights and brings to the fore.

2
WHITENESS STUDIES IN
THE CONTEXT OF THE USA

'Whiteness studies' in the USA is a broad, nebulous and multi-disciplinary field whose development has provoked a good deal of debate, since the early 1990s, on issues such as epistemology, reinterpretations of American history, and the ways in which dominant identities are constructed. In this chapter we provide an outline of the key areas of debate and the principal ways in which whiteness has been conceptualised.

What is whiteness? As with most social science concepts there is a lack of consensus around it. Whiteness is difficult to define due to the diversity of ways in which the term is implicitly and explicitly deployed. However, the problems of finding a definition should not eliminate the core problematic: whatever else, whiteness is about power and privilege – and legacies of inter-generational relative advantage. Any analysis must aim to disaggregate 'white' but not lose sight of the idea that however low they are in a given socio-economic order, white people benefit from being white, and not necessarily intentionally. Critical Whiteness Studies scholars seeking to re-evaluate feminism, labour historians, anthropologists studying the phenomenon of 'white trash', confessional writers describing their awareness of white privilege, or African-American writers dissecting the power relations they have been impacted by over centuries; each of these are examples of the standpoints from which whiteness has been approached.[1] What does white look like? That depends on what you're looking at, where you are looking from, and what you are looking through. It also matters not to be considered 'white'.

Let's begin with an example using Puerto Rico. The island had been annexed by the USA in 1900 and was granted 'unincorporated' status within the nation in 1917. Over the period since 1890, the Census recorded a steady increase in the proportion of people classified as 'white'. This proportion jumped between the 1910 and the 1920 Census: 65.5 per cent of the Puerto Rican population was identified as 'white' in 1910, but by 1920, this proportion had risen to 73 per cent. Mara Loveman (2007) and Loveman and Muniz (2008) ask whether this was because the section of the lighter-skinned population had experienced higher rates of growth than others. Only a small fraction of the growth can be explained by this. Was it because people identified *themselves* as white in higher numbers? No. In fact, they discovered that the Census Board in Puerto Rico had not only issued different instructions to enumerators in 1920 than in 1910, but also altered the data, after collection, to construct lower proportions of whiteness on the island. This was done primarily by classifying children as 'mulatto' (mixed) instead of white in cases where one of the parents was white and the other not. So the American rule of 'hypodescent' (if any blood relative is not white then that person is not white), which officially informed the Census inspectors' practice, militated against increased proportions of white subjects. Logically, the proportion of whites should have decreased if this practice were followed. The answer, argues Loveman, is that the enumerators used their Caribbean understanding of what white meant to resist what was seen as an 'inappropriately restrictive description of whiteness' (2007: 101). In the 20 years since annexation, Puerto Ricans' experiences of the US invasion led to a re-evaluation of the importance of 'race'. Moreover, the first wave of Puerto Rican immigrants to the USA (after the granting of citizenship in 1917) discovered the social costs of not being white, in terms of access to housing, employment, education and when serving in the armed forces during World War I. By the 1920 Census, enumerators were classifying large numbers of people who ten years previously had been classified as 'mulatto' as 'white'. This is before the inspectors attempted to overrule the enumerators.

In the first decades of the twentieth century, in the context of US military annexation, the stakes of being considered white *as a nation* placed Puerto Rican nationalists in a position of relative advantage. Their arguments would be listened to more seriously, as being put forward by white nationalists, than those made by people viewed as semi-savages, as Filipinos and later Haitians were (Go and Foster, 2003; Baldoz, 2004, 2008).[2] It had taken the Puerto Rican nationalists only a generation to realise the importance of being or becoming white.

This example illustrates four things: the constructed nature of racialised identities (there is no absolute consensus on what 'white' means); that such identities can be addressed at collective as well as individual levels; that the process of construction is fundamentally political (i.e. to do with power relationships); and that white identity is identified with holding power, decision-making and, crucially, problem-framing.

This chapter examines the way these issues have been approached explicitly and implicitly in American writing and research on racism. Here we have identified some significant *sociological* themes with which our fieldwork and analysis can engage, and which move us beyond the idea that white racialised identities, like all the others, are contingent and fluid. This chapter deals specifically and solely with work generated in the USA. The volume of such a corpus means that this necessarily involves the omission of work that others might feel is worth including. However, we hope here to convey a good sense of the key discussions and issues with which such literature deals, before synthesising where this might be specifically American. The following sections address work on whiteness in which it is conceptualised as: a form of 'terror' and supremacy; a type of invisibility; cultural capital, values and norms; a set of contingent hierarchies (involving class, gender, nationality, etc.).

Whiteness as 'Terror' and Supremacy

The conceptualisations of whiteness as a variety of socio-cultural forms that we will acknowledge below make sense only in the context of the historical and political argument that 'white' denotes a position of privilege. It is a location from which the Others of whiteness – 'blackness', 'Asianness', 'Jewishness', etc. – have been constructed, both psychologically (Fanon, 1967; Clarke, 2003; Seshadri-Crooks, 2000) and socially in a project going back centuries. Since the Enlightenment, white, European, middle-class and male norms have inflected the development of Western liberal philosophy on which contemporary democracy is founded (Eze, 1997; Mills, 1997). Goldberg (2000), for example, argues that the state itself is a racial institution based on its vision of order, rationality and mastery of nature, which corresponds to privileged male Europeans' self-image. The line of thinking that posits white as an identity with its own interests and political behaviour unsurprisingly developed out of the engagement of people who grappled with its impacts on a day-to-day basis, namely African-Americans. While knowledge of white behaviours and a complex grasp of the variety of positions occupied by white people in North America is clear from slave narratives such as those of Frederick Douglass (2003 [1845]), the first published analyses that can be understood as the origins of 'whiteness studies' were produced at the end of the nineteenth and early twentieth centuries. Ida Wells-Barnett (1893) published reports of lynching as part of her campaign against it in the 1890s. In her work is an explicit critique of white power. She maintained that lynching was not about protecting white southern women from rape (the justification put forward), but rather was a means of terrorising the free black population into acquiescence with segregation and institutionalised poverty. In the following decade, W.E.B Du Bois published *The Souls of Back Folk* (1903), which is usually seen as the reference text on whiteness. In it, Du Bois dealt with the social history of the post-abolition period, and harnessed this to an analysis of the position of black Americans, whom he argued had to develop a 'double consciousness', building an understanding of white people necessary for survival, and simultaneously a self-image that took into account what white society would see. He went on to write critically about white projects of European colonialism (1920) and American Reconstruction (1995 [1935]). This pioneering critique of white racialisation as global power is echoed in various fictional and non-fiction writing by African-American novelists and activists running from Langston Hughes through Richard Wright, Ralph Ellison, Malcolm X, James Baldwin and Toni Morrison to bell hooks.

Some of this writing will be looked at in the sections below, but in this segment we want to highlight the framing of whiteness as systemic power relations, because it is an element of American work that exceeds the British-based writing, and in so doing, provides a critique that will be useful when we come to set our findings in a broader context at the end of this book.

Terror

The terror referred to is that inspired by the imposition of physical and psychological violence by white Americans on black Americans, both within institutions (primarily lynching and slavery) and outside them in Reconstruction, Jim Crow and the segregated urban spaces of the North. Wells-Barnett's campaigns focused on lynching as a means of extra-judicial social control of black people in the post-slavery era. Du Bois' history of the Reconstruction South (1998 [1935]) emphasised the organised racist violence occurring in the interregnum between the Civil War and the restoration of white power in 1875.[3] Malcolm X (1969), for example, relates how his father died as a result of an attack by a white gang in Nebraska in the 1930s. The feeling of terror is due to the recognition that violence can be perpetrated randomly and with impunity. You do not have to have 'done' anything to merit retribution, except maybe go into an area of a town where you were unwelcome.[4] bell hooks tells of how she was terrified to walk through a poor white area of town to visit a relative in the 1950s (2000: 114–15) because of the potential for getting into situations where she, as a black person, could be blamed and held responsible for anything. She notes that she has since found academic work on travel as freedom to be profoundly blind to the idea that mobility is not equally liberating for all people. Fictional representations of slavery (Morrison, 1987) and the civil rights struggle (Baldwin, 1965), for example, amply demonstrate the horrific dehumanising impact of centuries of oppression, both on the dominated and the dominating. This is the context that created the exercise of power related by African-Americans, and which constitutes terror as the starting point for all consideration of the other means of conceptualising whiteness.

The level of both theoretical and empirical work on the systemic nature of these social relations, in simultaneously privileging whiteness and penalising non-whiteness, is a distinguishing feature of US research, and it is to illustrative examples of these that we shall now turn.

Systemic Supremacy

While there have been large-scale surveys of income (Massey and Denton, 1994) and wealth (Oliver and Shapiro, 1995), as well as of housing segregation patterns (Gotham, 2000), a short review that illustrates the mechanics of these processes is Lipsitz's (1995) notion of a 'possessive investment' in whiteness. Lipsitz's work covers a connected set of processes that produce segregation, and he argues that patterns of lending for house purchases are a significant factor in the development of segregated housing in urban America.

The background to urban-suburban residential segregation is lending by the Federal Housing Authority from its creation in 1934. The pattern of housing that emerged from this, contends Lipsitz, favoured white movement to the suburbs and prevented such mobility for non-whites. This broad pattern is then exacerbated by the practices of financial institutions and real estate agencies (such as 'redlining').[5] Even when he compares white and black working-class applicants, he finds that the former are offered bigger loans, and under more advantageous conditions than the latter. Moreover, in the post civil-rights era there is less job security for minority workers, who are disproportionately concentrated in the manufacturing sector and therefore suffer more from the lay-offs and de-industrialisation in the late 1970s and 1980s that affected these types of industry.

All in all, the creation of the general urban American pattern of white suburbs and de-industrialised minority-dominated centres reflects the structure of inequality as expressed through access to private and public-sector housing and all the issues surrounding that access. Essentially, Lipsitz shows that minorities have more hoops to jump through at every stage of the process.

Whiteness as 'Property'

Cheryl Harris' groundbreaking work, 'Whiteness as Property' (1993), is a treatise on the socio-embedding of white domination achieved through validating white European norms of ownership of both people and land in legislation and case law from the nineteenth century onwards. Space does not permit us to give the attention that Harris' subtle argument deserves, so we shall focus here on the last strand of the three upon which she builds her position: property in bodies, property in land, and property in expectations.[6] To a certain extent, the article's argumentation is cumulative, so I will begin by recapping the conclusions of the first two sections. Harris notes that under slavery, black bodies had been commodified in a way that white ones could not be, which granted relative privilege to all white Americans. The 'one-drop rule' meant that whiteness could be polluted in a way that blackness could not, which illustrates the privilege accruing to whiteness as a property of the body. The courts used definitions of 'race' that emphasised the biological at the expense of the social. When Homer Plessy brought a case against the East Louisiana railway company for ejecting him from the 'whites only' carriage in 1892, the decision was unfavourable and he took it to the supreme court, where in 1896 Judge Ferguson ruled against him on the basis that segregation did not constitute discrimination, and secondly, although he 'passed for' white, this was a lie that did not entitle him to compensation. In other words, what Plessy lost *in social terms* through being outed as black did not count in the law's eyes as worth addressing. Its view of the status quo was one where white dominated black *without this being discriminatory*, just normal.

Harris observes that property was conceptualised in solely European terms, as the right of an individual to acquire and dispose of. Native Americans did not own land in this way, rather they saw themselves as collective stewards of the land, managing it for the following generations. So if the courts only recognised European property-holding ideas, then only Europeans could actually 'own' property in this way. 'This fact', asserts Harris, 'infused whiteness with significance and value because it was solely through being white that property could be acquired and secured under law. Only whites possessed whiteness, a highly valued and exclusive form of property' (1993: 1725). She gives the example of the Mashpee Indians of New England whose case for ownership of land in Massachusetts was overturned in 1978. The Mashpees had mixed with black Americans, Europeans and other tribes, sometimes adopted Christianity, and remained mobile. Their definition of Mashpee involved a relationship to land and shared culture rather than racial purity (Harris, 1993: 1764–5). However, the court's definition of identity was based on racial purity and sedentarism: the ruling was that the Mashpees no longer constituted a tribe at the moment of conveyancing. Whiteness is thus revealed not only as the power to define property and means of ownership, but additionally, the power to define criteria for membership of collectivities to which non-whites belong.

Harris indicates that property is not restricted to the tangible, but can also come in the shape of expectations, e.g. those deriving from a belief in individual rights based on membership of the white 'race'. In three notable cases in the 1970s and 1980s (*Bakke*, 1978; *Wygant*, 1986; and *Croson*, 1989), she identifies the unifying element of the court's rejection of the past as having any impact on the current racialised status quo. In *Bakke*, the plaintiff's claim to have a place in a University of California medical school class where 12 per cent of the places were reserved for minorities is based on white individuals' claim on 100 per cent of the places (as in the past) due to centuries of discriminatory practices. Moreover, only two scores – Grade Point Average and Medical College Admission Test – were used in court to prove the white plaintiff's merit, whereas in the normal university administrative process, additional criteria are used to determine an applicant's suitability for a place. The *Bakke* ruling prevented the University of California from maintaining its minorities programme, while leaving in place the 5 per cent of the places reserved for the Dean's discretion (Harris, 1993: 1773) (which usually go to relatives of alumni without the grades to qualify through other routes), and the *de facto* age discrimination in medical school recruitment. In this case, the 'innocent white' *individual* is faced with the burden of compensating for past discrimination, and the court overruled the compensatory dimension of the university's programme.

The error in each of these three cases, argues Harris, is to conflate two types of claim: 'distributive' (fairness) and 'compensatory' (overcoming the past). In the context for the law's construction of rights as individual rather than collective, this confusions leads to the case being interpreted as one of the claim and counter-claim of minority person versus innocent white, with the court supporting the latter. The correct way to interpret it, however, maintains Harris, is by focusing on the salient issue as *prior advantage gained through a discriminatory system*, which is not individual but collective.

Harris posits a solution to this problem, arguing for the separation of 'whiteness as property' from 'whiteness' as identity. The idea of distributive justice focuses on introducing fairness into an unfair pattern of distribution that has a historical dimension, thus not focusing 'primarily on guilt and innocence, but rather on entitlement and fairness' (Harris, 1993: 1783).

Harris' thesis revolves around this discontinuity between past and present. She relentlessly draws out the idea of ongoing social inequality whose result is that the law at once makes 'whiteness' into an objective fact – although in reality it is 'an ideological proposition imposed through subordination' (Harris, 1993: 1730) – and makes blackness and Native Americanness, *inter alia*, into devalued identities. So even if for many white people in contemporary America whiteness is little more than a 'consolation prize', it still prevents its bearer from becoming something else. That is, it stops them from falling into a status to which further, broader penalties are intrinsic. The kind of property protected in affirmative action counter-claims is that of maintaining white people's unquestioned privileged access to resources and reduction of obstacles facing them in the labour and education markets, among others: 'In protecting the property interest in whiteness, property is assumed to be no more than the right to prohibit infringement on settled expectations, ignoring countervailing equitable claims that are predicated on a right to inclusion' (Harris, 1993: 1791).

'White Supremacy'

In a series of key publications (Mills, 1997, 1998, 2003, 2004; Mills and Pateman, 2007), Charles Mills has been working on approaches to racism from within the discipline of philosophy, sketching the contours of an understanding of whiteness as 'systemic'. Mills' attempt to break out of what he has termed the 'debilitating whiteness in mainstream political philosophy in terms of its critical assumptions, the issues that it has typically taken up, and the mapping of what it has deemed to be appropriate and important subject matter' (2004: 30) involves delineating a structure he provocatively calls 'white supremacy' rather than 'white privilege'. The former 'implies the existence of a system that not only privileges whites but is run by whites for white benefit' (Mills, 2004: 31). Moreover, Mills acknowledges the necessity of asserting continuity with the past – a central plank of Harris' arguments. By drawing attention to 'supremacist' structures in US history, this continuity is thus highlighted in the present, constituting 'no less than a fundamental paradigm shift' (Mills, 2003: 40).

Mills understands 'white supremacy' as being constructed as 'objective, systemic, multidimensional' and 'constitutive of a certain reality' (Mills, 2003: 48).[7] The systemic exertion of power and reaping of benefits, he contends, can be sustained only if whiteness requires its practitioners *not to see* the benefits as accruing from structural advantages, but rather as manifestations of individual failings on the part of those who are not white. Mills' emphasis on the collective acts of wilful not-seeing (under the cognitive-evaluative dimension), shows how, at best, racism is popularly viewed as something that at worst only disadvantages some groups, rather than simultaneously advantaging others. Mills' attempt to analyse the mechanics of this advantaging process (2004: 44–5) is portrayed as 'not a matter of a single transaction but … a multiply interacting set with repercussions continually compounding and feeding back in a destructive way' (Mills, 2004: 46). There is thus a form of exploitation analogous to, but not reducible to, class exploitation. So the importance of Mills' interventions is to underscore the systemic aspect of whiteness, and to suggest that it benefits white people regardless of whether they want to benefit. His *Racial Contract* explicitly states that:

> The Racial Contract is that set of formal or informal agreements or meta-agreements … between the members of one subset of humans, henceforth designated by … 'racial' … criteria … as 'white' … to categorise the remaining subset of humans as 'non-white' and of a different and inferior moral status […] in any case the Contract is always the differential privileging of the whites as a group, the exploitation of their [those who are not white] bodies, land and resources, and the denial of equal socioeconomic opportunities to them. All whites are beneficiaries of the Contract, though some whites are not signatories to it. (Mills, 1997: 11)

However, despite there being rationality to adhering to whiteness (for economic benefits), it is also clear that not all wages are economic, and there appear to be psychological bonuses available, as 'one can only be white in relation to nonwhites' (Mills, 2004: 52). Racial exploitation, here conceptualised as distinct from (although partly overlapping with) class exploitation, is posited as functioning within the economic, cultural and psychosocial domains.

Whiteness as a Type of Invisibility

Both Mills and Harris implicitly conceptualise whiteness as operating as a normative aspect of the norms of the legal system, the economic system, and the discipline of philosophy, for example, so that it ultimately defines what is marginal, what is mainstream and what is deviant. Mills has also affirmed that not-seeing is a learned and inherent element of 'white supremacy'. Other writers on whiteness have dealt with the theme of invisibility in similar terms. Richard Dyer (1997) sees whiteness as defining the normal and natural way to be. To be white in cinematic portrayals, he argues, is to be human: everything else is deviant. Whiteness becomes invisible in the act of invoking its opposites, while setting the framework for understanding what difference is measured *from*.

One effect of this kind of normalisation process (where whiteness disappears from the field of enquiry and joins the assumptions on which conjecture is made) is to make the individuals not racialised as white, invisible. In fiction, Ralph Ellison's eponymous *Invisible Man* (1952) is invisible as a human being, and visible only as a cipher of what male blackness means to the white American mind: irrationality, fecklessness, savagery and danger. As the white gaze 'blackens' the character, it saps him of humanity. This is a theme explored by a number of commentators on the functionings of whiteness. Fanon (1967) states that racialisation is a synonym of dehumanisation in the colonial relationship. George Yancy (2008) picks up on Fanon's work, asserting that the white gaze 'returns' the black body in a distorted state, as less than human. Janine Jones (2004), commenting on white responses to the Rodney King incident in 1991, maintains that white Americans can sympathise but not empathise with black Americans as they are socialised into not seeing them as fully human (covered in the 'metaphysical' dimension of Mills' schema). In similar vein, D. Marvin Jones (1997) uses the example of the Charles Stuart murder case in 1980s Boston to show how black men can be rendered collectively invisible. Stuart and his brother murdered Stuart's wife, then blamed the attack on a fictional black man in jogging pants. The police quickly stopped and questioned large numbers of African-American men in the area, and searched for the killer for days before detectives forced Stuart to admit to the deception. In that intervening period, argues Jones, black men had embodied threats to property and person, had encapsulated the fears of white America that any one of them could randomly and inexplicably kill a respectable white woman in front of her husband. Their individual characters no longer counted. They had become invisible as people and visible only as what Jean Baudrillard would call 'simulacra', countless copies of something that has no original, in this case collective anxieties about crime, invasion and brutality.

It is not only minority people who are made invisible as part of the 'whitening' process, but the set of norms that constitute 'white' at a given moment. Peggy McIntosh's fictitious 'knapsack' of privileges (1988: 1) is conceptualised as 'an invisible package of unearned assets that I can count on cashing in each day, but about which I was "meant" to remain oblivious. White privilege is like an invisible weightless knapsack of special provisions, maps, passports, codebooks, visas, clothes, tools, and blank checks'. Here McIntosh presents a list of privileges underscoring how whiteness can be unmarked. She explains the rationale:

> As a white person, I realized I had been taught about racism as something that puts others at a disadvantage, but had been taught not to see one of its corollary aspects, white privilege, which puts me at an advantage. I think whites are carefully taught not to recognize white privilege, as males are taught not to recognize male privilege. So I have begun in an untutored way to ask what it is like to have white privilege. (McIntosh, 1988: 1)

The list contains things that McIntosh feels she can do that colleagues who are not white cannot. They involve unnoticed, unharrassed, 'un-othered' movement through public space; being treated as an individual rather than as a representative of a group; and finding her experiences and needs catered for as normal. McIntosh's reflexivity allows for the focus to be placed on what accrues to white people rather than simply what disadvantages face Others. The act of making invisible makes other things visible. Toni Morrison (1993) argues that early American fiction makes black people invisible: Europeans are all there is to see in a struggle against nature and savagery (represented by Native Americans).

Whiteness as Cultural Capital, Values and Norms

One of the themes to come out of empirical fieldwork with white people is their general unease at thinking of themselves as white *per se*. This is borne out clearly in Ruth Frankenberg's (1994) pioneering interviews with American women. Many had grown up in small white Californian towns and never came to think of themselves as being raced until they moved to larger cities with more ethnically diverse populations. Despite the breadth of their class locations and the over-representation of feminists and anti-racists in her sample, Frankenberg suggests that they still manage concerns about their thoughts on 'race' by using what she labels three 'discursive repertoires' (or thematic narrative strategies): essentialist racism, colour and power evasion, and race 'cognisance' (1994: 188). The first involves popular biological and cultural understandings of 'race'. The second is the presentation of the innocent white self abstracted from history and the social relationships entailing discrimination, while the last means recognition that white is a raced social location vis-à-vis others. The women often move between these repertoires.

One of the recurrent 'discursive repertoires' in American fieldwork is the theme of contrasting industriousness and entitlement with laziness and dependency. This ostensibly de-racialised topic in fact condenses a host of ideas about 'race'. The section of Michèle Lamont's comparative study of the USA and France (2000) focusing on New York State and New Jersey demonstrates a clear distinction in the way her black and white respondents define themselves. Although there is a degree of overlap, in that their shared class values are family and solidarity oriented, there is also a gap. The black workers expressed greater attachment to group solidarity and generosity, the whites focused more on self-reliance and the work ethic. Neither group spurned the values of family and responsibility, but these were viewed as belonging more to the realm of the group by the blacks, and of the individual by the whites. Lamont refers to this relative difference of emphasis as expressing the 'caring self' versus the 'disciplined self' (2000: 20–1). Indeed, Lamont concludes that 'self-reliance, laziness and responsibility are important in framing whites' stig-matisation of blacks' (2000: 135). This works by fixing laziness and irresponsibility as natural characteristics that constitute a moral flaw, a flaw attached in the white respondents' minds over-whelmingly to blacks. So, when asked to identify traits that they liked and disliked in others, 70 per cent of white workers and 40 per cent of black workers stated that they did not like irrespon-sibility; and 59 per cent of whites and 40 per cent of blacks said they liked hardworking people (Lamont, 2000: 28):

> for white workers, moral and racial boundaries are inseparable from each other. Whether they focus on differences in the area of work ethic, respon-sibility, family values, or traditional morality, interviewees move seamlessly from morality to race, effortlessly extending these moral distinctions to broad racial categories. They view these moral boundaries as legitimate because they are based on the same universal criteria of evaluation that are at the center of their larger worldviews. They are thus able to make racist arguments and feel that they are fundamentally good, fair people. (Lamont, 2000: 68)

Indeed, the way in which white people construct 'fairness' is elaborated through Karyn McKinney's experiences of teaching an undergraduate course on 'race' and ethnicity in which she focuses on whiteness (McKinney, 2005). Her students keep a reflexive diary accompanying the course. There are two principal outcomes, one of which is the resentment exhibited by students confronting their whiteness as a raced identity, often for the first time. What this means in terms of structural privilege is frequently addressed through one of two forms of denial. The first is to argue that racism is either exaggerated or a question of individual prejudices not shared by the author of the diary. This constitutes what McKinney calls the 'golden rule' of treating everyone as an individual rather than as a member of a group.

The second outcome is a discourse asserting that whiteness is actually detrimental, rather than beneficial, to the bearer's life chances. Such discourse has a very specific American focus: affirmative action. McKinney's findings show that white students are concerned about quotas and other manifestations of affirmative action that they perceive as having a negative impact on a number of areas of their lives: university entry, obtaining grants, the size of the grants, and on their and on relatives' employment and promotion prospects. The young people here understand the slate as having been wiped more or less clean by the reforms of the civil rights era, and that minorities are now on a level playing field with them. As all the oppression happened before they were born, runs the argument, why are they now victims of quotas and the like? In their eyes, quotas mean they are unfairly discriminated against *as individual white people*. Just as Harris (1993) maintains, affirmative action is constructed by McKinney's twenty-first century undergraduates as 'reverse discrimination', with individual white subjects being held accountable for collective and historic practices that are not his/her sole responsibility. The failure of past patterns of structural disadvantage to be included in the equation that necessitates the establishment of affirmative action in the first place is usually absent from these students' accounts. The disjuncture between past and present is represented as all-encompassing: history begins in 1968.

Yet another facet of the multidimensional literature about white identities, however, demonstrates the continuities between past and present, through the reproduction of particular kinds of social relationships that re-introduce class in to the equation.

Whiteness as a Set of Contingent Hierarchies

The first wave of white writing about whiteness began in the 1990s. The work of labour historian David Roediger (1991, 1999), and his collaborative work with James Barrett (1997, 2004, 2005), is a principal reference point. Together they have elaborated the contested concept of 'inbetween people', which refers to a process whereby nineteenth-century Southern and Eastern European immigrants to America learned what the social value of whiteness was, and how to become 'white' socially. During this transitional period (which differed from group to group), they were not considered as fully white, that is, as civilised as other Americans and fit for membership of a democracy. The 'inbetween people' are therefore provisionally stuck in a status between the unproblematic whites who constitute the American polity, and the groups of non-white people: Native American, black and Asian, on its periphery. Barrett and Roediger are not alone in positing whiteness as an over-arching mainstream value of Americanness. A number of other historians suggest this (Horsman, 1981; Bernstein, 1990; Saxton, 1990; Allen, 1994; Almaguer, 1994, *inter alia*). However, Barrett and Roediger (1997) are the only ones to assert that in the period from the 1850s to the 1920s, incoming migrant Europeans were exposed to a situation where whiteness exerted forces constraining Europeans to claim whiteness and gain privileged access to resources, psychological and social capital (Du Bois' 'wages of whiteness'). The argument that incoming 'white' immigrants were not considered fully white is derived from exclusionary language, comparisons and images in circulation in the nineteenth and early twentieth centuries. We would add that the 1924 Immigration Act, whose quotas were based on eugenics-inspired understandings of the innate fitness and degeneracy of various racialised groups, is quite a clear expression of this: the quotas were most severe for Southern and Eastern European Catholics and Jews.

Yet it is clear that not being white does not equate to being black or Mexican, for example, as Guglielmo (2003, 2004) emphasises. Instead, we understand Barrett and Roediger's thesis (1997, 2004) as containing two connected substantive points. First, whiteness is to do with cultural, material and political power: those who appear phenotypically white are not equally incorporated into the dominant groups under those three headings. Second, migrants from the Catholic, Southern, Eastern and Central European countries were not immediately accepted culturally as white, even if they were politically accepted (with access to citizenship and the body politic). Differential access to this resource was sought by successive waves of migrants learning the rules of the American game, 'this racial thing', as one of their respondents puts it (Barrett and Roediger, 1997: 6).[8]

The corollaries of this form of categorisation were not a set of life chances equivalent to those of blacks, Native Americans or

Hispanics, rather the obligation to define themselves as 'white' in a society where that mattered a great deal, and where there was a social cost to not being white. In this sense, European immigrants became 'white on arrival' (to use Tom Guglielmo's (2004) term) in the New World because they disembarked into a new set of social identities, where their overarching identity was whiteness. This is supported by their legal definition as white (therefore not property), and as potential citizens and thus political subjects. However, for a sociologist trying to understand the problem of racialised identities, the law is equally fair game for deconstruction as popular culture: as Cheryl Harris (1993) argues, it is not a superior level of discourse. The legal domain was utilised from the nineteenth century to inject scientific rationality into decisions about who belonged to which race (Jacobson, 1998). The basis of the law on 'race' was 'spurious, reliant as it was on unfeasibly accurate records about people's ancestry, and understandings of definitions of "race" that were not empirically provable. The result of this was that the legal concept of "blood" was no more objective than that which the law dismissed as subjective and unreliable' (Harris, 1993: 1740). In sociology, the term 'white' can be interpreted as encompassing both non-material and fluid dominant norms and boundaries. Within the white racialised hierarchy were, as Guglielmo rightly points out, a number of 'races'. Using the definition of 'white' as an institutional starting point is a legitimate historical argument. Yet this sees the terms 'white' and 'black' themselves as naturalised *givens* transposed into law, rather than products of the processes of racialisation. So, there are various contexts – economic, social, legal, cultural, for example – in which meaning is attributed to types of difference.

We will now use a contemporary piece of ethnography to illustrate quite another aspect of the problematic: the intersection of race and class and how it works culturally. John Hartigan's study of the everyday realities of 'race' as understood in three neighbourhoods of inner-city Detroit (1999), and associated publications (1997, 2005), brings to the fore a number of factors that are not discussed with reference to empirical studies elsewhere. The accepted wisdom from studies focusing on working-class areas suggests that working-class subjects are less equivocal about racism and less guarded in their language and actions. Hartigan's self-styled inner-city 'hillbillies', however, are far more complex and ambivalent about their class location and their relationships with whites and minorities from better and worse-off neighbourhoods across the city. Hartigan notes that the inner-city Briggs area, where he was based for fieldwork, is one in which black and white residents are, unusually for the USA, permanently thrown together spatially, and that the generally peaceful co-existence is based on local understandings of codes about how to do 'race', class and gender. Commenting on the social mixing he observed in this area in public spaces, Hartigan concludes that the degree to which people were geographically and thus socially 'at home' greatly influenced the role that racialisation appeared to play in their interaction, in other words, the degree to which 'race' was salient in a given inter-personal interaction. When he told some interviewees that he was studying 'race relations', they directed him to a housing project across the highway, indicating firstly a place where 'race' was deemed an issue, and that it was a zone too dangerous for whites (1997: 191) vis-à-vis their safe mixed district:

> In this [their own] neighbourhood, they were one family among many, white and black, who held elaborate and lengthy knowledge of each other reaching back over the tumultuous past three decades. But across the intersection [i.e. in that particular project] they were simply 'whites', partly for their skin color and partly in terms of location and being out of place.

Hartigan's white respondents here thus predict their own racialisation – and social decontextualisation – as nothing but whites, in an area where nobody knows them. Long-term familiarity changes the rules. One of Briggs' black residents, Marvin, explains to Hartigan that people get along well there because so many of them went to school together and have known each other for 20 years or more (Hartigan, 1999: 96). In Hartigan's account, ethnography's capacity to demonstrate what people actually do, rather than what they say, allows us to appreciate the contingency of the extent to which 'race' is, or is not, interpreted as significant in a given situation, as well as the plural registers of language and action in which it is performed. Particular terms and behaviour are acceptable in some contexts and not in others.

All the way, 'race' and class are read through reciprocal frames. In the story of the multiracial baseball game (Hartigan, 1999: 139–44), class-related fault-lines in the family of Hartigan's main informant, Jessie, emerge. They are originally set to play against a team of local black people whom they had met the week before. As the afternoon progresses, however, more players join the game, and both teams end up multiracial. This provokes discord in Jessie's family. Jessie's son, David, and his girlfriend, Becky, are visiting for the day from Dearborn, a white suburb. They are both reluctant to play, and Becky does not want her equipment used by blacks. The resulting feud is interpreted by the family as being about Becky's incapacity to socialise in this surrounding, and their feeling that she, like David, thinks she is better than them. Upward mobility for working-class whites, suggests Hartigan, involves 'the need for careful racial boundary maintenance by avoiding interracial situations' (1999: 142). Part of being middle-class and white (the mutually constitutive suburban categories) is to live in isolation from where 'race' is seen to be an issue (Forman and Lewis, 2006).

Conclusion

Whiteness has therefore been conceptualised in a number of ways in the US literature. The starting point is systemic discrimination, verbal and physical violence, which has framed the major part of American history and, many would argue, continues to underpin the present. A few decades of highly variable post-civil rights experience does not trump more than three centuries of explicit institutionalised racism in the form of genocide, slavery and the Jim Crow laws, among other things.

In the field, scholars have identified that whiteness can be at times a form of invisibility and at others clearly remain visible. It can revolve around forms of cultural capital that translate into racialised privilege, which in turn concretises into a system comprised of a set of contested and contingent racialised hierarchies.

The type of questions this raises for us are to do with areas of further exploration. In American scholarship the focus has been predominantly the social relationship between white and black Americans. There is relatively little so far on the specifics of the relationships between the growing Asian-American and Latino populations and the dominant group, which would be revealing and possibly add further complexity. Moreover, how can these pieces of scholarship inform us about being white in the UK? There has to be an awareness of the historical and social distinctions between the two societies, as well as the similarities of colonial and post-colonial, commercial and linguistic domains. Where there are distinctions there are also similarities.

Both societies were profoundly implicated in transatlantic slavery, yet the type of implication differs. It meant a sizeable proportion of black people in the USA since the seventeenth century, most of whom were engaged in the production of wealth for a property-owning elite. Whereas the British slave population was primarily although not exclusively abroad. There is also the post-abolition history of Reconstruction, Jim Crow, wide-scale extrajudicial violence sanctioned by authorities, laws against intermarriage, accumulation of generations of privilege (even for those at the lowest level of the scale), and indeed the binary race relations conceptualisation of social relations. There is much less place for Latinos and Asians in accounts of social relations outside specific settings (California, Florida and the South-Western states).

However, while Britain's racial segregation (with a small number of exceptions) occurred within empire, the two countries' imperial histories provide possibilities of comparison in terms of racialising ideology. Next to Britain's well-documented imperial dimension are the USA's Spanish-American wars: the annexation of Puerto Rico; invasions of Cuba and the Philippines; the later occupation of Haiti and neo-colonial adventures in Central America.

Moreover, while affirmative action is clearly a central focus of contemporary American racial discourse it is absent from the European landscape. Yet the core notion of white Europeans as an emerging unprotected minority is certainly sporadically present in fieldwork. Indeed, what Paul Gilroy (2004) might include under 'post-colonial melancholia' is working- and middle-class white Europeans' construction of themselves as losing out in a new set of social hierarchies in which the indigenous find themselves unfairly sidelined vis-à-vis minorities. So at the other extreme of the idea of whiteness as being unmarked lies the possibility that it has become hyper-marked and transformed psychologically into a liability. The 'whiteness-as-a-liability' line is indeed being reproduced in the UK (see chapters 4 and 5).

In the next chapter we will set out, through engaging with empirical fieldwork, the areas of similarity and discrepancy between whiteness in the UK and whiteness in the USA.

3

EMPIRICAL RESEARCH INTO WHITE RACIALISED IDENTITIES IN BRITAIN

The intellectual project of using whiteness as a tool of analysis is not one that has taken root in the UK. However, there are a number of empirical studies that investigate the racialisation of white identities. This bears some comparison to the themes thrown up by the plethora of American work in the loose multi-disciplinary field labelled 'whiteness studies'. Indeed, that corpus is far advanced: Winddance Twine and Gallagher (2008: 5) label the empirical studies of localised whiteness as it intersects with class, nation and gender, as the 'third wave' of whiteness studies. This scholarly movement has been blamed for displacing the focus of inquiry from racism to the often class-based cultural variations of white identities (Field, 2001; Andersen, 2003). The marking of whiteness as a racialised social identity, rather than a normative, un-raced one, has also been critiqued for operationalising racist assumptions (Howard, 2004), and for being incapable of fulfilling an anti-racist mission within an academic context of white middle-class domination (Ahmed, 2004). Moreover, British scholars have frequently opted to avoid using the term 'whiteness' in relation to work that in the USA would clearly fall into the domain of 'whiteness studies'. Steve Fenton (2005) talks of 'banal majoritarianism', while in keynote addresses to a conference on whiteness in 2006, both Paul Gilroy and Les Back expressed profound ambivalence and reticence about pursuing whiteness *per se* as a topic of inquiry.[1] Indeed, there are good reasons to choose our language carefully. Conducting qualitative interviews with, and ethnographies of, white UK nationals around questions of community, national identity and immigration generates data full of implicit and explicit assertions of racialised difference often expressed through claims of the eclipse of traditional solidarity and fairness (Wells and Watson, 2005; Dench et al., 2006). Presenting such findings as fact, rather than perceptions to be critically analysed, actually endorses populist ideas of beleaguered white communities upon which far-right political mobilisation across Europe is based. Such communities may well be beleaguered, but 'race' is surely not the only variable that can help explain this perception. Problems arising from using whiteness as a framework therefore include the danger of lending credence to identity politics based on it, as well as the epistemological slipperiness of using a term that is not habitually used by respondents as a means of self-identification. This paradoxically broad disavowal of 'whiteness' on the part of UK academics working in the field of the sociology of racism therefore forms part of the context in which the following synthesis is produced.

In this chapter we aim to identify some of the themes to have emerged from the sporadic *empirical* studies of white racialised identity in the British context, from the early 1990s until 2006. There is no such review available in existing literature. Moreover, we go on to argue that while some of the themes identified in US corpus (Garner, 2006) are also present in the British work, there are significant differences that lend a specific national context to what we shall refer to here as the whiteness 'problematic' (i.e. how to conceptualise the racialisation of white identities). Finally, we outline how this work relates to contemporary political discourse on Britishness. First, however, we shall set out our understanding of the concept of whiteness.

British Fieldwork

Empirical sociological studies that contribute to a research agenda on 'white' identities in specifically British contexts have made sporadic appearances over the last decade and more (Hoggett, 1992; Back, 1996; Phoenix, 1996; Tyler, 2003, 2004; Byrne, 2006; Dench et al., 2006; Evans, 2006). The themes we have identified are: invisibility; norms/values; cultural capital;

contingent hierarchies; narratives of disempowerment and empire in the present.

It is not the case that there is no tradition of theorising British whiteness as constituting 'terror' in various forms (Puar, 1995; Bhattacharyya, 1997, 2008), nor is it the case that racialised minority academics have not written about whiteness in varying degrees of explicitness. Virtually all the writing on 'race' and ethnicity in Britain could in some way be understood as covering different aspects of whiteness, particularly in its articulation to Englishness (Hall, 1992; Young, 2008). Indeed, landmark work such as Hall et al. (1978), Carby (1982) and Gilroy (1987) are all partly about white British identity formation. However, this chapter concentrates solely on empirical fieldwork that explicitly illuminates aspects of the whiteness problematic *in its British forms*.

Invisibility

The assertion that whiteness denotes an absence of specificity, or is an invisible non-raced identity, is the traditional starting point for discussions of whiteness. Dyer (1997) argues that whiteness is normalised as universal and above all human: hence its potency. If white is human, everything else is deviant. So, to clarify, the argument is not that whiteness is actually invisible, but that it appears so unmarked to the majority of white people that in their eyes, it does not function as a *racial* or ethnic identity, at least outside of particular contexts. Dyer's work focuses on the visual and he is talking primarily about film. For those not categorised as white, whiteness is an all-too visible presence. Strong echoes of Dyer's argument are evident in sociological work (see also psycho-social work in this area by Seshadri-Crooks, 2000; Clarke, 2003). Ann Phoenix's (1996) interviews demonstrate how young white people enjoy the luxury of not thinking about racialised identity. They have the freedom to idealise egalitarianism, and assert that colour is not important in judgements of personal worth, etc. while essentialising blackness, which is experienced as a threatening presence in particular spaces. They are thus forced into the confrontation with the contradiction expressed by identifying themselves with non-racial identities, while recognising 'that being white signifies a social location, and as such, has a history and interconnections with other colours' (Phoenix, 1996: 192). This ideological impasse epitomises the idea of 'sovereign individuality' floated by Farough (2004: 244) (following Herman, 1999), whereby the white subject is always viewed as a non-racial universal individual, while the Other is essentially a raced member of a collective. Treating whiteness as a non-identity thus conceals racialised power relations and the ideas and practices that sustain them. Phoenix concludes that 'silence about "whiteness" implicitly serves to maintain the status quo of power relations between black people and white people' (1996: 196)

Yet some studies emphasising spatial awareness and mobility suggest that whiteness is *not invisible* to anyone. Watt and Stenson (1998) and Watt (1998) find that young white people in provincial southern England see particular spaces as dangerous for a number of classed, gendered and racialised reasons, i.e. fear of crime and violence, an experience heightened when they do not know individuals resident in the areas they are crossing. The other side of the coin is that young minority people avoid certain areas, and even whole towns, because they are seen as fearsomely white. Yet we should also steer clear of generalising this fear into a norm: other white subjects find that mixed occupation of space can become, or already has become their norm, and their ontological security is unbalanced by an excess of whiteness. 'Jim' in Tyler's (2004) study of Coalville in Leicestershire notes a big difference between Stoke-on-Trent (where he went to college) and his hometown, in that Stoke's multiculturalism pushed him to question prevalent ideas on 'race' when he returned to Leicestershire.[2] One of our interviewees, Darren (40s, Plymouth, mc)[3] is a public-sector worker who grew up in a Midlands city, and had black friends and was used to a 'racial mix in school'. Before moving to Plymouth, he had lived for a while in a small northern town, 'which is predominantly white ... I suppose my social radar had adjusted to that idea'. After years in Plymouth he got involved in a thread of work around diversity and realised he had become 'almost soporific on the racial front in living in Plymouth for that long'. The exposure to Plymouth's annual festival, Respect, saw him start to 'connect with that, you know, what were these communities, how big were they [...] discovering there was a very large Chinese community in Plymouth, but also myriad of other communities and I suppose over the years, becoming more and more involved with that, and aware within school when I was teaching, of kids' attitudes [...] that not being used to seeing black faces in the street, kids in school, perhaps one black kid in the whole school'. Darren's white habitus seems to have erased awareness of his whiteness, which was reawakened suddenly. This has led him to devote part of his time to anti-racist work around the city. Whiteness thus emerges from fieldwork as either marked (visible) or unmarked (invisible), depending on the location of the person doing the looking.

White Norms and Values in Practice

North American writers have suggested that whiteness has been constructed as a set of interrelated norms and values, ranging from a feeling of racial superiority, Christianity, through the work ethic, to lying and chronically unethical behaviour.[4] Dyer (1988) lists rationality, order and repression of emotions. Moreover, the process of constructing whiteness as normal and otherness as abnormal occurs through selective understandings of culture as static, and of these understandings being presented as acts of common sense by the interlocutor. In the British context, we might also highlight a distinction between urban and rural settings that emerges quite strongly.

Urban Settings

Paul Hoggett's (1992) study of Tower Hamlets, in the East End of London, demonstrates the predominance of values as a battleground in racialised inter-communal tensions.[5] The Bangladeshi incomers in this borough are perceived as embodying values that used to characterise the working-class East End communities. The sense of loss of such values thus coalesces around a physical presence of a group of new migrants and is thus the cause of a degree of jealousy.

> The resentment the whites feel toward the Bengali community is made poignant by the fact that the latter community has many characteristics – extended and intensive kinship networks, a respect for tradition and more seniority, a capacity for entrepreneurialism and social advancement – which the white working class in the area have lost. (Hoggett, 1992: 354)[6]

In local discourse, the physical presence of the Other in Tower Hamlets becomes embodied in the figure of the cockroach (Hoggett, 1992), when the modernisation of a tower block housing many Bangladeshis leads to an infestation. Here we return to more familiar notions of associating dirt, impurity and potential disease with out-groups (Douglas, 1966). The Bangladeshis' status as matter-out-of-place is thus emphasised, in contradiction to the social values and shared history of class oppression objectively binding them to local working-class white East Enders. The cockroach theme resurfaces in Dench et al.'s 1990s fieldwork (2006). This group of Others, because of the values they are seen to embody, constitute an identification rather than a self/other couple. The out-group seemingly assumes the values of the white working class, while simultaneously 'stealing' these values from them. Thus what follows is a series of projections and identifications. 'The local white is engaged in one sense in an envious attack upon the Bengali within him', writes Hoggett, 'an attack which twists and corrupts him into its opposite' (1992: 354). Indeed, the traumatic experience of racialisation evokes recognition of loss of place, standards and status in unpredictable locations. The journalist Lesley White even finds a local British National Party organiser in Oldham who concedes that 'we can learn something from the Asians about family values and looking after our own' (2002: 54).[7]

Rural Settings

Although 80 per cent of the UK population lived in urban areas as of the 2001 Census, this represents a 10 per cent shift towards rural living since the previous Census. The English countryside has long been constructed as a repository for pure English values, and a space of authenticity vis-à-vis the dangerous cosmopolitan urban centres (William, 1973; Neal and Agyemang, 2006). In his study of ideological interpretations of disorder in twentieth-century Britain, Rowe (1998: 176–7) makes this point by juxtaposing press coverage of the 1985 Broadwater Farm riots with former Home Secretary Lord Whitelaw's memoirs of that event. In these texts, urban inhabitants are constructed as implicitly culturally alien and their presence degrades cities, exacerbating their distance from the putative bucolic norm. Much could be made of the mass of hierarchical social relations binding city and country, which are glossed over in this ideological manoeuvre, but in the following section we will focus only on the mechanisms for demarcating rural space as defensible against alien encroachment.

Hubbard (2005a, 2005b) argues that rural landscape is racialised as white in the process of opposing the locating of asylum seekers in particular spaces in England. Alongside protests over land use *per se*, he identifies elements of discourse produced in campaigns in Nottinghamshire and Oxfordshire that construct asylum seekers, regardless of their geographical origins, as an undifferentiated (over-ridingly male) criminal, sexually threatening and alien presence in the English countryside. While elements of this discourse can also be identified in urban and semi-rural settings (Modell, 2004; Grillo, 2005), Hubbard identifies a specific narrative of white rurality dependent on implicit norms of location away from chaotic and dangerous multicultural settings. One complainant writes to the local planning authority: 'As a Bicester resident, I do not want to live in a multicultural community. Having lived in London and Surrey I have experienced the trouble this brings' (Hubbard, 2005a: 14).

Similar themes crop up in the letters written by residents of Portishead (North Somerset) in the 2004 campaign against the re-locating of an asylum office in a small industrial estate within a larger new-build housing district (Garner, 2007: 156–8). Among other topics is the theme of betrayal by local councillors, central government and the property developers who are seen as placing residents in a position where their house values will drop and their quality of life will be threatened by the proximity of asylum seekers visiting the office:

> Having moved to Portishead 18 months ago to invest in my families' [sic] right to a better quality of life I find all the past years of hard work, saving and moving to what I thought was an up and coming area, all to be taken away. The decision to be made by councillors, most of whom, probably do not live in the affected area. How would you truly feel if it was next to your home? Something you've worked for all your life to be wiped out from underneath you. (Garner, 2007: 156–8)

Alongside the complaints about noise, light and traffic pollution that the establishment of the asylum office is expected to cause, asylum seekers are imagined as sexual threats to women and children:

> Why is the proposed centre in the middle of a residential area? It is full of children, which at present can safely be allowed out to play. If the proposal goes ahead can you guarantee the safety of our children, I don't think you can with the sort of people you are planning to dump on our doorstep. (Garner, 2007: 156–8)

The defence of social space against the wrong kind of person is illustrated further in Tyler's 2003 study of the Leicestershire village of Greenville. Here, semi-rural space is defended using the development of middle-class values of belonging through adherence to ways of being and behaving. While not neglecting the class distinctions within the village, she concentrates on the ways in which racism is articulated there. The Asian families in Greenville are produced as 'abnormal' (2003: 394) because they lie outside notions of respectability and normality, such as not getting involved in charity activities or going to the pub. Indeed, Garland and Chakraborti (2006: 164–5) echo this finding, adding that those who are not Christian or secular also face obstacles integrating. While some ethnic minority village residents' professional status may obviate a degree of the hostility, they still cannot own the cultural codes required to function 'normally'. 'For community "insiders"', they contend, 'rural villages can be places where kinship and shared identities can be played out and enjoyed; for those subject to the "othering" process, such places can be cold and unwelcoming' (Garland and Chakraborti, 2006: 169).

One Greenville Asian family extended its house (against local opposition) and the anxieties of the villagers reveal the prism through which the Asians are (mis)understood: the potential over-use of space, as a residence, business and prayer room. One villager states that: 'They are very nice people but eyebrows are raised when the hordes of friends and relatives come from Leicester. It isn't done in Greenville' (Tyler, 2003: 405). Indeed, Tyler concludes that 'wealthy Asians are thought to live in extended families, are perceived to be excessively wealthy, extravagantly religious, run disruptive businesses from their homes and cook smelly foods' (2003: 409).

Daniel Miller's conclusion about cultural capital is worth noting here: 'The relationship between the two kinds of capital – cultural and economic – is uneasy [...] Society, then, is not to be understood in terms of a simple hierarchy, but as a continual struggle over the hierarchy of hierarchies' (Miller, 1987: 152). The hierarchy of economics can apparently trump that of culture: the Greenville Asians literally cannot buy the requisite cultural capital.

Cultural Capital and Respectability

One cultural battleground over which competing versions of hierarchy coalesce is the question of respectability. Of course, this varies from setting to setting, but its potency as a racialised border is undiminished. The Greenville Asians are seen as not respectable vis-à-vis norms of charity, religiosity and quietness. For the middle classes in semi-rural Leicester, tranquillity is a prized ideal. While solidarity (for the poor elsewhere) is demonstrated through the routines of charity work, the real test of belonging is to attain invisibility. Talking of a particular Asian family in the village, one resident tells Tyler (2003: 400): 'They are as good as gold ... we never see them'. Hiding oneself and keeping the noise down is viewed as the correct way to behave, a value that contradicts the justification for not forging more intimate relations: Asians 'don't mix'.

In terms of whiteness, cultural capital can involve among other things: shared expectations of behaviour on the part of minority groups; a belief that one is part of a tradition of dominance including empire; knowledge of norms and behaviour patterns that will produce intended outcomes in particular situations – including the right to question certain people's eligibility for various resources without this being countered, and the assumption of rationality juxtaposed with the irrationality of Others.

Nayak's 2003 study of youth subcultures in Newcastle provides a counterpoint to these more extreme views, and in doing so points to differing versions of whiteness. The 'Real Geordies' see themselves as the most authentic bearers of working-class culture. Their family and/or occupational histories and allegiance to Newcastle United FC tie them into the region's manufacturing and mining base.[8] This leads them to view the keystone of respectability as hard work, which subsequently grants entitlement. Yet they promote 'the values of a muscular puritan work ethic (honesty, loyalty, self-sufficiency, "a fair day's work for a fair day's pay") in a situation where unskilled manual *unemployment* was increasingly the norm' (Nayak, 2003: 309). In the eyes of the 'Real Geordies', the 'Charver Kids" unemployed status, involvement with petty crime, and relationship to black music and dress make them not respectable and, Nayak argues, virtually racialised. Wells and Watson's London shopkeepers (2005) also implicitly posit some of these respectable values. They perceive their position as jeopardised by groups receiving state resources at the expense of people like them, i.e. on the basis of cultural otherness *per se* rather than through hard work. Spaces that were seen as neutral, or as resources previously accessible to the whole community, have been turned into mosques, for example, indicating the neighbourhood's demographic shift away from Britishness. This 'decline' can be charted in alternative ways. One of Wells and Watson's respondents, a butcher (2005: 269–70), narrates the area's transformation through the types of meat available. The white working-class clientele's demand for rabbit has long given way to the appearance and proliferation of halal, and before that, kosher butchers. The expectations of civilised and classed familiar meats have been overturned by 'smelly' and alien meat preparation methods: a microcosm of the invasion narrative that is told in the rest of the interviews. Byrne's interviewee Emma also depicts a struggle for Englishness against such a background:

> if you go round the back there are some … in the marketplace you get all this halal meat and all sorts of stuff. I wouldn't touch that with a bargepole. Not because it's different, or because of anything. But just because I think it smells funny. (Byrne, 2006: 149)

Thus we have a similar response to the one found in Hoggett's (1992) study. Despite good material reasons given for the cockroach infestation in Tower Hamlets – improvements in ducting and central heating that caused a veritable breeding ground for cockroaches – the psychological othering takes precedence. In the butchers' case, many local outlets had been forced to close down because of competition from supermarkets, so only those who specialise, for example, in organic meat or halal, can survive in a niche market.

We have argued so far that the paradoxical nature of white identity requires both strategically and ideologically procured and maintained invisibility (a denial of raced specificity), and the performance of values and norms that are reflexively juxtaposed against competing and inferior ones. What sustains these norms? They require ideological upkeep. One answer is provided by cultural capital that fuels and helps reproduce this form of labour. Indeed, part of this is knowing how to behave and speak in particular contexts in order to make oneself fit in unproblematically. This is the strategy adopted by two Caribbean migrants in Broomfield, our Bristol estate, as related by community worker Tom (60s, Bristol, wc). In a conversation about when immigrants stop being immigrants, he contrasts a couple (Richard and Carolyn) with a single man (Shafiq):

> You see one of the reasons I think of Shafiq as being an immigrant is that, for all his kindness and his carefulness, you feel that he is still having to work

> very hard at negotiating across the boundaries. With Richard and Carolyn, you don't feel that, well, they do it without you noticing it.

Tom explained that he had tried to talk to Richard about the cricket, but he was not interested unless the West Indians were playing:

> Now you could argue, couldn't you, that he would be supporting England if he was really English … I don't think that, you see. There is something about the way they [Richard and Carolyn] go on that makes me feel that they don't need to do that, they're comfortably part, they make great efforts to be. I mean, Carolyn is the sort of person who turns up with stuff when there's an event at the church; she has ways of making sure she has become part of the community. She's actually, somebody said, [*whispering*] 'I'm going to invite Carolyn to stand for the church council this year'. Now they've been coming for two and a half years, I think. In Broomfield terms, most of these people have been coming for 30 years! So you kind of feel, you know, don't you, she's worked, she's being seen as part of the thing.

So these two migrants have utilised their cultural capital to insert themselves seamlessly into a space that other migrants have trouble doing. They can make their presence 'invisible', in a way.

However, there are other sorts of cultural capital. In Watt and Stenson's (1998) exploration of the contingency of racialised space and young people's leisure-related mobility, some places, especially more rural Buckinghamshire small towns and villages, are viewed as 'whiter' (i.e. more dangerous for minorities) than others. So the cultural capital of non-whites includes security-oriented knowledge of dangerous, excessive whiteness. Moreover, minority spaces, however safe, are not always emancipatory for members of the minority, e.g. for young Muslim women, who prefer to go somewhere more anonymous for nights out, an experience echoed by young Sikhs in Kaur's (2003) study of Southall. Watt and Stenson's young people's leisure itineraries are shaped by intersections of class, raced identities and gender. Their middle-class suburban white youth are fearful of both white working-class neighbourhoods and an Asian area in the town, whereas non-whites steer clear of particular areas in Townsville unless they know white people who inhabit them through school or shared leisure activities. Indeed, most of the inter-ethnic friendships were among the working-class respondents on estates (Watt and Stenson, 1998: 256). The middle-class youth, more advantaged in many areas of cultural capital, are in this respect impoverished in (multi)cultural capital that they have not accrued (in contrast to their working-class peers) from 'personal contacts across the ethnic divides which were so important for moving confidently about the town' (Watt and Stenson, 1998: 257).[9]

Contingent Hierarchies

Where the British-based work most acutely pinpoints the complexity and conceptual fluidity of white identities is in identifying where conditional alliances, allegiances and loyalties that blur the black/white binary emerge.

In Broomfield, we were told by a number of respondents that the most pertinent distinction made by locals on the estate was not between white and black or Asian, but first, between 'Broomies' (residents of the estate) and people from outside, and second, between the established population (including African-Caribbean and Asian residents) and the newest arrivals, the Somalis. 'I don't like Somalians, to be honest', says Pauline (40s, wc), who has also lived in a different part of Bristol, in an area with many Jamaicans:

> I think they're ignorant people. They don't, um, you know, if you're on a bus stop, you've got to get out of the way, mate, they sort of do that. They done it to us, so I done back and said, nah, I was here first [...] Now Jamaicans, I think they're lovely, but I don't like Somalians at all [...] They seemed to have all come at once. You know, a couple of years ago, I never even heard of Somalians, and now they're here, wearing what they wants to school, that's wrong as well.

Another man, Luke (20s) talks of encountering Somalis in school:

> I mean, you know, in my junior school, there was one Somalian that I knew and I think that she was Brit ... You know, I think she was over as long as I had been here. And when you when you went to Broomfield School, it

was just [*making a wide gesture with his arms*]. It just sort of, I didn't know what a Somalian was until I went to Broomfield School, but you've got to remember that there's other people, loads of different junior schools that they've obviously been to in the past, and then they've decided to go to Broomfield, but then you know, you just started seeing new students that all were Somalians starting school, ones that weren't even speaking English, do you know what I mean?

The focus on cultural clashes between Somalis and everyone else is not confined to Broomfield. In a later piece of fieldwork elsewhere in the city (Hoggett et al., 2008) a similar, if more intense version of the same story (which runs: lots of Somalis came here very quickly and they get better treatment than everyone else, even though they don't get on with other people) was told numerous times.

So a series of trajectories of whiteness emerge from the white actors in ethnographic studies. Nayak's 'White Wannabes'; the youths on Back's 'Riverview' estate; Watt and Stenson's Townsvillers; Byrne's white mothers of 'mixed' children; and Kaur's white Southall sisters, all negotiate themselves across cultural and geographical terrains with varying degrees of ease and intimacy with black and Asian people from their neighbourhoods. While there is frequently tension, there is also frequently alliance, through personal relationships drawing on shared knowledge and experiences.

Indeed, the majority of the British studies here are micro-level ones. This is simultaneously a strength and a weakness. It is a considerable challenge to locate the complex, contradictory and elusive personal testimonies of 'defended subjects' (Hollway and Jefferson, 2000) within long-term structural processes. However, from the studies by Back (1996), Watt and Stenson (1998), Nayak (2003), Tyler (2003, 2004) and Byrne (2006), it becomes apparent that white actors can be highly reflexive about their racialised identities, and that complex and contradictory ideas can be held.

Katherine Tyler's (2004) inter-generational dialogue among smalltown Leicestershire inhabitants shows how the contingency of personal biographies may shape how people perceive Others. Among the interviewees, no homogeneous representative voice is expressed: white superiority is contested by some, just as it is accepted unthinkingly by others. Identification can take the form of empathy, for example, as in 'Sarah's recognition of her own narrative – the experience of *her* Czech immigrant father's struggle to run a business – in critiques of Asian businesses' (Tyler, 2004: 304).

Les Back's (1996) ethnography of young people on south London estates suggests that values determine the salient borders of identity, as culture becomes the modality through which they are racialised. Black and white youths put aside differences to ally against Vietnamese and Bangladeshi newcomers on their estates (1996: 240–1). While the black youths are well aware that in other circumstances they could be, and indeed have been, the victims of such aggression from their white counterparts, in the context of defining authentic membership of the estate, their secular, linguistic and music-based coalition with white youth in the Riverview estate appears to predominate. They thus become what Back terms 'contingent insiders' (1996: 240), while their counterparts in Southgate, another nearby estate, seemed to enjoy a qualitatively different relationship with their white peers, who had 'vacated concepts of whiteness and Englishness ... in favour of a mixed ethnicity that was shared' (Back, 1996: 241).

Hoggett et al. (1996) remark on a similar set of provisional allegiances, noting the large Afro-Caribbean presence in an East End demonstration following the fatal stabbing of a white schoolboy by a local Bangladeshi boy:

> The paradox is that whilst Afro-Caribbean soccer players can still be the object of crude racial abuse at nearby Millwall Football Club, Afro-Caribbeans can nevertheless also be included in an imaginary community of English-speaking Christian Eastenders which stands opposed to the alien Muslim threat. (1996: 113)

Indeed, a recurrent topic in ethnographic studies is the heterogeneity and elasticity of the category 'white' in its members' affiliations with black and Asian cultures, to the point where terms such as 'black' or 'white' culture become ideal-types.

Kaur's focus (2003) on white *women* in Southall, and Byrne's (2006) on south London mothers, is therefore unusual, given the content of other studies. Kaur's subjects' identities are juxtaposed with those of both women and men from other minority groups. She argues that they stress gendered experiences more than racialised ones. Conscious of being a minority and seeking to avoid drawing attention to their whiteness, the women also realise they have to perform particular versions of femininity to obtain respect and ward off the frequent accusations of loose morals they either experience or perceive among the Asian men with whom they come into contact. Byrne's mothers negotiate 'race' through complex narrations, often eliding 'race' to instead focus on culture, nation, class and gender. 'While whiteness was largely undiscussed', concludes Byrne (2006: 172), 'it was at the same time defined through difference'. As a consequence of the identity-juggling and erasure practices noted in both cases, the women's gendered experience is always raced, their raced experiences always gendered. Indeed, an early attempt to tease out white British women's whiteness (Lewis and Ramazanoglu, 1999: 40) noted that: 'Rather than speaking the unspeakable, most women dealt with the discomfort of a white identity by slipping out of it'. Women deployed strategies to avoid talking about 'race', including retreating to other terrains of more comfortable identity:

> Women could mark their whiteness as absence rather than substance by defining everyone as individuals, by claiming not to see difference, by denying the specificity of a white culture or by slipping into other facets of identity: especially gender, sexuality, nationality, ethnicity, region. (Lewis and Ramazanoglu, 1999: 40)

Imogen Tyler's (2008) study of the use of the term 'Chav' as a proxy of 'underclass' in contemporary Britain demonstrates the gendered nature of this process of hierarchical division, and how it intersects with racialisation. The subjects of this discourse are white working-class British people. The use of 'Chav' and its regional variations since the early twenty-first century has now become, for Tyler, 'a ubiquitous term of abuse for white working-class subjects' (2008: 17). She argues that the Chav has become a representative 'figure' of classification accumulating power through repetition. The disgust that is a central feature of class relations (Ahmed, 2004; Lawler, 2005) is attached to bodies of white poor people who are not normal, but made abnormal in the constant repetition of the themes that 'make' the Chav. They are instead for Tyler, transformed into 'hypervisible "filthy whites"' (Tyler, 2008: 25). The bodies of female Chavs (Chavettes) are most explicitly objects of disgust. Here the figure of the Chavette begins to absorb a number of 'disgusting' practices: wearing garish and excessive clothes, revealing too much flesh, being overly sexualised, having children out of wedlock and frequent 'race' mixing.

We could observe that whiteness appears to reveal itself more fully when the ostensible object of discourse is something else. Repressed complicity with systemic racism is refracted through talk of discrimination and difference in evidently more manageable discourses.

Moreover, Wells and Watson (2005) find in their survey of shopkeepers in a London borough that not all those championing white values are white, while some champions of white rights include their black neighbours in their embattled and beleaguered 'we'. In those cases the Other is Muslim/Asian, which reverberates with Back's configuration of Afro-Caribbean + White versus Asian. Clearly, the power relationships at a personal and local level allow for whiteness to be stretched to incorporate those not phenotypically white beneath its cultural canopy.

Narratives of Disempowerment: Empire as Presence

The working- and lower-middle-class subjects in these studies often position themselves as facing deprivation: the appropriation of 'their' values and territory is viewed as a physical and cultural invasion in which the state (local and/or national) may well collude. 'Jim' (in Coalville) reports that his uncles had been upset by the purchase of his grandmother's former house after her death: 'The presence of Asians in the home where they were brought up signifies an intolerable and unacceptable transformation' (Tyler, 2004: 299). Just as the link is frequently made in popular discourse between racialised minority presence and the physical degeneration of an area, so the Asian presence in Jim's uncles' home retrospectively degrades their status. It is the retrospective element here that is striking, leading us later to examine the relationship with empire. An interviewee in Modell's (2004) documentary on a community split by the asylum issue expresses concerns about potential settlement in Lee-on-Solent (a small town on the south coast). Recalling his time living in Reading (a medium-sized town west of London), he states that 'our colonial friends' had moved into a set of streets, 'we moved out and I don't know how many roads they've taken over now'. He specifies that these people were Jamaicans: 'I've got nothing against them, not one little bit, cause there are some nice guys, but it lowers the price, the value of your property as soon as they move in'. There appears to be an acute awareness of disadvantageous social change that is attached in narratives to the arrival and entrenchment of racialised minority groups. Not only do they 'occupy' territory, in the military jargon often used, but they usurp traditional values of patriarchal family, industriousness and solidarity.

Elsie (70s, Bristol, wc) talks of a trip to visit her daughter in East Anglia, which necessitates a coach trip along the A11 (Mile End Road) that first shocked her:

> When you leave London and then go on to Norfolk, as far as Stratford ... When you go along there, it's all sort of market, sort of all the way along, and you don't really see an English person, it's all like Muslims and you know. The first time I did that on that coach, I mean, I got a bit more used to it now, I thought, oh my, it was just as if you were in a different world, you know. Once you got past Stratford, it was okay of course.

Later on we returned to this topic:

> Q   So it's not a shock anymore?
> A   No, it's not a shock anymore, but I don't think even now, I wouldn't like to walk among them myself on my own, I think I'd be a bit wary, even

though I, you know, got used to it now. Yeah, it was quite a, I didn't really think that, yeah.

As Elsie had survived power cuts and bombing in Bristol during World War II it was in one way rather odd to hear that she was made anxious by what is essentially a large market. Yet this pushes us to reflect that a different type of insecurity is triggered by being momentarily caught out of place socially, than by a physical threat she had been expecting and which turned out not to be as frightening as she had imagined.

We argue that communities can express nostalgia for particular values, relationships and uses of space. Yet the precise nature of the loss, we contend, is shaped by the actors' location of themselves in a downward trajectory or at best a fragile and threatened slot in the post-empire world order: whether or not empire is explicitly invoked (Gilroy, 2004). During the period of research for this book, one controversial study of white identities that relates to this implicit colonial relationship was briefly in the media limelight. Dench et al.'s *The New East End* (2006) provoked a range of responses, from endorsement by Trevor Phillips and *Guardian* columnists, to a series of critiques.[10] The work was developed from a study in the late 1950s by Michael Young and 'updated' in the mid-1990s.[11] The authors found among the white East Enders they interviewed a set of attitudes not completely dissimilar to those we found ourselves, in that they paint a picture of a solid white community disrupted by local authority intervention in social housing to the benefit of the incoming Bengali immigrants. The authors claim that the policy shift from contributions-based welfare to needs-based welfare advantages the Bengalis, a far higher proportion of whom were living in overcrowded dwellings and therefore granted priority for rehousing. White communities are thus dispersed to outer London boroughs.[12]

Michael Keith (2008) maintains that the authors 'conflate three contentious assumptions: an historical amnesia around whiteness; a confusion of selective histories and absent geographies; and debates about welfare rights and migration'. Indeed, while giving voice to people's complaints about Bengalis, local authorities, etc., there is little economic contextualisation and the comments appear to be taken at face value. The political implications of the racist view that sees Bengalis as permanent non-contributing outsiders (regardless of their presence in the East End for up to four decades and the contribution they have made in terms of taxes) are that it triggers an understanding of deprivation based on 'race' alone rather than the complexities of class and 'race', and confers legitimacy on the idea that the white working class are institutionally placed below all other groups. The problem is constructed not as a shortage of social housing *per se*, but as one in which Bengalis get 'unfair advantage' in access to housing. Both white and Bengali East Enders are pathologised: the whites trapped in a nostalgic culture of defensiveness and the Bengalis marginalised from ever being equal members of a community defined by what it had been (in empire and especially World War II), and not what it is at the point when the research is undertaken. Whatever the other problems in conducting such research, one is to convey messages and findings in a way that simultaneously acknowledges the sincerity with which people hold opinions, but reiterates that the comments made in interviews are *perceptions* of reality, just like those of any other actors.

The evidence that empire has a direct relationship in the way people think through social relations gleaned from qualitative interviewing is less compelling here, but this relationship is crucial, at least for the theorisation of putative British versions of a global white identity.[13] Explicit references to empire are quite rare in qualitative fieldwork carried out in Britain. The context, however, is the post-colonial nation, in which norms are contested and expressed in a discourse of loss, eligibility and belonging. Here, the shift from colonial to post-colonial involves a leap of faith for the researcher in terms of interpreting white British attitudes. Early studies written from within the 'race relations' paradigm assumed the continuity of the coloniser–colonised relationship (Banton, 1967; Rex and Moore, 1967). However, by 2007, the justification for not examining such an important assumption is far less easy to sustain. Ware (1992) has explored historical relationships in this field, while Caroline Knowles (2003) is a rare voice seeking to clarify the nature of how the imperial bond informs actors' identities in the present. She concludes that reading the post-colonial through the colonial does not necessarily make sense without further theorising based on empirical studies. Indeed, she has followed up her appeal for the structures and mechanisms of post-colonial British whiteness with studies of white migrants in Hong Kong (Knowles, 2005).[14] Yet the question she raises is all the more pertinent in relation to Britain itself. How exactly does the colonial heritage impact upon white identities, particularly at the border adjoining its relationship with people descended from former colonial subjects in the metropolis? Tyler reports one of these rare moments of explicit juxtaposition and its interesting uses. Commenting on a retired, former Raj, client in Greenville, self-employed Mike first situates himself as neither a racist nor a snob. He then describes the situation:

> He has got Indians living to the back and side of him ... The house with the mosque thingy ... So you can understand it from their point of view. They have worked hard all their lives to achieve whatever bracket of wealth or status, to enjoy their retirement in a quiet village, and all of a sudden you get three families moving into one house and try and run a business from it. Transporter vans coming and going and they probably have a couple of sewing machines running in the garage. Women doing a bit of machining and then multiples of kids running around the garden, as he is sitting out on a nice sunny day, and it all drives you mad. It is very difficult for them. (Tyler, 2003: 402–3)

Mike's musings on the Asians' activities make his phantasies explicit, realigning him as an ally of the Raj man: worship, business and noise will erupt. It is tempting to think of this as revealing the projection of some contemporary British fears: secular doubt in the face of faith, where the latter is seen as communal, self-effacing and irrational; guilt over others' industriousness that threatens your supposition of laziness and incompetence; maybe combined with unfair competition (through unwaged family labour). Finally, there is the plague of large noisy families and expressive communities, the hint of high birth-rates and the ultimate assumption of power by the 'hordes'. In addition, this example shows that whiteness is classed, even when stressing the external border. Moreover, the locations of the actors, at least in this hierarchical imaginary, stem at least partly from the reconfiguration of the coloniser–colonised relationship.

Yet it could equally be argued that the younger actors, particularly in working-class areas (Back, 1996) do not utilise the colonial relationship for interpreting their locations, at least not reflexively. Some questions that require further research are clear: to what extent are younger actors, in comparison to older ones, aware of the colonial past? If the parasol of whiteness shades both villages in middle England and urban estates, then do we need to qualify the salience of the colonial legacy? How does this legacy work exactly, even where we can see it referred to? In the case of Modell's film about Lee-on-Solent (2004), and Tyler's Greenville research, the legacy appears to provide a pool of interpretative frameworks, associations, supposed knowledge of Others, and a blueprint of hierarchy. When this hierarchy appears open to change, anxiety and tension are exhibited.

Conclusion

In this chapter we have argued that white identities involve the construction of contested sets of interlocking values, which neither coincide systematically with skin colour, nor pertain exclusively to all members of a group. In empirical sociological, ethnographic and anthropological fieldwork carried out in Britain, people emerge as more complex than the black–white binary allows for: the white subjects display a range of degrees of critique and reflexivity towards the dominance of whiteness *on an individual basis*. Yet this conclusion in no way disturbs the *structural* domination of whiteness: individuals cannot alter this, but they can and do question and critique it, even if this is a minority position. The unwelcome conclusion that white people are complicit in systemic racism as beneficiaries and contributors appears to cause the avoidance of direct references to this arena, so people end up talking about other areas of identity and/or by expressing this recognition 'very neutrally, so that the agency of people practising discrimination is lost' (Lewis and Ramazanoglu, 1999: 33). Is this really unconscious, or an effect of power?

Whiteness is emphatically not an ethnicity or identity like any other: it is the dominant normalised racialised location in British society. White people's lack of awareness and evasion of discussions of their 'racedness' demonstrate the over-riding potency of this location. Themes identified are invisibility, norms, loss and empire, contingent hierarchies and cultural capital, with terror an underplayed theme vis-à-vis the US literature. The common themes of invisibility/visibility, cultural capital and contingent hierarchies are expressed in local accents, while the major basis of difference is the discursive focus on affirmative action (in the USA), and the context of welfare, empire and re-evaluation of Britishness (in the UK).

It is clear that the research focus has so far been primarily on young, mainly working-class people, principally men in urban England. More studies of middle-class subjects and/or women, outside England and/or in rural settings, would be welcome additions to this corpus, while the theme of empire is clearly a vernacular seam to be explored in future work. Our study focuses accordingly on both middle- and working-class respondents (with a gender balance in the sample) in two English provincial cities.

4

BRITISHNESS

Among the questions we asked our interviewees in 2005–6 was what being British meant to them. Their responses reflect the precise historical moment in which this project took place: the end of the first decade of devolution, the recent 9/11 and 7/7 attacks and bombings, an intense focus on asylum and immigration, and an attempt to reinstate Britishness as an explicit point of collective identification. Starting by outlining some of the theories of national belonging, we will go on to present and analyse responses picked up in our fieldwork. We argue that the way identification is performed suggests that people are evacuating from the space of Britishness to that of Englishness, and that this discursive switch is in part racialised. The way this functions can be seen in the ways people talk about immigration and perceived threats to national identity.

Context

Leading on from the previous chapter, we explore the way in which using whiteness as a lens for understanding the construction of identity enables us to link discourses about belonging to various communities: local, regional, racialised, national, etc. The ideas of racial inferiority and superiority that were prevalent in public discourse prior to the late 1970s have been reconfigured. Ideas about difference are now voiced in complex combinations of adherence to values, expressions of culture and entitlement to resources, which are all linked to origins, residence and integration (Barker, 1981; Taguieff, 2001). Broadly the same constructions also serve to identify particular groups of white Others such as

Irish Catholics, Travellers, Jews and 'Chavs' within the nation at various moments (Kushner, 2005; Garner, 2007; Tyler, 2008). One important function of these discourses is to constantly reformulate and justify boundaries separating the national 'we' from the foreign and/or abject 'they'.

In recent years, a series of opinion polls and qualitative surveys have demonstrated a more hostile turn in British public responses to immigration and asylum (MORI, 2003; YouGov, 2003, 2004, 2007; Lewis, 2005; CRE, 2007). Our project was aimed partly at exploring the why and the how in this equation. Why are attitudes to minorities becoming more hostile, and how are they articulated outside the confines of opinion polling, which produces particular types of response to usually very direct questions?

Our work took place against a backdrop of a process by which social class has been largely evacuated from British public culture (Skeggs, 2005). The erasure of explicit reference to class includes an aspect of culturally pathologising working-class behaviour on a number of fronts (including its putative propensity for racism). This can range from the televisual confrontation of good (middle-class) with bad (working-class) models of personhood in reality television shows (Skeggs and Wood, 2008), to the othering of white working-class students as less valuable agents of capital vis-à-vis Black and Asian Minority Ethnic (BAME) children in school selection (Reay et al., 2007), and the development of the figure of the 'Chav' (Haywood and Yar, 2005; Tyler, 2008), through which contemporary anxieties about disorder are focused on white working-class bodies. Indeed, the trailer for the BBC's March 2008 season of films entitled 'White', showed social anxieties literally being inscribed on a man's face, until the face was obliterated by the names of social issues. The films showed exclusively working-class people, as if there is no need to examine middle-class attitudes, or that integration only happens and should happen only in specific residential areas. In our study, however, there is a much more nuanced picture of the role class plays in attitudes towards immigrants, immigration and Britishness. There is a large area of overlap in concerns that both working- and middle-class interviewees talked about in relation to immigration, and the differences are more about the framing of perceived competition as a more or less abstract experience, depending on social location. As we give the class position of the respondents along with their quotes, this overlap will become clearer over the next two chapters.

The Nation and the Nation-State

The nation is both a territory – a special space protected and managed by a state – and a people who owe solidarity to each other and allegiance to that state. Thus, blood (genealogy) and soil (territory) combine to make nationals who 'belong' in that place, to that group. Being part of a nation necessitates a collective act of imagination and emotional investments in belonging. People construct nation-states. They are not natural units. Etienne Balibar argues that the link between 'race and nation' is actively made by the state (Balibar, 1991a). Nations are constructed as 'natural' entities, as we have seen above, in which the human race can be broken down into homogeneous groups. Through its institutions, particularly the legal and education systems, the state 'produces' both 'nationals' and 'non-nationals'. This happens by socialising them into the idea that people in a given nation are intrinsically different from those of other nations, and that any internal divisions are less important than this principal one. This idea is approached from a different direction by social psychologist Michael Billig (1995), who argues that nationalism is not all about wars and flag-waving, but also the innumerable ways in which the idea of belonging to the nation-state is transmitted and picked up by the nation's population on a daily basis through maps, oaths, school curricula, language, official procedures, the use of 'we' to talk about the nation, etc. He terms this 'banal nationalism'. What both he and Balibar underline is that nations are necessarily *exclusive*, established as they are in permanent opposition to all other nations, an ongoing process of othering that functions differently in specific economic contexts, hence the term 'crisis racism' (Balibar, 1991b: 219) for example, to cover what is referred to elsewhere (Barker, 1981) as the 'new racism', emerging from the period of de-industrialisation following waves of developing-world post-colonial migration to Europe.

Ours was primarily a qualitative interviewing project, and we want to focus on what people themselves said about being British rather than forensically examine theoretical takes on nationalism and Britishness.[1]

Persuading people that they legitimately belong to a community so large that they will never know all its other members, but to which most have a strong allegiance, and for which many are prepared to die, necessitates a potent set of emotional investments. The language of the *nation* is all about this emotional response, whereas that of the *state* is more about rationality and interests. Using the language of essences and the natural world to understand the social world are key elements of 'race', and we find them all in the discourse on the nation. The language of nation is permeated with references to communities and kinship, bloodlines, sameness and purity. The nation is an implicit presence in how we frame our talk about identity and social problems, for example. Using 'we' and 'our' to talk about teams, problems, solutions, history, etc., locates the interlocutors as participants in the construction of bonds with people alive, dead and unborn. From this perspective, we have a series of undeniable bonds with the other members of the nation, as an extended family, with whom we face other nations, equally constituted, in the global competition of nation-states. As part of that bond we owe allegiance to the state, which 'protects' borders against incomers, and provides us with signs and symbols of membership, such as passports, currency and tax returns.

The New 'Britishness' Project

In 2004, a year to the day before the London bombings, the then Chancellor Gordon Brown gave the British Council's annual lecture (Brown, 2004). In it he attempted to put forward a vision of a Britishness based on shared civic values rather than ethnicity (we read this as 'race' as well as ethnicity, as in the Census categories), in a project aimed at winning back Britishness from the right, and restoring cohesion to a social arena understood to be divided by class, ethnicity and religion. The principal values he outlined were liberty, duty and a commitment to tolerance. Brown pursued the theme throughout early 2005, declaring on BBC's *Newsnight* in March that Britishness needed to be redefined in a positive way (Kearney, 2005). In a speech on the same day, the then Home Secretary David Blunkett launched an initiative to revive the concept of Englishness (IPPR, 2005). The Commission for Racial Equality (CRE) also commissioned a major piece of focus group-based research into Britishness in 2005 (CRE, 2005) and a major conference on Britishness, attended by leading politicians, was held by the British Political Studies Association in November 2005. Months after the outcry at the so-called failure of multiculturalism that had followed the London bombings (Mirza et al., 2005: 43–9; Modood, 2005), the project had become imbued with a different level of urgency. With multiculturalism withering in the public discourse, Gordon Brown gave a keynote speech at the Fabian Society's 'Future of Britishness' conference in January 2006. While there seemed to be a critical mass of interest in Britishness, it should not be forgotten that as long ago as 2000, the then Prime Minister, Tony Blair, had put forward his vision of the values holding the country together:

> Qualities of creativity built on tolerance, openness and adaptability, work and self improvement, strong communities and families and fair play, rights and responsibilities and an outward looking approach to the world that all flow from our unique island geography and history. (BBC News, 2000)

This moment of interrogation of the meaning of these national identities is not a coincidental one. Devolution for Scotland and Wales had completed part of what Tom Nairn (2003 [1977]) had predicted as 'the break-up of Britain'. The huge protests against the Iraq war, the trauma of 7/7, the 'war on terror' and the electoral revival of the British National Party had altered Britain's view of itself. It is perhaps unsurprising that intellectuals should pose these kinds of questions at these kinds of moments. It is also unsurprising that political leaders might be attracted by an overarching master vision of solidarity in the face of so many potentially destabilising forces. The values that the various commentators put forward are so many and the overlap so nebulous (tolerance, hard work, decency) that there is nothing specifically British about them.[2] These are surely universal: you can hear a similar discourse in any country. Does any nation define itself by intolerance, laziness and unethical behaviour?

In the next two chapters, two main problems with the Britishness project emerge. One is that the assumption of cohesion among the white UK portion of the population over Britishness is questionable. In other words, it does not correspond to the ways in which people actually identify themselves on the ground. The second is the redrawing of history that such a rapid treatment requires. This necessarily leads to important elements being omitted. What is glossed over in Brown's (2004) version and some later ones is extraordinary: Britain had no revolution, and abolished slavery. The former is not true, and the second misses out the two and a half centuries of sustained British involvement in the slave trade that preceded abolition. How such omissions feed into the way people talk about Britishness is alluded to here and explored in greater detail in the next chapter. We begin however, with the positive response towards being British.

Britishness as Positive

The paradox of the New Labour 'Britishness' project is that it seems to be focused on the wrong ethnic groups. Stone and Muir's study for the IPPR (2007) found that 52 per cent of minorities identify with being British compared to only 29 per cent of white UK nationals, who prefer their constituent nations as primary points of identification. Moreover, in the 2001 Census, people ticking the box 'Bangladeshi' were the ethnic group most likely to say that they identified with the label 'British' (more than 80 per cent). This trend of white dis-identification was commented on by Heath (2005) in relation to Scottish and Welsh identities, but at that point, the attachment to Britishness among English respondents appeared to be holding up.

However, our survey seems to indicate at the least, a growth of ambivalence toward Britishness among our English cohort since the Census. However, we shall begin this review of the responses with a methodological and substantive point about another response to our probing on Britishness that we had not predicted: indifference.

Our methodology involved reflection on our methods as an intrinsic part of our work. Team meetings discussed issues arising as well as findings. One of the early points of concern was the type of flat response we were getting to the original question: 'What does being British mean to you?' It became clear early on that this was a difficult question to answer. But why it was difficult is more interesting. It seemed to be a question that few of our interviewees had given much thought to, which in turn produced the response that Britishness did not mean much. Fenton (2007), whose study was more or less contemporaneous with ours, argues that indifference and even hostility towards identification with the nation casts doubts on the assumption that national identity is a normative component of modernity. Like Condor (2000), he sees some thematic equivalence in the distancing from nationalism observed in his interviews, and self-distancing from racism. His study focused on young adults, whereas ours was more demographically weighted to the middle-aged. Condor writes of one of her respondents, taken as illustrative, that 'her concern appears to be focused on the possibility that to be heard to speak about what is "different about this country" might automatically stigmatize her as prejudiced' (2000: 183). Strategies for avoiding potential accusations of racism involved 'relaying', that is, restructuring the answers so that they represent what an outsider might see (2000: 185). Indeed, the relationship between respondents and the nation emerged as thorny and problematic. There was an overall disavowal of national identity (2000: 186–7). We found that the identifications with Britishness focused on a mixture of institutions, legacies and perceived characteristics, all underpinned by ambivalence about the perceived discrepancy between the more glorious past and the tricky present. The foci for *feeling* British (our revised question) emerged as moments of national danger, or the rare sporting successes:

Q   Can you think of times or events when you've felt more British or English than you normally do?

A   Yeah, it's a good question. Well, I did enjoy winning the Ashes last year [2005], I thought that was good. I thought it was about time we did something for the cricket pitch for a change and I think sport is probably mainly the area when one becomes conscious of it. There's something about the way we operate with our law, there's something about the judicial system that feels particularly British to me, maybe even English. You know, like when I hear the way certain things are handled overseas, like in some of these countries, you think thank God we've got the kind of system we've got. (Tom)

Tom's stress on law and order is picked up by Les (50s, Bristol, wc):

Q   What pleases you in Britain?

A   … You've still got your freedom of speech, still in most cases you've got freedom to demonstrate … You can voice your opinion. If you don't like the government, you can still vote against them, whereas in, say, 80 per cent of the world, you can't do that sort of thing. There's votes and you've only got one person to vote for, things like that. And then they say that's rigged … People don't realise just how much we are free, is the word I suppose.

We suggest that imagined freedom to move around in space is one of the constituents of McIntosh's (1988) 'knapsack' of white privileges. Non-white respondents (Watt and Stenson, 1998) seem to have an awareness of dangerous racialised space that is to be avoided. However, this central theme of freedom/democracy is the one cementing diverse lists of what is good and bad about being British. An ambivalence about the positive elements of free society versus the recognition that other things were changing negatively permeates the answers of our sample group. One of the methodological advantages of our open-ended questioning is that it allows the respondents to associate the elements of what they think is important in a way that is impossible in opinion polling, and even in more structured interviewing. The question on Britishness in the next case triggers an exemplary confusion of positive and negative:

Q   What does it mean to be British?

A   Years ago, everyone used to be proud to be British, but I don't know about so much now [...] It's something that you don't sort of like think about, but when you get all the politics and everything on there now, you're thinking ... in a way you are proud to be British, in another you're thinking, no, no, I need to get away. There's nothing left here now. Everyone's coming in, not that I've got anything wrong with asylum seekers and immigration, nothing like that, I've not got a problem with it, but they're coming in and trying to dictate what we should and shouldn't do, like religion in schools and Christmas and you know, I think, was it a while ago that they weren't allowed to put, not putting decorations in one part of it because that upsets Muslims or whoever it is, I don't know. And I think that's so wrong. I think if they come here, they should adapt to our way of life, you know [...] being British, yeah, okay, but I don't think it's something it's something you're so proud of as what you used to be. (Les, 50s, Bristol, wc)

So for this person, Britishness is intimately connected to the cultural battlefield we shall examine more closely in the next chapter, 'national culture' in post-colonial Britain. However, we might suggest that one element that does recur in positive accounts is democratic openness. Adam (20s, Bristol, wc) answers the question about what he likes about Britain:

Things like the fact that we still have a national health service, that our police still remain unarmed and despite all the criticisms of the law system and the police system, it seems to work most of the time, the fact that we are still reasonably democratic compared to a lot of other countries anyway.

Like most of the responses we got, they can be placed on a continuum rather than distinctly and neatly categorised. The national character was infrequently referred to in general, but in Fiona's (50s, Plymouth, mc) account it is the major element:

I'm proud of the, if there is such a thing as a national character, I'm proud of my Britishness in that I think that British people tend to be caring, compassionate, traditionally, you know, when there's a disaster, the British are very often the first on the scene. They're very generous and they're giving, that kind of thing, I'm proud of it from that point of view. I'm ashamed of some of the things that some of my ancestors did in the past in terms of exploitation and colonisation and so on. But I think I'm proud of the British characteristic in our, there is the sort of almost caricature of the British bulldog, you know, quite stiff upper lip and determination and the eccentricity of the British race, all those kinds of things.

Fiona's line is drawn from a vision of the national community that imputes a distinct set of characteristics to each nation. This is indicated in the work of theorists referred to at the beginning of the chapter. The idea can be deployed to galvanise a nationalist movement or fuel nationalist sentiment, as well as to bolster, in a 'banal' way, a sense of national identity. The most positive end of the spectrum is represented by retired businessman, Mike:

I'm very proud to be British. I have no hang ups at all about being British. I have no hang ups about empire, about Britain's past. I have very few hang ups about Britain at all, about British history or about being British ... yes, I'm proud to be British. I'm fairly patriotic.

Note how Mike pre-empts the issue of Britain's imperial legacy being something that one should be at least ambivalent about. This legacy is a more or less tangible presence in many people's thoughts about Britishness. That will be explored more in the following chapter. However, Britain's historical role is one of the poles of discourse about being British, alongside democracy, legal system, defence of values. The values seem, by default, to be to do with the expression of a secular/Christian culture.

Britishness as Negative

Kiely et al. (2005) show a diversity of ways in which Britishness is constructed contingent on place, time and context: in their case, twenty-first century Scotland. This basic point is also illuminated in Jacobson's (1997) and Hussain and Bagguley's (2005) interviews with British Pakistanis for example. Whatever Britishness means, it does not mean the same thing to everyone. Indeed, the interviews with British Pakistanis reveal many of the younger people resentful at their exclusion from this category in terms of their experiences of civil society rather than indifferent to being British. While it seems to represent a source of as yet unattainable formal equality for minorities, Britishness is subject to a number of negative discursive probes by our white UK respondents. Our fieldwork indicates some of the constructions placed upon it by our white UK (virtually all English) sample in the south west.

> Proud to be British, I suppose, not so much nowadays. I mean, we used to be good at things, we used to make the best films, we don't do that anymore because the Americans do all that, they got the money for that. Our little Ealing Studios and things like that don't seem to work so good no more. We used to have the best film starts, comedy people ... They're all dying off. (Les, 50s, Bristol, wc)

The recognition of lessening, worsening experiences may be part of what Back (1996) refers to as the construction of a nostalgic 'golden age', in which everything was better than it is now, especially for older respondents. However, even when people begin to talk about what they like about Britain, the dialogue soon slips to what they don't like, and the explicit comparison with the past. Within a couple of sentences, Jacqueline has intertwined the positive with the negative in this way:

> I am very happy that we have a monarchy in this country. I like all the trappings that go with the ceremonial, I suppose. [...] What else is British? I don't know, because it has all got watered down rather a lot. [...] I'm thinking of my own and others growing up, children in the school where I am. Security has gone. In some ways, that's right, because things should be fair for all, and for people who haven't been in the country, well, who've been here one or two generations, three perhaps, it's right that it becomes fair for all, I would feel.

Again, the association between Britishness, fairness and immigration is made, although at this point in the interview, the term 'immigration' has not been introduced by the interviewer. Britishness moves people to an evaluation of advantages and disadvantages. One option many took was to shift towards Englishness.

Englishness as More Meaningful Than Britishness

> Q   Just taking the whole theme of identity – you're British, aren't you?
>
> A   English, actually, sorry.
>
> Q   That's okay. Do you make a distinction between being British and English?
>
> A   I do, I do now for the first time in all these years, yes I do.
>
> Q   You are saying for the first time. Why?
>
> A   Because I am just, well, this is going to sound really racist now, I am just fed up with all the British that aren't, you know, the non-British that are now British, and I just think that in so many years time, the English, we're just going to be the minority. I think the government should have put a stop on how many foreigners they were letting in. (Denise, 30s, Plymouth, mc)

This vision of drowning under the weight of larger numbers of immigrants is a trope that goes back at least to the Book of Exodus. What is interesting for us is the interplay between Britishness and Englishness as spaces that offer different resources for people. Sally (40s, Plymouth, wc) answers 'I'm English', to the question, 'What does it mean to you to be British?':

> Q   Do you make a distinction between the two?
>
> A   Yes, I do, because not to be politically correct, I get really, not annoyed, that's the wrong word. British can be so many different things now. I'm English, and I want that put down that I'm English. That sounds like I've got a racist problem, but it isn't. I just think we're all entitled to our own individuality. People who come to this country, they want to keep their individuality. Well, I actually come from this country originally and I'm English and I want them to know, whether that's because it's on forms now, you have to state, and British can be so many. But maybe it does matter to me, it's almost like saying I'm white and I was born here, isn't it, but I don't intentionally think of it. I just think of it as I'm English.

This ambivalence towards the diversity and inclusiveness associated with 'British', and the notion of exclusivity linked to

'English' was a common thread across classes and genders. They even link people who are generally more critical about the class and racial domination to others who are more favourable to nationalism and less open to immigrants. 'Tom' is a community activist who has worked on working-class estates for much of his life. We shall hear more from him later, but his response to the question on Britishness is very revealing:

> A   Oh, no, I'm okay about being British. I kind of have this secret hankering to be English [*laughing*].
> Q   Tell me about that.
> A   Well, I don't know what there is to say about it really. It just feels right to me.

'There seems to be quite a strong Welsh and a strong Scottish and Irish identity', he remarks, 'and I'm kind of a bit jealous of it really'.

> Q   What aspects are you jealous of?
> A   [*Hesitates*] I don't know, I haven't thought that out enough, but it just feels like to be able to say you're Scots or you're Welsh or something is something that's stronger to me than saying you're English.

Others noted that to emphasise their Englishness could be constructed as jingoistic, even extreme, with associations of far-right parties.

In general then, there seems to be a preference for developing Englishness as a point of reference as opposed to the more formally understood Britishness. This is tied to a sense of identity injustice and deficit compared to other more 'identity privileged' groups, which of course includes the 'culture-rich' Scots, Welsh, Irish and BAME. The problematic nature of identifications with Britain, because of the perceived relative identity deficit vis-à-vis the Celtic nations, is often expressed as a cry of frustration and inequality.

Perhaps this sense that English culture is somehow 'weak' drives the feeling some people have that it is being over-ridden. Denise again:

> I think that, you know, we should allow for different religions, but not when their religion takes precedence over ours, because we certainly can't go to a Muslim country and have the same rights. And to call, I think, was it in Leicester, I'm not sure, the Christmas lights winter lights because of an offence, see, and it's that that's becoming really annoying to most people that I have spoken to lately anyway. I think it's just that enough is enough now.

The ever-present external force of 'political correctness' is used as a shorthand to articulate a variety of English anxieties about losing ground, both economically and culturally, vis-à-vis other groups. The retreat into Englishness and the repeated reference, even by secular people, to Christmas as a festival that has to be defended, cropped up in the narration of distinctions between the majority and minority communities. Indeed, the passage of time for those older respondents revealed a pattern of decreasing purchase on the idea of Britishness. As Les makes clear:

> You can't be as British as you used to be. Going back to the thing that people are just for themselves now, what I want, number one and that's it, people don't seem to want to put in and be a community [...] If one person stops flying the flag, no one else sort of flies the flag.

He recalled that when he was little, most churches and buildings had a Union Jack or the cross of St George, or if it was the Queen's birthday, 'we'd have a fair few flags, or anything like that. But now they don't have flagpoles on buildings no more, I don't think, not even school buildings or anything. I mean, if we put a flagpole up here and put a flag up, there'd be an outcry I should imagine, spoiling the view or something like that ... You can't go on about it like you used to, people say you can't do that and you can't do that'.

As frequently observed in our interviews, the associations lead from Britishness to manifestations of negative change, into un-Britishness, if you like. Later in the same conversation, Les argues that 'you should still be able to say Christmas and send Christmas cards with the theme on them of the manger and things like that, but a lot of people have stopped doing this'.

Q   Have you experienced that yourself?

A   No, it's only I read in the paper and things like that ... Down the schools, the kids don't have school Christmas plays like they did, say, only six years ago ... They don't seem to do that anymore. It's all multicultural sort of things.

Q   How do you feel about that?

A   What I don't like that is some of the lessons they have ... They don't learn about David and Goliath or anything like that like we used to at school; they're doing about Judaism, and something like that. And I think, what's this? And they say, oh we've got to do that. And there's a bloke with 15 arms, summat like that, like a Buddha, things like that.[3]

Les's concern that children should be taught the kinds of things he learned at school is another indicator of how Britain is slipping away from the English – understood in this way that sees cultural change as subtracting from national identity rather than altering it benignly.

Beleaguered Englishness

The way in which Britishness is evoked by our interviewees is paradoxical. On one hand there are few accounts of substantive Britishness (giving the world the English language, wartime resilience, independence), but a strong narrative of whatever it did mean having been weakened in the post-war period. Britishness seems to be defined more by what it is not.

People generally agreed that it was not something they had thought much about, apart from at very significant moments of national history, such as during World War II, or in the days following the 2005 London bombings, or when they were abroad and had to define themselves nationally. Yet there was more identification at sporting events (the Olympics, football, rugby, cricket) at which point the locus was Englishness rather than Britishness. Several expressed embarrassment about the behaviour of British people abroad and anti-social behaviour at home, but more interestingly, about the historical legacy of empire. This haunts people's statements about the desire for a more tangible and substantial Englishness in the face of the 'dilution' of Britishness. Martin (60s, Bristol, mc) has adopted a long view:

> I think English is somewhat purer or somewhat filtered, I suppose ... I would say that English goes back to, you know, Norman times, whereas British might be a British subject from the Caribbean or the Far East or whatever. One is not making racist judgements. One is merely saying that English has a longer history in this island that British does. [...] Yeah, I just feel that English is somewhat older and somewhat purer and somewhat more filtered.

It is not merely that English has a genealogy distinct from the Scots and Welsh, but that the latter are perceived as being free to celebrate their distinctiveness in a way that the English are not. 'I think of myself as English', says Stella (40s, Plymouth, mc), 'mainly because I get very annoyed when you get Welsh people and Scottish people who seem to be allowed to celebrate their identity and in fact it's praised, it's praised the fact that they're proud of being Welsh and proud of being Scottish, but you say you're proud of being English, and kind of almost BNP connotations to say you're proud of being English, which annoys me, because you should be able to say that'.

Indeed, in post-devolution Britain, the celebrations of Welshness, Scottishness and Irishness are viewed enviously by many who feel caught between the acknowledgement that the St George's Cross and the Union Jack have become symbols linked to the political right, and the perceived 'political correctness' that involves not celebrating Britain and England's imperial past for fear of offence. It is interesting that much of the anger expressed about 'pc' derived from the administrative banality of filling in forms and not having anywhere to stipulate an English identity. Denise angrily recounts the story of how her son had brought a form home from school:

> some census that they're doing and it had every nationality, every denominal [sic] mixture, anything that you could possibly think of, except English. And I just think, the Scots can be Scottish, the Welsh, you know, they're Welsh,

but we have to be British [...] I had never bothered about it before, but I am bothering about it now.

She is not the only one bothered. Les is vehement that: 'you're not allowed to be English. You got to say you're British or white British or black British or Irish. [...] Every form you fill in ... there's no English, it's British, British'.

There is a definite sense that you have to resist to be English and be like the other constituent nations, perceived as having fun and, to use Žižek, stealing the 'enjoyment' of the English (Žižek, 1993). The imagined act of stealing pleasure, attributed to some group against whom the national 'we' can be defined, is painful because it underscores the impossibility of actually attaining that pleasure oneself. In the act of stealing enjoyment, the 'thieves' become unlike 'us' and the objects of jealousy. 'My old Dad', says Les, 'still crosses out summat and he put English. But you can't do that, they just send the form back. [...] But sometimes you got to stand up yourself: like St Georges Day is meant to be an English day, St David's Day, St Patrick's Day, St Andrew's Day – you all have your own days. But your Scots celebrate St Andrew's Day, your Welsh go overboard on St David's Day, your Irish actually have a week off for St Patrick's Day. And then St George's Day ... It's not flags out, national holiday sort of thing'.

Yet even this is open to different configurations of interpretation. Mark (40s, Plymouth, wc) had noticed at work that there was no 'English' under the ethnicities code that they use. Most people, he says:

don't like the idea of having it said that they're just British ... You have to be very careful because there is a fine line between national pride for the history and all of the wonderful things, and that next little step people take and become nationalistic and quite insular. And as far as I'm concerned, that couldn't be further from the truth. I like the whole idea of being able to be English within Europe.

However, this is a distinctly minority viewpoint. Stella's (50s, Plymouth, mc) more representative response reveals the identity deficit/identity envy expressed in terms of unfairness. This leads us to the place in which our diverse group's emotional identities were focused.

Q   Some people have told us they think Britain is losing its identity. How do you feel about that?

A   I think it's possibly a strong way of putting it maybe, but I mean, there's been a lot of talk among my colleagues at work recently when you've got these Muslim councillors who have started to say we'll cancel Christmas in this borough and we don't have Christmas and you can't have Christmas lights and things like that, and people were sort of saying, we're losing our identity as a country because of this. And I think nobody's got any problem with freedom of speech, freedom of worship, human rights of anybody who comes to this country, but, you know, I do feel that we should be able to celebrate Christmas or whatever it might happen to be in our own way and not feel that we have to not do that in case we upset someone else.

The ubiquity of the 'banning Christmas' theme is a remarkable element of our fieldwork, as the actual incident that generates it may be apocryphal: a number of sources are cited for doing away with Christmas cards, or banning the term 'Christmas' or holding nativity plays, yet they seem not to correspond to anything that has actually happened (Burkeman, 2006). It is a religious and secular festival that seems to occupy a space on the other side of what is open for debate. Its function is to define the zenith of irrationality (banning something so normal and natural), and to assert that Britishness is only flexible up to a certain point. Some institutions and elements of national life cannot ever be challenged. Yet the fact that it is not actually challenged means that talk of losing Christmas becomes a mythical point of no surrender, a kind of thin-end-of-the-wedge logic that suggests in an apocalyptic moment that Britain's Judeo-Christian basis will be erased by something else. Is the banning Christmas discourse a surrogate, like many of these other resource-based discourses, for a wide-ranging set of grievances, impotences, frustrations and perceived injustices that cannot be compellingly articulated in another way? The most common picture to emerge from our question about Britishness was of a beleaguered Englishness, which has a problematic colonialist dimension triggering defensive responses. The annoyance, frustration and sense that the celebration of Englishness is judged according to different criteria permeate the interviews. There is a real sense that being English is a social location of relative weakness that now has to be defended. The idea of defence is nowhere clearer than in discourse about immigration.

Immigration: Crisis and Productivity

In answering the question 'what is your opinion on immigration', the notion of 'control' was important in many responses. Yet the discursive construct 'immigration' appears emblematic of a variety of problems to do with a downward spiral in behaviour and living conditions in Britain whose relationship to immigration was not made explicit. Liz (30s, Bristol, mc) summarises this:

> there is an element of me that thinks you have to kind of get your own place in order to a degree before you can expand and start sort of allowing huge numbers coming in. You know, we've got huge homeless numbers and those kind things, well, they're quite distressing really, aren't they?

Or more broadly, the idea was frequently floated that everything had been going downhill for decades. While the topic of immigration was sometimes referenced with numbers and skills, there was also an appreciation of it as a historical phenomenon, and interestingly, the moment at which immigration became a 'problem' *per se*, was identified:

> And when you think of all the people who have come from the Caribbean and India ..., we couldn't actually have survived. Like the 1950s, they came over and were all bus drivers and all sorts of things, because the English people, there weren't enough for them to do it, etc. ... But I suppose, what did upset me really was when the tide seemed to turn a bit, when we got all those people trying to get through like the Channel Tunnel and things like that. I think it was when there was loss of control of it. I think it was the government I didn't have faith in because they didn't have the right facilities, the right training and the right finances and things [...] so it seemed to go out of control. (Katherine, 60s, Bristol, mc)

The historical record shows that things did not go smoothly for immigrants trying to integrate into local economies and other institutional structures prior to the turning of the tide referred to above (Rex and Moore, 1967; Fryer, 1984). Moreover, the period prior to the 1990s is viewed as one in which immigration served a specific (i.e. productive and economic) function, while the iconic images of people climbing onto the Eurostar train as it leaves France for Britain were mentioned by a number of respondents. The context into which immigrants now arrive is viewed as qualitatively different from that of the post-war period. The Channel Tunnel immigrants emerge into Britain bringing chaos, over-burdening both the welfare state and the physical space of Britain itself.

There is no absolute consensus on immigration among our sample, rather a spectrum ranging from those who think there has been too much immigration, at one end, to some critical voices who question the parameters of the discussion at the other. However, the majority position is qualified acceptance of immigration and immigrants.[4] The qualifications are to do with productivity (allied with no claims being made on the welfare state without contributions), and making an effort to integrate.

Indeed, a striking element of the general talk of immigration is its 'scripted' (i.e. routine) nature (Edwards, 2003): respondents preface their comments with ritualistic references to an immigrant's duty to contribute (add value), and to finite resources (evoked explicitly as spatial, economic, etc.), which are threatened by uncontrolled immigration. Even Kerry (30s, Bristol, mc), who is admirably uninterested in the topic, says of immigration: 'It's not something I feel especially strongly about ... what's the problem if they have something to contribute? The amount of political hoo-hah over it seems daft'.

It is a big 'if' expanded upon by many other interviewees. However, a more representative comment is the following, linking recognition of migration as a way of improving life chances, and tolerance contingent upon a foundational quid pro quo:

> If people want to come and live here, then they want to live here because they like the British way of life, the democracy, and they do want to integrate. I mean you can't blame people wanting to come from a really, really poor, poor country, just wanting to come for a better way of life for themselves and their families, but I think they have to feel that they can give something back as well, not just take. (Sue, 60s, Bristol, mc)

The anxiety evinced by unspecified numbers of people accessing services often leads people to retreat into rationalisations of welfare finance, summed up by Martin: 'Resources are finite, so one has to be very careful'. Liz, again, is concise:

> Potentially I think it [immigration] is a huge problem, mainly down to what I kind of call realistic issues surrounding numbers in hospitals, numbers in schools, you know, job situations, so you know, more from a pure practical reason ... you know, the more and more people we allow into the country, clearly you don't need to be a rocket scientist to understand that it's going to have some potential issues.

Like Liz, most people placed a premium on productive immigration as the key justificatory criterion. While images of inundation and overwhelming numbers seem to generate the logic of 'added value', it also leads others to perceive crisis point as more imminent:

> Q   What are your views now about immigration?
> A   The population density in this country is only exceeded by Holland. I think I'm right in saying that ... Yeah, asylum seekers in genuine need, need assistance, but economic migrants do not. Our hospital services are under enormous pressure, our education provision is under enormous pressure, our social services are under enormous pressure. I don't really see that we can put them under more and more and more pressure just for egalitarian ideals. Yeah, I mean immigration should be very, very carefully restricted. (Martin)

Not only is the focus on productive immigrants, but there is a suggestion that national interests might be better served by reconfiguring priorities in terms of the right of immigrants to come to Britain at all. It is worth pointing out that both Martin and Liz live in our middle-class Bristol neighbourhood. Their take on resources being threatened is shared by our working-class respondents, but their focus is on specific stories of how things relate to them:

Adam (20s, Bristol, wc) is feeling resentful about what he sees as immigrants' 'leapfrogging' of nationals in the queues for social housing:

> if I wanted to go out and get a house or get a flat, I would be put further down the list for someone that is not a British citizen to say, someone that has come over into the country, they get everything handed to them and it's people that have been living in this country since they were born that are not getting the same benefits as other people in this country. I could understand with pregnant women and with couples, but I can't understand with people that have hardly been in the country and they are getting more rights than what we are. As I say, I don't want to go too into it. But you know I look at it like that.

Throughout the second interview Jake had stated that he did not want to talk about the issue, but ended up returning to it, particularly in relation to the unfairness of access to resources. He finally repeats himself in an intense response to a question on what picture he has in his mind of an immigrant.

> Q   What picture comes to your mind if I say the word immigrant?
> A   Someone that's come over to the country and is living in our country.
> Q   Do you have a picture?
> A   I don't know ... when I think of immigrants ... I think of just someone that's come into the country, that's obviously not allowed to come into the country but they're living like what we are. That is what I think and what I see. And I think it's unfair on British citizens, established British citizens, do you know what I mean. It's not fair, it's not fair at all, just don't like it.

Helen (50s, Plymouth, wc) continues the theme of unfairness, this time when asked what 'displeases her about Britain':

> I don't like all the immigrants coming to this country. And you're in the Post Office waiting for your pension which you've worked for. And you're standing there, and immigrants come in, go to another counter and they're seen right away, and you're standing in a big queue, and you're feeling tired

and that and then you see other people getting better treatment than what you are because you've still got to wait. And when these people come into the country, I think they that they should be tested in some way to see that they really need to come to this country because they're having all the things that we've worked for, especially housing. You go in a lot of places in Devon and Cornwall and the people are crying out for houses and their children have got to move away because they just can't afford it. And then they get a load of immigrants come and they're pushed on the scene and they get housing. Well, it's not right.

Such stories of unfairness and leapfrogging pervade the second round of interviews. The advantaged group slips between immigrants, asylum seekers and white welfare claimants. The specific examples given are either first-hand experiences or picked up from the media. Together the narrative patterns comprise what Hewitt (2005) calls a 'counter-narrative', a way of talking about social hierarchies in a way that questions the dominant framework, according to which ethnic minorities are the major victims of discrimination. In the stories we heard, and have continued to hear in other projects since this one (Hoggett et al., 2008; Garner et al., 2009), it is the white working-class who are the major victims. These stories express the conviction that there are not enough resources to go round and that they have a more legitimate claim on them than minority groups. The status of 'immigrant/ asylum seeker' (and people consigned into that status) has come to represent a rival competing with an unfair advantage. While the white working-class have to contribute before they can draw out, runs the argument, and often with complications, immigrants have more rights, go straight to the front of the queue, or in the case of the Post Office above, have their own queue. However, some are aware that there is a layer of historical complexity to the shortages of resources, such as Elaine (30s, wc), a social worker on the estate in Bristol, who says:

We were talking about asylum seekers [...] the misconception that they come straight away and get housing, and that's a very emotive issue. I was talking to an old lady, her grand-daughter can't get on the housing list, because she's working and they're saving up to get married and they're not entitled, and she said, oh, it's because of all these asylum seekers. And I said, actually, it's not, it's because of people like me, people who chose the right to buy and bought their council houses, so the council don't have, they have very little housing stock.

Only two other respondents out of 64 refer to this issue in terms of the housing supply. The view of dwindling resources from the estates may merge with that of residents of the leafier suburbs, but the stories are to do with impotence ('it's not fair and I don't like it'; 'it's just not right') and Denise captures this growing sense of beleagueredness:

And the more you speak to people, the more stories you hear of how, I do think we are penalised in this country, how much more we do to accommodate and yeah, we will lose our identity [...] *they* can have their cake and eat it, I think, but we can't. (speaker's emphasis)

Conclusion

While Britishness can hold more than the sum of its constituent nations, there is an identity deficit within it. The English are increasingly withdrawing from Britishness and doing so largely to occupy a defensive and (in the terms of our methodology), 'defended' space. The normativity and power-holding location that is Britishness may well sometimes inspire indifference, but in our study it generates anguish and frustration. In responses to the question of what Britishness means, our respondents appear to be inverting the dominant constructions. Britishness is in turn irrelevant, positive and negative. Britishness is weak and open to minority occupation in a way that Englishness is not.[5] Englishness is a source of more effective and meaningful identity, and it is the poor relation within the UK. Just as the white working class in the counter-narratives about immigration emerge as the real victims, so do the English emerge as the put upon majority whose culture is not recognised, and whose rights are not equivalent of those of other national groups.

Britain's boundaries are culturally meaningful because their existence draws attention to the history of colonial power within the British Isles that leaves England as the dominant source of Britishness. Within the space of Britishness come people without roots in Englishness (allegedly) so it becomes too diverse a space for some English people to cope with ('non-British that are now British').

The clear twin equivocations, about what the term 'Britishness' actually covers and whether to be proud of Britain, enable us to assert that the very least that can be said is that there are definite policy implications here. Rather than comprising the bedrock of Britishness, the group that is not targeted in the Britishness project (that is, the 90+ per cent who tick the box 'white UK' in the Census) appear profoundly ambivalent about it. In the discourse of the people to whom we spoke, the whiteness of contemporary Englishness is usually implicit: a set of associations about who is entitled to what and why.

There is no consensus on values or norms, and it is also apparent that many associate the contemporary 'immigration-asylum' discourse with a threat to Britishness. Here, paradoxically, Britain cannot be defined except in its threatened state, thus provoking the strategic withdrawal to a less tainted, purer and more defensible space. The conditions for this ideological secession is that England is a beleaguered nation within a larger union. It is under attack (from minorities and the underclass with the aid of the politically correct ruling elites), as in wartime, but without the community spirit. Yet this secession from Britain is also partly an evacuation from the historical legacy, which we shall explore more closely in the next chapter.

5

WHITENESS AND POST-IMPERIAL BRITAIN

It is *assumed* rather than *demonstrated* in some key work in the field of post-colonial studies that British identity is still inflected by the experience of empire in twenty-first century Britain (Knowles, 2003). This also provides the backdrop for the work of critical race theorists such as Paul Gilroy, who grounds *After Empire* (2004) and its inter-related arguments about Britishness, loss, 'conviviality' and 'melancholia' in this idea. What we do in this chapter is look at data from fieldwork on identities in Britain, and advance a tentative argument about the presence of empire in people's construction of identity in post-imperial Britain. This involves understanding the foundations of the discursive strategies used, as much in terms of what is *left out* of accounts as by what is included. While there is relatively little explicit reference to empire, there is plenty of use of historical empire-related argument in narratives.

We also argue that the assumed cultural and racialised hierarchies that emerge from interviews and ethnographies in Britain are anchored in the imperial period and *vicarious* empire experiences. Ideas outlive the structures that generated them, and emerge in messy, non-linear and sometimes contradictory ways.

Of course, the current demography of the UK is clearly influenced by the country's imperial history. The BAME[1] population at the 2001 Census stood at 7.9 per cent non-white, the majority of whom are descended from former imperial subjects, plus the 1 per cent of the population in the white Irish category.

We begin by looking at the idea of 'segregation', which to an extent informed our choice of topic and the geographical location of our fieldwork, before examining how our respondents talked about 'integration'. We then take five individual stories from our participants in the discourse about empire who demonstrate a range of positions, informed by a variety of engagements with empire as a theme in their discussions.

Sleepwalking Into Segregation?

During our fieldwork, the then Director of the Commission for Racial Equality, Trevor Phillips (2005) made a speech in September 2005, a few weeks after the London bombings, in which he argued that Britain was becoming more segregated: 'The fact is that we are a society which, almost without noticing it, is becoming more divided by race and religion'. Particular communities, those of Pakistani and Bangladeshi origins, were becoming more ghettoised than others, he asserted.

> Residentially, some districts are on their way to becoming fully fledged ghettoes – black holes into which no-one goes without fear and trepidation, and from which no-one ever escapes undamaged. The walls are going up around many of our communities.

Phillips leant on a paper given by geographer Mike Poulsen (2005) in which *it was reported that he* claimed[2] that using indices of segregation, Birmingham, Leicester and Oldham had entered the top division of ethnically segregated world cities, joining those in North America such as Miami and Chicago. Phillips later apologised for using the term 'ghettoes' (BBC, 2006). British geographers agree there are no such things as 'ghettoes' in the UK (Peach, 1996; Simpson, 2004; Dwyer and Bressey, 2008).[3] Moreover, Danny Dorling (2005) and Ludi Simpson (2005, 2004) have both rejected the claims of increasing segregation, arguing instead that levels of ethnic segregation are decreasing nationally because minorities are dispersing into previously white areas. These are key claims, because the frequent association made in talk about integration is of minorities self-segregating in 'their own' areas. Moreover, based on the work he did on the 2001 Census (Dorling and Thomas, 2004), Dorling asserts, that: 'We have not been sleepwalking into segregation by race, but towards ever greater segregation by wealth and poverty. That matters most to the life chances of people in Britain' (Dorling, 2005). He argues that the claims of ethnic segregation are thus a red herring, distracting us from the far more compelling data on the geographical patterns and trends of poverty and social class. Simpson claims that the idea of self-segregating Asian populations 'gained the status of a legend' (2004: 677) after the Cantle Report (Cantle, 2001) into the rioting in Bradford, Oldham and Rochdale in 2001. He goes on to remark that: '"Flight" is the term used to describe White movement, while self-segregation is reserved for other groups' (Simpson, 2004: 677). In any case, Johnston and Poulsen (2006) later published a more detailed version of their interpretation of Census data using a different typology from the single-figure segregation index. They argue, in reference to trends in London, that:

> There was thus a process of what we might term 'depolarised segregation' in London between the two censuses. Fewer whites lived in the predominantly white areas in 2001 than 1991, and fewer nonwhites lived in the areas where their own group predominates. Instead, more whites and nonwhites lived in relatively mixed areas. (Johnston and Poulsen, 2006: 2198)

This is more or less what Dorling (2005) and Simpson (2004, 2005) suggest is the case nationally. Moreover, in explicit relation to the Asian groups that are allegedly self-segregating, they also state that in London:

> Members of the various nonwhite ethnic groups especially those claiming South Asian ethnicity are no longer congregating into enclaves which are not only almost exclusively nonwhite but also dominated by their own ethnic group [...]. Instead they are moving into more mixed neighbourhoods, in which whites are, however, a minority. (Johnston and Poulsen, 2006: 2198)

Regardless of the technical arguments about measurement indices, there are also qualitative elements of segregation and integration that cannot be captured by quantitative methodologies. Phillips's study of Bradford (2006) for example demonstrates that there are a set of structural factors heavily influencing British Asians' decisions about where to seek housing in Bradford: affordability, fear of racism, proximity to mosques and families, proximity to places of employment and knowledge of the area, all play a part.

The overall trends show a more qualified pattern than the assumption of 'increasing segregation' that seems to underpin public discourse on integration. We examine this now because it is important to realise that, like much of the talk about immigration and 'race' in Britain, it is not based on empirical evidence but fictions fuelled by imprecise or misleading political discourse and sensationalist and sloppy journalistic practices (Buchanan and Grillo, 2004). In Simpson's 2005 report, he argues that against a long-term trend of diminishing segregation, groups with high segregation indices in 2001 (African-Caribbean, Pakistani and Bangladeshi) are among those dispersing. The various groups' movement patterns are similar – that is, leaving urban areas. There are 118 (1.8 per cent) of the country's 6,500 electoral wards where whites are in a minority, but only 14 wards have a majority of a single ethnic minority group, half of which are Indian. More non-white residents leave areas where whites are a minority than do white residents. White flight is therefore a 'misnomer'. Moreover, even moving to more mixed areas (implicitly seen as a step forward in the discourse on integration/segregation) does not necessarily benefit minority groups: 'male Bangladeshi, Pakistani and Caribbean unemployment is double the White rate in wards with mainly white residents, just as it is in inner city areas' (Simpson, 2005: 7).

However, the vast majority of white UK people still live in wards with fewer than the national average BAME residents. This is demonstrated using the index of isolation (which measures the probability of meeting someone of your own group): whites in the UK score around 95 per cent on that index, while it is below 10 per cent for all the other ethnic groups.

We chose our research sites because they had relatively low BAME populations and the idea was to gauge attitudes in areas that were like the mainstream majority white experience (of relative residential isolation) rather than the more multicultural urban centres (London, Birmingham, Leicester, Manchester, Leeds, Bradford, etc.) where the majority of British sociological fieldwork on 'race' and ethnicity has been carried out. Our project differs in that we were searching specifically for white provincial milieus, something akin to what Bonilla-Silva and Embrick (2007) refer to as the 'white habitus', social and geographical spaces in which minority presence barely registers. These can be conceptualised as the opposite of places in which conviviality is woven (Back, 1996; Gilroy, 2004). In these types of spaces, it is assumed that talk of integration is necessarily of a different order from that in more mixed areas.[4]

Integration

The principal issue here is the perceived distinction between integration and self-segregation, in other words, to what extent should people change when they come to Britain? The most frequent argument in our interviews deploys the 'when-in-Rome' logic, which emerges as a discursive 'commonplace' (Billig, 1991), as well as a clinching argument. First, this sets out a general principle of equality that must be respected. Second, it posits an equivalence between the structural position of Third World migrants in Britain, and British migrants elsewhere, thus glossing over a central part of British experience: colonialism involved *making* other people play by British rules in their own countries. By arguing that the migrants whose culture is seen as causing a problem are on a level playing field with the British, respondents are performing two ideological manoeuvres. First, they are casting the past as finished business that no longer has an impact on the present, in which language should be learned, culture should be embraced, and failure of immigrants to do either of these things had led to the dilution or retreat of British culture. Second, the equivalence erases the power differential, so that white is just another ethnicity rather than the location of dominance for the past 600 years. Here total agency is attributed to the non-integrated communities (named nationally by city, or locally by district), and no consideration is afforded to structural factors. This form of logic sees integration as a set of individual choices, agency and failings, rather than taking into account any systemic discrimination or obstacles placed in the way of it. In its US incarnation, this type of explanation (for racism, poverty and gender inequalities, for example) has been labelled 'power-evasive discourse' (PED) (Frankenberg, 1994). Such discourses, it is argued, have become the hegemonic ones for explaining the social world. These frames are much more freely available to individuals than those involving reference to structural disadvantage. While in the US fieldwork (Lamont, 2000; Lewis, 2003; Bonilla-Silva, 2006) it is minorities who are more likely to hold counter-hegemonic understandings of structural impediments, they are not immune to the prevailing PED. Similarly, very few of our sample saw integration as anything but a simple choice, to be made on an individual basis.

This choice expresses itself in a number of ways, which are often combined in our respondents' stories. One of them is dress codes. While Sam (60s, Bristol, wc) believes foreign dress codes to be understandable and acceptable 'for granny', he cannot see why grandchildren would still want to dress like this (Asian clothing). The theme of cultural distinctiveness is thus central in the responses to questions on immigration.

> Q   What does the word immigrant mean to you?
> A   Not necessarily an ethnic thing. Basically someone from another culture who's come into our culture and who should adapt to our culture [...] If they want to integrate, they have to learn English. The idea of, you know, great swathes of people in Bradford or Southall or Birmingham or Bristol or wherever, not speaking English is absurd, if you're going to have integration. Otherwise, you do have cultural and racial ghettos, which is no good to anybody. (Martin)

Here we can identify a number of strands of discourse. The idea of ethnic being divorced from culture indicates a popular understanding of 'ethnic' as the politically correct word for 'racial'. Second, the monolithic and static model of 'our' culture and the 'we' behind the 'our' alerts us to assumptions about how people live their lives in segregated ways. Third, we have the identification of geography with otherness (here denoted by absence of English language), which actually corresponds to current political discourse on segregation. Lastly, although it is not an 'ethnic thing', Martin was specifically envisaging Asian immigrants. This may be an attempt either to say 'Muslim', or to indicate that the variety of Asian faith communities (evoked by Birmingham, Southall and Bristol) suffers the same problem. Indeed, the language barrier is not seen solely as a sticking point by the 'domestic population'. In the BBC's poll (2005), 82 per cent of non-Muslims and 90 per cent of Muslims stated that command of the English language was vital to integration. As those who do not think it is vital are clearly a small minority there is not necessarily a conflict over this. It is not clear, however, whether this concern is really about language acquisition, or more about perception and imagination, as a proxy for less openly discussable matters. For example, the idea of the cultural ghetto is raised by one respondent:

> And I must admit I don't have much patience with people who choose to come to live in this country and then decide they're going to live in a little self-enforced ghetto where they don't even have to make an effort to learn the language of the country that has accepted them. I think that if you are coming to Britain, then you are part of Britain. And it is no issue whatsoever about keeping your own culture and your own beliefs, but I do think that can be taken rather too far, because you're part of Britain. You have to interact with Britain. But as long as someone is interacting with not just their little local clique, then surely then they're not an immigrant any more ... Having said that, by that logic, somebody who does only interact with their little local clique and doesn't know any English at all and hasn't made any effort to, it doesn't matter if they lived here 30 years, they're still an immigrant. (Kerry)

Integration is still presented as an unhindered choice. The point at which one's own beliefs can be retained and when it is 'taken rather too far' is unclear until the end. There is no place in this account for external hostility to partly explain the 'self-enforced' ghetto (Phillips, 2006), or for comprehension of the relationship between economic hierarchies and access to housing (a relationship that is clearly understood in relation to social housing).

However, it is not simply a case of keeping themselves to themselves, but of imposing their values on the mainstream that provokes anger. Denise refers to Muslims in the context of what she sees as the unfair prioritisation of their needs over those of Christians (she is a churchgoing Christian):

> They have their own mosque inside a factory. Would we have our own little chapel inside a factory so we can pray? As non-Muslim, you wouldn't, though, would you? And you couldn't even get away with demanding it, but they have. Some Muslims in the factory found it offensive that some women in the factory wear T-shirts, because they were exposed, but if they don't like it […] go back to where it is not bloomin' offensive.

Although much of the discussion is to do with cultural difference, there are occasional shifts into the territory of the body. Ray's (40s, Bristol, mc) vivid account of his trips to London, like Elsie's trip through London in chapter 3, brings in some additional perspectives.

> Q   If I say the word immigrant, what picture does it conjure up?
> A   Oh it conjures up negative images, I hate to say it, but it does. It conjures up East Europeans or Africans, Soweto, not Soweto, what do you call them, what's that place, there's a lot of them in Cardiff [Somalis?]. It conjures up bad images. It conjures up spongers, people living off us who are not destroying our way of life, but having an effect on the British side, I suppose […] This is why we're partly being diluted. It's not being diluted by Indians or Pakistanis who've been here for 55 years or whatever. It's by people coming in, and I've noticed it, I go to London once a month, and I do find it, I'll be honest, mildly irritating because you hardly see what you would call a normal white British person on the street, because it is just full of foreigners, Foreigners in inverted commas, sorry.

In this account, foreigners have engulfed public space in London. Ray experiences embodied difference as disruption, like Maggie, upset that the mosques in Kensington two decades after she had left her job there, meant that 'it wasn't my London'. While careful to distinguish between welcome and unwelcome bodies (the former having resided here for a requisite period), Ray is obviously using racial markers. How can you tell, just by looking, what nationality, immigration or employment status a person has, or how long they have been in Britain? So the rarity of Ray's 'normal white British person' activates his own sense of whiteness and otherness when transplanted to a different setting. He attributes cultural dilution and economic parasitism to people on the basis of physical appearance, thus racialising Britishness as white, industrious and cultural. Ray's directness is rare, as is critical reflexivity about this process. Tom observes: 'one is hoping that, I mean, with two mixed race adopted children, you're super conscious that some people who make a fuss of being British are actually talking about being white and all that, and you don't want to go down that road, not really'.

Definitions of the British community, into which particular immigrants are seen not to be integrating, involve ideas about belonging bound up with both phenotypical and cultural difference. The norms from which difference is measured are not always, but usually and implicitly exclusively white (based on periods of residence that place them well before important post-war extra-European immigration), and contain unsubstantiated assumptions of language ability and cultural closure that lock the subjects (including the British-born members of these communities) into permanent exclusion from the national 'we'.

One element feeding into the overall confusion around integration may well also be the lack of understanding of the different statuses entailed in the positions of people as labour migrants, asylum seekers, refugees and UK nationals who are not white. In our interviews, these groups tend to be amalgamated, or the lines between them blurred. This ambiguity emerges in the examples of good integration that are sometimes provided.

James (50s, Plymouth, mc) gives us a model integrator who is 'going up to Liverpool on a stag weekend that he's organised because he's a passionate Everton fan, he's a second-generation Asian, but you just wouldn't know it because he's a Scouser, and he waves the flag for England for the cricket [...] That's my kind of immigrant. If everybody was like that, there would be no problem'. Denise has two model women in mind:

> My husband's cousin is Indian. Her family are Indian and have been here nearly 40 years, but they're very Westernised. They don't, you know, they do wear their saris at special occasions and things, but they're not here demanding to bring a bit of India or, you know, to be Indian in this country ... The children's godmother is from Jamaica ... Janine is just as English as I am because. Well, she was born here, but not because of that, because she's not, you know, they're just the same as me and anybody else. They're not trying to be different.

Yet this construction of integration is problematic. James's friend is of Asian origin, but actually born and brought up in Liverpool. Similarly, Denise's friend is born in Manchester of Jamaican parents. So the generation for whom integration begins seems confused. Two of these three integrators are actually UK nationals, so why give them as examples?

As we saw in the previous chapter, a set of opinion polls has charted the growth of negative responses and their spread into previously more tolerant sections of the population. The socio-economic breakdowns show *relative* greater hostility towards immigrants among the C2, D and E groups (semi-skilled, unskilled and unemployed), however, what we can say about the responses given in our interviews is that there is an area of overlap, an inter-class discursive 'hinge', which is the idea of 'bending over backwards'. James (50s, Plymouth, mc) and Sally illustrate this. 'I get very annoyed about issues', states Sally, 'the way rules and regulations are changed in Britain to accommodate people who are visiting this country, who have come to live in this country, when I know if I went to live in their countries, nobody would accommodate me'. She returns to this point later in the conversation, and asserts that: 'They're bending over so much to not offend people that you're actually offending the people that come from this country'.

The image of tolerance being stretched past the point of reason-ableness, the 'pendulum having swung too far' (Sam) is one of the most frequent devices supporting the 'when-in-Rome' argument. It is often reached rapidly from questions about Britishness. Indeed, in response to the question: 'What displeases you about Britain?' James replies:

> I have to say that while I am terribly cool about people coming from all over the world and living here, I feel to a certain extent that if people are going to be here, they should play by our rules rather than we should bend over backwards to let them play by their rules. I wouldn't expect to go to a foreign country and totally live out my culture if it wasn't the way people did things there. So I think we're a bit soft in that respect [...] I think if people want to embrace our culture, they should embrace our culture and if they don't want to, then don't live here. It's simple.

The assumption in this discourse is always that minorities are not trying to integrate on the whole but only some individuals. Second, the unseen actor in this equation is central government or local authorities, the 'they' whom Sally accuses of damaging relations between British and immigrants, and whom others identify as the source of political correctness and unfair advantage in allocating resources.

Fairness

We saw in the previous chapter that fairness was invoked around different types of resources. These include culture and the capacity to impose norms, as seen in Denise's example of Muslim attitudes in factories. While as much resentment was expressed towards the idea of non-nationals accessing resources and being afforded cultural preference, there is also antipathy towards white British people viewed as unproductive and/or dangerous. This is true of middle-class and working-class respondents. For many of our sample in the Bristol residential area, the large estate on the other side of a main road bordering their 'village' is the source of the anti-social behaviour that occurs there, including drug-dealing in a local pub. One resident calls the road 'a big divide you have to cross'. On the Bristol and Plymouth estates, the non-respectable working-class inhabitants are identified as benefit scroungers, people who could work but don't want to, people who deal drugs, don't discipline their children properly and neglect them. The slippage between minorities and unproductive white nationals is often very smooth, as the examples below illustrate. First we hear Janice (60s, Plymouth, wc) talking about who should be let in as immigrants:

> I suppose if we've got a shortage of skills and they want to come here and work and again, it's being useful members of society, innit? And let's face it, there's plenty of white English people, or not just saying white, but English people in this country, or British people in this country who really, if you set the criteria of not being useful members of society, you'd kick out of the country anyway.

The experiences of Maggie (60s, Bristol, wc) link minorities and unproductive whites around housing. First, she tells a story of her confrontation with Bristol City Council housing officers:

> There was a case about an Indian family staying in a hotel and they just kept paying for them. And I said to them, if I was black or wore a sari and had half a dozen kids, I said, you'd put me in a place right now. They said, that's not very nice. I said, no it isn't, but that happens to be true ... And I'm not prejudiced, but we should come first, we are British, we are born here.

Maggie's comment 'if I had half a dozen kids' is aimed also at her neighbour. She and her husband live next door to a young single mother. According to them she has had a series of boyfriends, one of whom burgled their flat in broad daylight. She and her husband are dismissive in their interviews about the ease with which young single mothers access housing and boyfriends, and some of their talk is of the difficulty of finding alternative housing. They say they were offered a council house ... but it was in Hull!

Read against the emotive responses of our interviewees in the previous chapter, the discourse on integration seems to be premised on the idea that integration is actually the same thing as assimilation (a unilateral abandonment of cultural difference). Moreover, the cultural core of Britishness, represented by tolerance and fairness, is seen as being undermined by the lack of integration that minorities engage in as active agents resisting Britishness and seeking to impose their non-Britishnesses on the indigenous host society. The 'host' metaphor really addresses what people speak about, because terms like 'accommodate' and 'bending over backwards' indicate the assumptions surrounding the various roles. Worst of all, in the logic here, the perceived failure to integrate is not sanctioned but rewarded, by dwindling public resources being spread increasingly thinly, displacing the white working-class's claim on what they see as theirs.

Empire

We shall now briefly look at five engagements with the imperial legacy, which range from positively unashamed through to critical.

Terence and Brenda: 'That's History'

Terence (60s, Plymouth, wc) served in the armed forces, and his concise statement neatly encapsulates one of the ambivalences that surface when referring to national identity. There is an awareness for most of our sample that Englishness is seen and historically experienced by other groups as oppressive. 'I'm of an age', recalls Terence, 'that can still remember the British Empire, and when we were at school, there was lots of pink on maps or atlases of the world, so in some ways, I'm a bit old fashioned in that respect, but again we exploited all these countries going back then, not that I feel in these days, that's history and we shouldn't have to be apologising to everybody all the time for what we did'.

In the public discourse, the idea that Britain is constantly apologising for past actions resurfaces from time to time. Gordon Brown explicitly said so in a trip to Africa in 2005 (Brogan, 2005) for example. However, there are no official public apologies for human rights abuses under empire (except the apology for the Irish Famine, by Tony Blair in 1997, and some civic ones around the Abolition of Slavery in 2007). Like the spectre of banning Christmas, the frequent apologies that have never taken place assume a symbolic role in the discourse that maps out parameters for discussion: they tell us that in the speaker's opinion, the pendulum has swung too far away from the ethnic majority. It is a way of drawing a line in history that severs the present from its social and economic moorings. Like the 'color-blind' racist public discourse in the USA, it asserts history as finished business, with no explanatory role to play in discussions about inequality that might be argued to stem from past structures. One of our Bristol interviewees, Brenda (60s, mc) argues:

> I got into furious arguments with some people about a question of how did one teach the business about the British Empire and there was kind of a desire almost to have a denial that it happened because people started to feel ashamed that we had oppressed other races and refused to look at the other side of the coin, at what we actually did to open up trade and the globe and everything else, because there's always two sides to every story. And yes, we oppressed and we exploited, but we also improved and educated and spread the English language.

From this basis, Brenda's frustration with foreign students she met when doing seasonal work in Britain follows logically:

> they started griping about this country ... this is the way it is here, and you're welcome to stay if you knuckle down like the rest of us do. But stop whingeing. You know, if it's that bad, well go and find somewhere else, because this is what it is here, you know. And I still get that feeling of anger sometimes, especially when I hear a lot of these people recently, moaning and groaning about things and about the fact that they're not accepted and they can't have this and they're disenfranchised and I think, is it not because you disenfranchise yourself by demanding to be different? You know, with Muslims, for example, they want their mosques, they want to keep their women at home, they want their girls to wear burqas and God knows what for school, well, okay, we've said they can do that, and then they say, we're different, you don't accept us, we're not integrated with you, and you think, well, just hang on a minute, you know, you want your cake and eat it, either you want to integrate and be part of the way this country lives or you don't.

In this model, the act of integration is unhindered by any structural experience of exclusion, here reduced to the issue of dress codes and generalised to cover all Muslims. Muslims are most readily used as the example of a non-integrating minority, and Brenda's critique summarises the areas that receive most attention. Complaints about the experience of (unspecified forms of) exclusion are refuted out of hand, and the criteria for integration include the values of industriousness and phlegmatism. Alien dress ('God knows what') precludes integration. Yet what is actually being integrated here? The examples are all cultural and none economic. The focus on the cultural sphere, particularly the exploitation of women and the wearing of garments understood to be unequivocal signs of oppression (Delphy, 2006) are not specific to Brenda, but general aspects of Western interpretations of Islam. While there is a variety of forms of dress opted for by Muslim women and girls in Britain, often chosen strategically (Dwyer, 1999) from no headwear or a headscarf to niqab and burqa, the one furthest from the Western norm is selected as the representative one. It fixes Islam as alien and unchanging rather than diverse and dynamic, with integration meaning cultural assimilation only. The 2001 Census shows Muslims (particularly of Pakistani and Bangladeshi origin) as economically worse off on a number of indicators, yet all of the comments about failure to integrate that we picked up were organised around the religion and dress. Indeed, Brenda's unconcealed frustration was shared by a good proportion of the sample, especially in relation to religious norms (see above). Yet this was not confined at all by class, gender or age. Indeed, one of the staunchest critics of contemporary racial discourse was one of our oldest interviewees, Sheila.

Sheila: Eyes Wide Open

Sheila (70s, Plymouth, wc) has had a difficult life: frequently moved by the authorities (evacuated, re-housed), losing husbands and finally taking professional training and working with children. She purchased her council house under the right-to-buy scheme in the 1980s, and expressed regret that more social housing was not built to accommodate people since then. When asked what displeases here about Britain. Her response is unequivocal:

> I really don't like some of the racist comments. I really ... that ... I don't join
> in with that because I can't, it's all out of context, I can't relate if people
> carry on about that for a long, long time, and as I say, that irritates me a
> bit, because it has always been good and bad, hasn't it? If you have read
> enough history books and whatever, okay the British knocked each other
> around didn't they?

Sheila says she has a problem answering questions about being British because she doesn't think about it. However, when she does begin, the story focuses on her having tried to explain Empire Day to her daughter:

> I had no idea what Empire Day meant, but it was a lot of flag-waving
> and whatever, and she [her daughter] said, oh dear me, Empire Day, we're
> British, you know, we're the top of the tree, we are, we celebrate our Empire
> Day, all those empires we conquered with cruelty and savagery and you
> know, and now we're getting a bit back and we don't like it, we don't like it.
> I know she was quite surprised to think that schools, that we all celebrated
> our great empire founded on wealth ... and India and the Caribbean and
> whatever ... and the Slave Trade and all that money that people made off,
> you know, we weren't blameless, by any means. We were just as bad as
> some of the dictators now.

Indeed, Sheila's sense of history is vividly contemporary. She has travelled a lot since retirement, and talks about having been on a cruise whose itinerary meant they had a few days in the Dominican Republic, where she was horrified to see people working in sugar-cane fields, oxen pulling ploughs, and ragged children holding their hands out for food. 'And then you go back on the ship and you think there is something wrong with this world today, somehow, isn't there? That we've got all this food and all this, then half of it thrown away. That made me feel uncomfortable'.

Sheila is very unusual, however, in that she does not seem to mind reflecting on what has made her uncomfortable. Instead of burying or rationalising such experience, she treats it all as an education. The key phase for her seems to have been the friendship she struck up with a young African artist. Her daughter made friends with 'Michael' at art college in London, and he later became friends with her oldest son too. Sheila met him a number of times. Sadly, Michael had sickle cell anaemia and died in his 30s. Sheila has nothing but praise for Michael's warmth and resilience, and felt she had to attend his funeral, even though it wasn't what she was used to:

> I remember being at his funeral and it was this wonderful happy-clappy ... his Mum was Pentecostal, something like that, and the street was absolutely full of people and we had to sit in the aisles, and then he was carried to the cemetery in Birmingham with that song, 'We Shall Meet at the River', and I thought, am I really here? You know this little girl from a North Devon farm. Am I really here? And I said to my oldest son, you know, what am I doing here? And he said, Mum, there's a big wide world out there. You know, it's just ... So all these little things would ... so get out ... and meeting people is best, isn't it, if you can get a better judgement? I think perhaps if I had stayed here all the time and hadn't mixed with lots of different ethnic cultures and whatever, maybe I'm ... I've seen, been lucky enough to have met someone like Michael.

Sheila's image of being carried by communion and song, literally to a different psychological and social place, in a context of so much emotion is very striking, and perhaps enables us to make sense of her positions. Already she had experienced turmoil and grief and managed to overcome it, and Michael's example of tolerance seems to have added to this resilience and sparked Sheila's inquisitiveness. The brief story of herself she narrates seems to embody some shifts in Britain's recent history. From North Devon farm, through World War II; the struggle against class structure to qualify for a professional job and raise children despite losing her husbands' incomes; the purchase of a house; and finally the immersion, the 'meeting at the river' of urban multicultural Britain. A mile away, at the other end of the same estate, lives 'Frances', whose story is quite different.

'Frances': First-hand Experiences

Frances (20s, Plymouth, wc) grew up in Hong Kong. Her experiences of empire were thus first-hand, and they appear to have given her a particular empathy with minorities:

I felt as if I blended in then, but there were times when I went back on holiday, when I moved back to England, I went back to Hong Kong to visit my Dad and things, then I felt a bit out of place, especially as I was getting taller. I was sort of a head or two taller than everybody else and I used to get strange looks and it used to be a bit uncomfortable because other people looked at me as if I was a tourist, that was how I perceived their looks anyway, but I wasn't, it was my home. But I didn't look the same as everybody else, so I suppose that's affected my attitude towards other immigrants into this country. I don't see them as ... especially down this part of the country, people can be very separatist, can't they [...] you know, 'send them back where they came from', and comments like that. I don't think I've got the same attitude because I'm used to being on the other side of the coin, if that makes any sense, used to being the one who doesn't really fit into the country that they live in, if that makes any sense at all.

Frances is enjoying living in the part of the estate where she lives, where there is an explicit effort being made to develop a community. She like many others is sensitive to people she sees as 'working the system' and getting resources that she and her husband have to work for without contributing. However, she displays a different kind of reflexivity about 'race'. When she found that one of our research themes was white identities, she commented: 'It's almost more politically correct, isn't it, to be looking at other groups rather than white groups. You know that big box for ticking 'White British' – it's as if you don't have to be analysed quite as much as everybody else does'.

Indeed, she analyses white responses to immigration within her own workplace and Plymouth itself:

I don't like the fear that's going on and the seeming escalation of fear, whether that is media-fuelled, and I think that has something to do with it, but the perception that most people have and they start being afraid of other people and other cultures and other coloured skins and other people's religions, I don't like how that's evolving and it's not heading in the right direction [...] And just people at work starting up conversations in the canteen that are very, very one-sided and their voices are always raised so that other people then join in and it gets quite heated. And I think, well, hang on, just look at the other side for a moment, step back and see what you're saying and why you're saying it. I mean, it's generally sparked out of fear, a conversation like that.

The description she gives could be a sparse one fitting the whole discourse about immigration drawn from a cultural perspective, and is shared by both Patricia and Valerie (below). Is there a formative experience that determines people's individual propensity to buy into the available identity narratives of 'race' and nation? We wonder whether developing empathy is as simple a process as this. Narratives from former combatants for example (Rogaly and Taylor, 2010) suggest that the specific position someone held vis-à-vis the imperial subjects one came into contact with is more important than merely being among them. An interesting case of this is Patricia, who is married to an Asian national.

Patricia: Intimate Empire

Patricia's (40s, Bristol, mc) story reveals awareness of whiteness and empire growing through the experiences she has had since marrying her husband, whom she met at university. When she went to his country for the first time and met his family (before they were married), she was exposed to a more critical construction of Britishness, and began to realise that there was more at stake for his family than she had at first thought. They were strict Catholics and she was the son's foreign girlfriend.

Q Has there been any occasion when being British has really mattered to you?

A I think there have been times when I have been conscious of it like going to [his country] for the first time, when I was John's girlfriend, and a lot of his friends sort of jovially making anti-British remarks because of course they've got a long history with the empire and the colonies and so on, and I started feeling very defensive about it, sort of cumulatively because I was there for a fortnight, and I did get quite fed up about it. So that was a point when I was acutely conscious of being specifically British, but that effect wore off as they got used to me and I got used to them.

She was also affected by the levels of poverty she encountered: 'you just feel big and fat in this country where people are small and thin and dark, so big and white and fat'.

The experiences were thus becoming embodied, and after reaching a point where John's friends' remarks were no longer taken personally, she returned with a reflection on the enduring imperial relationship: 'We've no idea of the residual impact of our culture on places all over the world which still think British and talk British and so on and feel linked, and we've got absolutely no idea of their affiliations and our shared history with them'. She now sees links between this shared history and the social geography of Bristol: 'there are huge divides, some of them are economic, some of them are cultural, and when the two combine it is quite a staggering difference'.

She uses one particular area of the city as an example of this combination. The district has a substantial BAME minority, and in specific sections of the ward there is a majority of brown-skinned people. They go shopping there occasionally, and it signals a reversal of roles for her and John. In that place, he 'isn't looked at twice', whereas she feels conspicuous, and realises that this is the position for John in the other, white parts of the city that they frequently move around in.

The racial 'epiphany' generated by the experience of being in an intimate individual relationship, or of moving into proximity to racialised Others, is a recurrent element of fieldwork done with white respondents (Frankenberg, 1994; McKinney, 2005; Byrne, 2006). What was 'unseen' for our white interviewees, that is, the salience of being white, shifts into the realm of the socially visible and prompts insecurity. This is resolved to varying degrees, as a process of interrogating self and society ensues. This is particularly interesting in the story of Valerie.

Valerie: Reflection and Mobility

Valerie's (30s, Bristol, mc) start in life encompassed a set of overlapping national habituses and hyper-mobility. Her grandfather (mother's father) lived in Switzerland, and her mother was born there, but came back to England as a small child with her mother (Valerie's grandmother), while her father re-married in Sweden. Valerie therefore had a second family there. Moreover, her husband is a national of another European country, and she travels there frequently.

> Q What kind of impact have those international links had on your identity?
> A I think it has made me interested in things in a wider area than just on a small scale and it's made me interested in the fact that different people do things slightly differently. Sometimes that might be better or worse.

A more recent, but equally formative experience for Valerie was the two-year period she spent in Africa as part of an aid programme.

> Q And how did you feel when you were living there? Did you feel like a visitor or a stranger?
> A I felt like a visitor. I felt like a stranger. When you're a European, people are very polite to you and sort of put you at the front of the queue and things like that which is quite a … so it was the first time in my life I had been aware of my skin colour, I suppose, because that was why I stood out.

It is not so much the experience of discovering she was 'white', and what that meant in an African country that is interesting about Valerie, but the way she has reflected on her life in Britain as a result. She is vehement that the question of immigration 'is poisoning our culture at the moment, our national identity, this anger and resentment of other people and therefore I have to think what do I really feel'.

She observes that media coverage of such issues makes it difficult to think rationally because it is so manipulative. Commenting on British responses to it, she states:

> we have to link asylum to immigration because we like to believe ourselves as a nation of being very fair and kind of good people, and therefore the only way that we cannot want people to seek asylum here, or refuge, is to make them out to be some kind of financial sort of … stealing and therefore we can feel good about ourselves for rejecting them.

Given the value of productivity (immigrants must contribute) that is cited so often by people in their discussion of immigration in the previous chapter, Valerie is extremely perspicacious. Moreover, she links immigration discourse directly to resource competition. She works in the healthcare sector, sometimes providing services on a large estate elsewhere in Bristol.

> *Q*   You mentioned [name of area] earlier and that some people were saying immigrants took their houses. Did they really perceive that and is that related to social housing?
> *A*   I think it is very difficult. It's like the idea that the government has endless money, the government has endless housing stock, and that therefore if you have to wait for a year, it must be because somebody else is getting priority over you, and therefore who are these people? Well, I presume it is the immigrants. You know, I think it is a little bit 'filling in the gaps' and the fact that it might just be that there isn't that housing stock, so you have to wait for someone to die, I mean that's a ... People don't really think through the whole problem. It's more a kind of a quick response.

Of course it is very hard to 'think through the problem', precisely because its various strands overlap with each other. None of what we have been researching is *only* about 'race', any more than it is only about nation or class, or political economy or culture. However, what we have tried to show in this chapter is that when people in provincial urban Britain talk about 'integration', there are a number of aspects to take into consideration.

Conclusion

Empire provides an awareness of hierarchy, which might be denied by some as a justifiable way to organise society, but is nonetheless understood as having been the dominant model within living memory. Balibar (1991b) suggests that all forms of racism include the idea that the world's cultures are hierarchically related. While cultural forms of 'new racism' proclaim themselves egalitarian but separatist, Balibar notes that the idea of superiority pervades it. All integration or assimilation of people whose origins lie outside Europe is seen as progress for the latter.

Visions of segregation (especially self-segregation) as the opposite of integration (assimilation) emerge as the backdrop against which progress is measured. This progress consists solely of 'not trying to be different', or joining in without whining, or some other subjective measure. What is worth thinking about is how the phenomenon of BAME/immigrant segregation is assessed using rules different from those governing other types of population concentrations and processes. We have noted that social geographers agree that Britain does not have actual ghettoes in the North American sense of such high physical concentrations of minority groups (although presumably Johnston and Poulsen, by using the indices they specify, would argue that some British cities are heading towards that model). In this context, why is it so easy to assume and talk about minorities self-segregating, which indicates a process of choice and absolute agency on the part of the minority groups (Massey and Denton, 1994)? It is already assumed for example that residential distribution is chiefly determined by income, as property prices preclude different strata from purchasing in various areas. There is a market for housing and the outcomes demonstrate how that market functions, hence the 'wealthy areas' and the 'poorer areas', and those in between. Working-class people in Plymouth and Bristol are never accused of self-segregating, or even being segregated, although according to Dorling (Dorling and Thomas, 2004; Dorling, 2005) segregation by socio-economic group has a far more robust empirical basis than segregation by ethnicity. More importantly, the dominant positions ('middle-class' and 'white') are seldom linguistically constructed as segregating, although again, the case for arguing that they do might be strong. It is virtually a doxa of American studies of 'race' that white Americans select white suburbs to live in once they have accumulated sufficient capital, in order to avoid encounters with minorities and send their children to predominantly white schools (Johnson and Shapiro, 2003; Feagin, 2006; Forman and Lewis, 2006; Johnson, 2006). The segregation index (which measures what proportion of each group would have to move in order for there to be equal distribution) is only 5 per cent for whites at the 2001 Census. This shows that the vast majority (98 per cent) of British electoral wards are primarily white. Yet the index of isolation is 95! If one was seeking to use sensational language, is that not a ghetto-like figure?

However, if we were to assert in a report that Britain's ethnic population distribution is characterised chiefly by self-segregating white ghettoes, many of them middle-class, there would undoubtedly be a rapid and dismissive response. That interpretation of the statistical evidence is only shocking because the terminology and logic are strangers to the dominant social locations in British society.

Indeed, our findings raise questions about how the debate about integration is actually being conducted in public discourse. Most people we spoke to seem to understand integration to be a synonym of assimilation, a finding replicated in further work (Garner et al., 2009), and which must have some consequences for public policy. The integration of people into a not particularly consensual British culture is seen in these discussions as a set of fractures. The first is around productivity and contributions by migrants in order to access welfare, but also by local whites who are viewed as not putting into the system and only taking out. There is little appreciation for the different rights and statuses of the migrants referred to, and they are understood as all being able to access the welfare state as easily as, if not more easily than British nationals.

The second is the racialisation of class. Non-whites are associated with advantage and privilege and at the same time with poverty, backwardness and lower class positions. As an outcome of this process, culture has become a battlefield on which Britain is coming under threat in the domains of language, traditions, religion and dress codes. Women wearing various types of scarf over their heads generate anxiety. We should 'stop apologising for Britain's colonial past'. Christmas has been 'banned', by someone, somewhere and it makes me upset. What do these kinds of discursive figures really mean? Are they signs of a crisis? Or is crisis the norm, and it is simply that various aspects of it take precedence at different moments? The focusing of concerns and anxieties is not upwards towards decision-makers, but sideways and/or downwards on the socio-economic scales towards minorities (mainly 'elsewhere' for our respondents), who absorb resources.

Britishness is thus losing out to Englishness, which provides a haven for those vacating the former's more diverse and abstract space. Is this abandonment of Britishness a characteristic of the post-colonial UK? We argue that the imperial legacy still informs ideas of Britishness. It is a presence affecting how people see contemporary Britain and its relationships with the outside world, as well as the relationships between the people in it. It provides a racialised framework for weighing up how far Britain has come or fallen since it held a dominant position in the world economy.

6

PSYCHO-SOCIAL INTERPRETATIONS OF CULTURAL IDENTITY: CONSTRUCTING THE WHITE 'WE'

The social construction of white identity, or indeed identities in general, can offer us a real insight into how we perceive the self and others. In this chapter we argue that a psycho-social dimension goes beyond traditional analysis and allows us to understand the emotional, affective and visceral content of identity construction. Drawing on psychoanalytic ideas and concepts, we unravel the psychological dynamics involved in the construction of the white 'we' in relation to the otherness of the Other. Cultural identities are marked by a number of factors – 'race', ethnicity, gender and class to name but a few – yet the real locus of these factors is the notion of difference. The question of difference is emotive; we start to hear ideas about 'us' and 'them', friend and foe, belonging and not belonging, in-groups and out-groups, which define 'us' in relation to others, or the Other. In the following chapters on media representation and community we also see this emotive aspect of identity construction, which spans a range of fields from the human imagination to concrete ideas about community. To further complicate this matter we could also ask whether identity is a social construction or part of a psychodynamic process. We argue that it is a complex amalgam of both (Clarke, 2008b). We start this chapter then, by examining some of the sociological literature on identity through the work of Erving Goffman and Michel Foucault before going on to look at psychodynamically informed accounts of identity construction which form a backdrop to the proceeding chapters on media constructions and community. It has also to be noted that the question of what we mean by identity is contested and confusing; often the idea of identity becomes a 'bucket' into which all ideas are thrown. Identity, as we have argued, is emotive and marked by factors such as ethnicity and class, but it should also be noted that identity can, and often is, both situational and contextual. So, for example, given a certain context or situation, someone could identify themselves as British, South Asian or Indian. In the course of our research we have found that white identities are often very local or regional, but in another context different. So, someone may feel very strongly that they have been born and brought up in Cornwall, but in a different context while travelling abroad they identified themselves as British. It is, as Goffman would say, about the presentation of self in everyday life.

Socially Constructing the Self

> You can't lose an identity anyway, you can only change it and gain a new one. That's how I feel anyway.

That quote is from a 74-year-old respondent and we think she was very much talking about the performative self. For Goffman identity is a dramatic effect, the self is an effect of a performance, the way in which we present our selves in everyday life. In Goffman's (1969) *The Presentation of Self in Everyday Life* we have what has become known as the Dramaturgical model. For Goffman, life becomes a performance:

> When an individual plays a part he implicitly requests his observers to take seriously the impression that is fostered before them. They are asked to believe that the character they see actually possesses the attributes he appears to possess, that the tasks that he performs will have the consequences that are implicitly claimed for it, and that, in general, matters are what they are appear to be. (Goffman, 1969: 28)

Identity is therefore projected at the target audience in a theatrical performance that conveys self to others. The performer on the one hand can be completely immersed in his or her own act and sincerely believe that the version of reality being projecting is actually correct. On the other hand the performer may be cynical, not quite taken in by his or her own performance, indeed in some cases fully aware that the impression being fostered is but a mere act. It is not always the case, argues Goffman, that this is done out of self-interest, but rather in the belief that it is for the audience's own good. Think of politicians, they do this all the time, educators often project a cynical sense of self to get over a point, and we often talk about putting on a brave face in spite of adversity, many of our respondents did. These, for Goffman, are the two poles of performativity that are little more than simple continuum: 'Each provides the individual with a position which has its own particular securities and defenses, so there will be a tendency for those who have traveled close to one of these poles to complete the voyage' (Goffman, 1969: 30).

To convince people we really are who we are we use certain mannerisms and project certain characteristics within a given setting that will convince people that we really are a writer, lecturer or even a member of a community. A front for Goffman helps to induce or add 'dramatic realization' (1969: 31) to a performance. There is, however, a paradox for Goffman, or at least a dilemma between expression and action. The dramatisation of the part may well stand in the way of the action. For example, Goffman quotes Sartre's example of the schoolboy who is so keen to seem attentive in the eyes of his teacher, ears and eyes wide open, that he exhausts himself playing the role and is no longer able to listen. This is why, argues Goffman, organisations often delegate the task of dramatising the meaning of action to someone who does not perform it. So, for example, a sales representative may dramatise the role of the quality of workmanship in a particular firm promoting a product, just as the marketing department may sell a degree course to a potential student. Thus, for Goffman, performances are not only realised but idealised, shown in the best possible light to conform to cultural and societal norms, in other words cultural identities are often an idealisation set in opposition to stigmatised identities – made distinctive. One respondent gave this example in response to a question about white British identity:

> Everybody else is a problem [*laughing*], if you know what I mean. I'm not in the least bit racially prejudiced or anything like that, but there is something about, I don't know, the fact that we're an island, I suppose, and we're isolated. I know we're part of Europe these days and all the rest of it. We're an island and have had to depend on ourselves more so. And so I think we're a little bit more distinctive in some ways and have a different sense of humour to most other countries, I think, and stuff like that. We're just different, that's the best I can do.

In *Stigma* Goffman (1968) describes three types of identity – social identity, personal identity and ego identity. For Goffman society characterises people and produces attributes that are normal in this given categorisation. Social identity is about the category and attributes that a person is deemed to possess in relation to others. Often, when we meet a stranger, we make assumptions about the nature of this stranger and attribute what Goffman calls a virtual social identity. Stigma is based in a discrepancy between actual and virtual social identity, an attribute that we perceive as a shortcoming – 'in the extreme, a person who is quite thoroughly bad, or dangerous or weak' (Goffman, 1968: 12) leads us to discredit and stigmatise an individual. Personal identity for Goffman is about a person's biography. It is about something that is unique to a person and makes that person an individual within the social. 'By personal identity, I have in mind ... positive marks or identity pegs, and the unique combination of life history items that comes to be attached to the individual with the help of these pegs for his identity' (Goffman, 1968: 74).

So, this is not about our inner essence, how we feel we are and exist in the world, it's about a complex and continuous profiling about who we are in relation to society that marks us as an individual. Goffman identifies a third form of identity – ego identity – but as Tom Burns (1992) notes, Goffman only mentions it to make it clear he is not dealing with 'ego' *per se*, but is more interested in socially constructed interactional identity. Ego identity is about our subjective sense of who we are and how we exist in the world, in other words how we feel about our self. Indeed, if we return to the notion of stigmatisation, then Goffman clearly differentiates between these three types of identity: 'The concept of social identity allowed us to consider stigmatisation. The concept of personal identity allowed us to consider the role of information control in stigma management. The idea of ego identity allows us to consider what the individual may feel about stigma' (Goffman, 1968: 130). In this then we have quite a strong constructionist view of how the self and identity are both constructed by and maintained in parallel with societal norms (Garfinkel, 1967; Berger and Luckmann, 1971; Gergen, 2000; Burr, 2003).

The first thing we could ask is where does the role of emotion reside in Goffman's model of self and identity? The emphasis placed on social and personal identity draws away from the feeling self and in some sense negates identity as a felt state of being, it ignores our inner world, our unconscious feelings and desires. In largely affirming Mead's (1934) work the idea of a sense of cultural identity from the position of the subject is rather overwhelmed by the normalisation of self by society. If we look at the Dramaturgical model then as Manning (1992) notes life is just reduced to a set of performances, there is very little analysis of intention, motivation or even how the self is created. Identity becomes so performative we lose all sense of subjectivity and reflexivity. Indeed, for Manning, 'Goffman's dramaturgical perspective over-extends the notion of acting or performing, that it offers an inadequate account of the intentions of actors and that it imposes its solution onto the phenomena it purports to explain' (Manning, 1992: 54). Anthony Elliott (2001) also highlights the lack of psychic dispositions in the acting self, maintaining that an undue concern with impression management might actually be symptomatic of deeper concerns surrounding the self. Questions of desire do not enter into Goffman's framework and at the same time, argues Elliott, the self as performer throws doubt on any notion of 'true' self that 'modern culture valourizes, and which is evident in many forms of social thought' (Elliott, 2001: 36). Indeed for Elliott, Goffman's idea of the performative self might actually be a precursor to post-modern ideas of the self. This we would contest and indeed in chapter 8 we contest the view that there is a post-modern self. So, despite these criticisms Goffman's model offers us some positive insights into identity formation and notions of the self. Although we cannot realistically see the whole of social life through the metaphoric lens of theatre we also quite plainly do play roles, put on fronts and perform in different ways in different social contexts. Goffman's ideas around organisation and normalisation bear an uncanny resemblance to Foucault's later ideas, and as Tom Burns (1992) argues it is almost as if Foucault has used Goffman's ideas and interpretation and expanded them into a much wider context around power and social control. It is then Foucault's work that we want briefly to examine next before looking at a more psycho-social approach to identity construction.

Constructing Self and Identity in Discourse

As we have already seen, social and cultural identities, indeed white identities, are grounded in difference and, as Goffman has shown us, in relation to societal norms. In Foucault's exploration of the mad, the criminally insane, the history of the deviant and of sexualities we see how self is created in relation to expert discourses that define normal and pathological as well as trying to drive us back towards a norm; to make our sense of self align with a rational model in a process of normalisation. In *Madness and Civilization* (1995) Foucault takes us on a critical voyage from the 'ship of fools', a strange 'drunken' boat that glides along the calm waters of the Rhineland and Flemish canals, a time when madmen had an easy wandering existence, to a very different existence – to disciplinary society (Foucault, 1995: 7). In doing so, Foucault questions the very notion of what it means to be mad, to be a delinquent, and in his later work, the way in which expert systems have tried to construct sexuality and identity. Foucault explores the processes and historical circumstances that give rise to the modern person, to the creation of 'rational man' and the objectification of the Other.

Much has been written about Foucault's work on madness, deviancy and sexuality (Clarke, 2005), but we can draw some strong themes from *Madness and Civilization* (1995), which gives us a clearer picture of one of many forms of identity construction. Foucault argues in *Madness and Civilization* that there is a discourse on madness in Western civilisation that has four distinct stages. So, in the medieval times the madman was considered almost holy, in the Renaissance, the madman was not feared but had a different form of high reason. At the end of the seventeenth century madness started to become more clearly delineated from sanity and we saw the start of confinement, of hospitals. The mad were not excluded but confined. Towards the end of the eighteenth century the asylum was developed together with psychiatric discourse, which further separated reason from unreason. Finally, argues Foucault, all nineteenth-century psychiatry converges on Freud, on psychoanalysis (Foucault, 1995: 277).

For Foucault in the classical age, we could say the rational man was created by locking away all the people who did not fit the picture of rationality and morality of the time. Our sense of self is created in relation to historic discourse. In the asylum, the subject is objectified. The objectified subject would be described in greater detail later by Foucault in *Discipline and Punish* (1977), but the principle remains the same. The subject is constantly observed and made aware of the error of his or her ways. The mad are made to see their transgressions and brought back to the rational norms of society by restraint, retraining and discipline of the body and mind (Dreyfus and Rabinow, 1982: 9). It is perhaps the most significant development for Foucault, that when the doctor enters the asylum, we have the birth of the doctor–patient relationship and the expert discourses of psychiatry. Foucault shows us how expert discourses develop systems of knowledge that sustain power relations and domination in society. It is through the personage of the doctor that madness becomes insanity, and thus an objectification for investigation in medical discourse. If *Madness and Civilization* gives us a clue as to the construction of the modern self and identity in relation to the Other, then *Discipline and Punish* (1977) describes in detail the processes through which this transformation is attained.

In *Discipline and Punish* Foucault charts a history from the idea of sovereign power and public spectacle to the idea of the prison or penitentiary, and from public mutilation to private transformation. Again we see the development of an expert discourse of criminology that on the one hand identifies those who are deviant and on the other pulls us back to the norms of society. Prison becomes a transforming apparatus whose rules and processes, argues Foucault, we can also apply to most institutions and organisations. Schools, colleges, hospitals, factories all follow the principles of 'panopticism' that mark disciplinary society.

We then move on to the prison – Bentham's Panopticon. For Foucault, the panoptic effect reverses the principle of the dungeon, it disposes of the deprivation of light, and the idea that you hide the prisoner retaining only the function of incarceration – visibility becomes a trap. Each inmate is confined to a cell, only the supervisor or inspector can see him, he cannot communicate with fellow inmates – 'he is seen, but he does not see; he is the object of information, never a subject in communication' (Foucault, 1977: 200). For Foucault, this highly visible invisibility ensures there is no communication with fellow inmates and therefore no likelihood of further criminal dealing, or mass escape. If the inmate is a patient there is no possibility of contagion, if they are mad, then no risk of violence, if they are school children, then there is no hope of copying. Order is maintain through the gaze, no noise, no chatter, no wasting time, in the office, the workshop, the factory. Crucially for Foucault, the major effect of the Panopticon is to: 'Induce in the inmate a state of conscious and permanent visibility that assures the automatic functioning of power' (1977: 201). This is achieved by making the prisoner think and feel that he or she is the object of constant surveillance, of the eye of power.

The Panopticon, as Dreyfus and Rabinow (1982) note, brings together power, knowledge, control (of the body, and of space and time) in an integrated technology of discipline. Although the Panopticon was never actually built, the idea and ideas that surround it make up disciplinarity, and the techniques permeate the whole of disciplinary society, from the speed camera to the arrangement of timetables, rooms, examinations, students' records in the university, in the temporal, spatial, observational organisation of our lives. This is also the essence of Goffman's social and personal identities where we are pulled back to the norm and our personal identity is very much about information about us rather than how we feel. Famously we have Foucault's 'Gaze' – observation, judgement, normalisation, examination. Thus for Foucault there is a shift from the memorable man to the calculable man, from individuality to normalisation. Our identity and sense of self, we could argue, is illusional, it is a pseudo self created in the midst of a normalising discourse. The white 'we', 'me' and 'I' are a product of power and discourse rather than feeling and emotion. Just to add a twist to this debate at least one of our respondents (in her late 70s) would not agree, but we feel that's Foucault's point. She says:

> And, in the same way that in the Middle Ages, the two duties of the King then, when the King was government, was to provide defence of his realm and defence of his people and justice, so it was known as the King's Peace, and the King's Peace resided in those two things. That was the reason for having a head of state, the father figure who would defend against attackers coming into the country or settle squabbles between individuals within the country and stop them fighting and make territorial rules and then provide justice for those people who were done down. Now we've added to that, to my mind, a further extension of the concept of the King's Peace is the provision of education and health care so that every citizen has the right and the opportunity to get the best out of life and shall not suffer because they cannot afford to have their injury or their sickness repaired.

Foucault also draws our attention to the construction of sexual identity in *The History of Sexuality* (3 volumes: *The Will to Knowledge* (1976), *The Use of Pleasure* (1984), *The Care of the Self* (1989)). Rather than taking it as a natural given – the idea of sexuality becomes a discursive practice – sexuality was constructed, argues Foucault, through discourse. Foucault starts his examination of sexuality by questioning the role of repression, or the power of repression in the Victorian era. In some sense he is not calling into question the historical existence of repression; rather he is questioning the role that the repressive hypothesis has in terms of explanatory power when examining the relationship between power and sex. What we actually saw for Foucault was the social construction of sexuality – whole new discourses about perversion, homosexuality, deviance, that simply did not exist before they were invented. Indeed, for Foucault we saw a 'discursive explosion' in the eighteenth and nineteenth centuries around what constituted a legitimate alliance between people. For Foucault, the medical or psychiatric examination functions as a mechanism with two sides – pleasure and power. First there is the pleasure that comes from the monitoring and outing; exercising a power that searches out and exposes. On the other hand there is the pleasure that comes from evading this power.

The central concept in the scientific study and increasing admin-istration of sexuality was the confession. Although originating in the Christian confessional, the confession itself became one of the West's foremost ways of producing truth. For Foucault, the confession now plays a part in all our everyday lives – we have become a confessing society. We confess to our teachers, our friends, our doctor, in public, in private, we even pay to confess. Although the form of confession may have changed over the years, it is, for Foucault, still the general standard by which a true discourse on sex is produced. The confession has lost much of its ritualistic elements, and is no longer located merely within the church or the torturer's dungeon. It has spread to wider society and exists in the relationship between doctors and patients, parents and children, delinquents and experts, and of course for Foucault in the very practice of psychoanalysis. Through technologies of the self there is the idea that with the help of experts we can know the truth about our sense of being, of self and identity. Bio-power, the exercise of power of life and bodies, was thus born.

Thus we have a strong argument that cultural identity is linked to dominant discourses and power. Something that Judith Butler (1990, 1993) builds on in her notion of performativity, where a discursive practice enacts and therefore produces what it names. Performance, gender identity and sexual power are inextricably linked. Thus, the social construction of identity is tied in with notions of rationality, discourse and power. With the help of experts we can work on our self, change our identity or even discover who we actually are. Now we have looked in some detail at who we are, we can pose the question who are they? In other words, the analysis thus far is strongly centred on the construction of identity within a given culture and lacks any referent to passion or emotion. But we must ask how are identities, and particularly white identity, constructed in relation to other cultures? This really is the crux of the notion of all identity, the notion of the construction of identity in relation to some other becomes stronger when we start to define our 'selves' in relation to a cultural Other and is at the heart of racism(s), hatred and the construction of the 'white' we.

Psycho-Social Interpretations of Self and Other

In this section of the chapter we want to introduce what we term a psycho-social approach to understanding cultural and white identities. Psycho-social studies is very much an emerging tradition in the social sciences, which challenges traditional models of human rationality that opposed reason to passion. It places an emphasis on the inner world of the subject and while not dismissing discourse and cognition it gives equal weight to emotion, feeling and affect. In the next chapter, for example, we use a psycho-social interpretation of Bauman's (1990) and Žižek's (1993) work (referred to in an earlier chapter) to address the way in which the refugee as 'stranger' represents all our own fears of displacement, of chaos, of the ambiguity of living in the modern world and the impact this has on white identity.

A psycho-social approach therefore draws on multiple disciplines, on the sociological, the psychological and the cultural to analyse and synthesise the impact of the political and socio-structural factors that influence human behaviour and the construction of our identities. It uses psychoanalytic ideas to breach the gaps between these disciplines and as such places an emphasis on the inner world of the subject while recognising that the familiar split between individual and society is not helpful if we are to understand phenomena such as racism, hatred and fear of the Other. In a recent paper in the journal *Sociology* (Clarke, 2006) we outlined what psycho-social studies could offer sociology. We argued that it represents a synthesis of both worlds, rather than an opportunity to stake a position and stick to it in an inflexible way. We all know that there is a social construction of our realities as much as we know that we are emotional people who construct our 'selves' in imagination and affect. Neither sociology nor psychoanalysis provides a better explanation of the world than the other, but together they provide a deeper understanding of the social world. The use of psychoanalysis within sociological and philosophical enquiry is not new, but earlier models were quite crude in their understanding of the nature of the human subject and have led until quite recently to the tensions between the disciplines.

As we have previously noted (Clarke, 2003), psychoanalysis has not always enjoyed an easy partnership with sociology as a discipline. There are various reasons for this, based mainly in epistemology, the nature of the unconscious mind and doubts around Freud's ideas that misleadingly couch psychoanalysis as a science. Another tension has been the nature of psychoanalysis and the tension between biology and constructivism in which the idea of innate or inherited biological drives is simply at odds with a sociological viewpoint. For us this represents an inflexibility in thought as there quite clearly is both a social construction of our social reality and a psychological perception or construction of reality and who we are, that we may not always be aware of. Ian Craib (1998) has noted that the dismissal of Freud's work is based on positivistic notions of science, rather than the interpretive nature of psychoanalysis. Freud largely brought this upon himself by claiming throughout his life that psychoanalysis is a science and thus leaving himself open to constant criticism from both medical and philosophical disciplines. The debate around whether psychoanalysis is a science, as we have noted (Clarke, 2006), is expressed in the views of Popper (1983), Gellner (1985) and particularly Grunbaum (1984) and exploded in 1993 when the *New York Review of Books* published Frederick Crews' essay 'The Unknown Freud'. This rather critical report on psychoanalysis and Freud's theory describes psychoanalysis as an explanatory worthless hobbyhorse, thus detracting from what psychoanalysis might offer in terms of interpretation for the disciplines of sociology and psycho-social studies.

Craib argues that a hermeneutic reading of Freud opens up many new possibilities. Using the work of Paul Ricoeur (1970) and Jurgen Habermas (1968), Craib argues that philosophers can learn from Freud rather than trying to teach him – 'they do not destroy psychoanalysis but take it beyond itself' (Craib, 1998: 133). Habermas uses psychoanalysis as way of maintaining a hermeneutic approach to his philosophical sociology and pointing to forms of ideological domination. Ricoeur uses Freud's ideas to point to the unconscious distortion of meanings in tandem with a more traditional hermeneutic approach to conscious interpretations and meaning. There are many more interpretations of Freud's work than mere biology. These range from the philosophical discussions mentioned above to Lacan's reconstruction of Freud with his emphasis on language, to the writings of 'third wave' feminists, for example Juliet Mitchell's book *Psychoanalysis and Feminism* (1974) and in the work of Julia Kristeva (1989, 1991) and Luce Irigaray (1985). As Alvesson and Skoldberg (2000) note, after Ricoeur (1970), the entities that Freud discovered in the psyche, the id, ego and super ego, are not entities at all, but interpretations: 'the unconscious becomes something that does not really exist, but is an ascribed meaning' (Alvesson and Skoldberg, 2000: 94). Alvesson and Skoldberg argue that the history of hermeneutics has been a history that has been devoid of any suspicion; psychoanalysis adds another dimension on the periphery of the hermeneutic tradition seeking the irrational elements behind societal phenomena. So, we have in some sense the notion that psychoanalytic ideas can be employed within a hermeneutic interpretive method. This is a far cry from the biological nature of Freud's early work and we would suggest far more palatable for sociologists.

The Early Years: From the Frankfurt School to Frantz Fanon

If we look back historically it is the early work of members of the Frankfurt School which produced a real synthesis between sociological and psychoanalytic thinking both in theory and practice and which represents the very basic genesis of a psycho-social tradition which looks at the construction of self in relation to the Other.

Horkheimer and Adorno's (1994) *Dialectic of Enlightenment* and in particular the chapter 'Elements of Anti-Semitism' is written in anger and while they were in exile from Nazi Germany. It is a considered, critical and emotional attack on racial ideology, hate crimes and German fascism. It pulls no punches and is arguably borne itself on the shockwaves of Auschwitz and the programme of human destruction in Nazi Germany. The Jews in Nazi Germany were viewed not as a minority group but as an opposing race that had to be exterminated to secure the future of National Socialism and the Aryan race. This is particularly pertinent to this book as it examines the constructions of whiteness in a given historical epoch. Horkheimer and Adorno describe the elements of anti-Semitism well, its blindness and murderous ethos: 'attacking or defending blindly, the persecutor and his victim belong to the same sphere of evil. Anti-Semitic behaviour is generated in situations where blinded men robbed of their subjectivity are set loose as subjects' (Horkheimer and Adorno, 1994: 171). For Horkheimer and Adorno anti-Semitism is a deeply imprinted schema, it is a ritual of civilisation, indeed the very act of killing simply conforms to the way of life of the anti-Semite. There is, for Horkheimer and Adorno, a measure of truth in the idea that it is an outlet – anger is discharged on defenceless victims. Interestingly, they make the point that both the victims and persecutors in this type of dynamic are interchangeable. There is no such thing as a born anti-Semite, so gypsies, Jews, Protestants, Catholics may all take the place of the murderer as the norm. Horkheimer and Adorno use psychoanalytic ideas – projection, sublimation, mimesis – to explain the plight of the Jew in Nazi Germany.

Horkheimer and Adorno's work on anti-Semitism is a critique of capitalism, positivism and scientific rationality on the one hand; on the other, it provides us with a basis for the explanation of how we form our idea of self, our identity in relation to others, and our changing relationship to nature. It provides one of the first psycho-social accounts of racism by addressing both social structure and affect and if you take Horkheimer and Adorno's *Dialectic of Enightenment* (1994) and Horkheimer and Flowerman's *Studies in Prejudice* (1950) together then they provide both a theoretical and philosophical account of social conflict in tandem with empirical social research. This is one of the major threads we have seen developing in contemporary critical theory although the emphasis for many theorists has moved away from psychoanalysis to more eclectic psychological ideas – for example Bauman's (1989) 'stranger', which we discuss in the following chapter. Other members of the school are also well known for their psychoanalytic contributions to sociology: Eric Fromm's *Escape from Freedom* (1941) and Herbert Marcuse's *Eros and Civilization* (1956) are among the classic texts of critical theory. It was perhaps Jurgen Habermas more than any other social thinker who revitalised the idea of using psychoanalysis as a form of social philosophy.

Habermas's 1968 book *Knowledge and Human Interests* is an attempt to analyse the connections between knowledge itself and the interests of the human species. It is also a critique of science as the dominant and only form of knowledge. It is Habermas's contention that systematic self reflection is the path to self knowledge; self knowledge helps us free ourselves from ideological domination and unveil our 'true' self. Self reflection therefore leads to emancipation. The key to this is to think about a hermeneutic method in terms of reflection, which is why Habermas turns to psychoanalysis. Habermas's notions of the cognitive interests are well discussed elsewhere (Held, 1980; Outhwaite, 1994; How, 2003), but briefly: all knowledge for

Habermas is founded in cognitive interests. These interests are the basic interests of the human species and are the underlying modes through which reality is disclosed and acted upon. They delineate a general orientation that yields a viewpoint – from which reality is constructed. Cognitive strategies are determined by the conditions and problems governing the reproduction of the human species. So we have the technical interest with the according social sphere – the world of work; a practical interest embedded in the social domain of interaction and communication; and finally the emancipatory interest and the world of power relations. The corresponding types of knowledge are empirico-analytic, historico-hermeneutic and critical theory. For Habermas, it is very much the idea of psychoanalysis as a hermeneutic interpretative science based in self reflection that lends itself as a model for the mapping of the cognitive interests. Habermas argues that initially psychoanalysis appears only as a special form of interpretation, but on closer inspection we can see that psychoanalysis involves a much deeper form of hermeneutics, in other words a depth hermeneutics that addresses both conscious forces and unconscious or unknown memories that make up historical life, our sense of being, who we are.

Habermas outlines the method and role that psychoanalysis can play in uncovering distortions and meanings in everyday language, in linguistic expressions and text. Of course for Freud the royal road to the unconscious was through dream analysis and as Habermas notes, for Freud the dream was the 'normal' model of pathological conditions. The dreamer awakes, but does not understand his or her own creation – the dream. Psycho-analysis goes beyond the hermeneutic because it tries not only to grasp the meaning of distorted text, but also the meaning of the text distortion itself. Transposing this to society we can start to see a method for uncovering distorted communication and ideology. The emancipatory cognitive interest aims at the pursuit of reflection – 'in the power of self-reflection, knowledge and interest are one' (Habermas, 1968: 314).

Therefore for Habermas freedom equals knowledge of the real processes underlying human consciousness and motivation.

What makes us 'unfree' is that we are driven by both internal and external forces that we are not aware of. Internal forces are covered by repression; external forces are masked by ideology. Self reflection can free us from both these internal and external constraints. There have of course been some major criticisms of Habermas's work which we have outlined elsewhere (Clarke, 2005, 2006) many of which he addresses in an additional postscript to *Knowledge and Human Interests*.

What we now term as a psycho-social perspective can be seen as developing from these early ideas of the Frankfurt School, and for the authors, in terms of identity construction in the work of a very different writer – Frantz Fanon. Fanon, in his book *Black Skin, White Masks* (1967), saw the construction of colonial black identity and oppression as the product of both a political economy of hatred and a psychodynamic of racism. Fanon was influenced by both Freudian and Sartrean existential ideas, in what he terms 'psychoexistentialism'. The main feature of Fanon's understanding of the psychology of oppression is that inferiority is the outcome of a double process, both socio-historic and psychological: 'If there is an inferiority complex, it is the outcome of a double process: primarily economic; subsequently, the internalization, or better, the epidermalization of this inferiority' (Fanon, 1967: 13). There is therefore a link between the sociogenesis and psychogenesis of racism and these processes are violent and exclusionary. When Sartre talks of anti-Semitism as a passion it is not the Jewish person who produces the experience; rather, it is the (projected) identification of the Jew that produces the experience. Fanon illustrates this internalisation of projection: 'My body was given back to me sprawled out, distorted, recoloured, clad in mourning in that white winterday. The negro is an animal, the negro is bad, the negro is ugly' (Fanon, 1967: 113). If we apply a Kleinian (1975, 1997) lens to Fanon's thinking and understand the reference to the breaking up of bodies, to being sprawled out and distorted in terms of more than a mere metaphor, then these processes which have consequences on the sociogenic level are the outcome of processes of projective identification (see Clarke, 2003). The white person makes the black person in the image of their projections, literally forcing identity into another, as Fanon notes: 'the white man has woven me out of a thousand details ... I was battered down with tom-toms, cannibalism, intellectual deficiency, fetishism, racial defects, slave ships' (Fanon, 1967: 112). The black person lives these projections, trapped in an imaginary that white people have constructed; trapped by both economic processes and by powerful projective mechanisms, which both create and control the Other. This, of course, highlights the paradoxical nature of projective identification. White people's phantasies about black sexuality, about bodies and biology in general are fears that centre on otherness, otherness that they themselves have created and brought into being. This is what Fanon means when he says that I was 'battered down', 'woven out of a thousand details' – black identity is a stereotype of the black person constructed in the mind of the white person, and then forced back into the black person as the black historical subject (Macey, 2000; Dalal, 2002). This is a false consciousness. Fanon shows us, like Foucault (1977, 1995), how power is an important element in the constitution of our identities and how this is often an oppressive force.

The Emerging Psycho-Social Tradition

Thus, these authors form the theoretical backdrop to our own psycho-social position, albeit one that is influenced by Kleinian (Klein, 1975, 1997) and Relational (Clarke, Hahn and Hoggett, 2008) thinking rather than the Freudian ideas of these earlier thinkers. For us though the most important thing about psycho-social studies is the emphasis on empirical research in which the emotional life of both researcher and respondent are explored. This enables, after Habermas, a critical and sustained self reflection on our methods and practice. So, for example, how are we to understand identity if we do not look at both the socio-structural determinants of a person's life and the way in which they impinge on the inner world of emotion and vice versa? After all, we live in a world where one person's fiction is another's fact; one person's rationality is another's irrationality.

We think perhaps the idea of relationality is best seen and developed within psycho-social research methods where the form of sustained self reflection advocated by the Frankfurt School leads to a critical examination of the relationship between researcher and researched; this we discuss in the final chapter of this book. Although wide ranging inroads have been made into social science disciplines by psycho-social perspectives this is a relatively new area of research. These inroads challenge masculinist notions of rationality not only structured in positivism but in the social sciences in general and can be seen as a relativist challenge to the duality of the researcher as the purveyor of all known knowledge. Thus, the emphasis is on the co-construction of data and the research environment. This can be seen by example in Hollway and Jefferson's (2000) work, which we discuss later in this book, in work by Stephen Frosh et al. (2002, 2003) on young masculinities, and in Valerie Walkerdine et al. (2001) *Growing Up Girl* (see also Lucey, Melody and Walkerdine, 2003). More recently Hoggett et al. (2006) use a psycho-social method to understand the nature of personal identifications, for example class and gender, that underpin the commitment of welfare workers to their jobs.

In looking at a psycho-social construction of white identities there are some key psychodynamic ideas we can draw on, both in theorising and method. Theoretically and practically we see the use of projection, that is attributing feelings and thoughts that are our own onto, or into, some other person as if those attributes belong to the other. In other words projecting, often unconsciously, how we perceive others to be which is actually a construction of our own imagination and delineates our identity from that of the Other. This is one respondent's view of immigration:

> What frightens me is they don't walk around in twos, they always walk around in fours and fives. You never see one on his own, four or five and I've always said, in a car, if there's three blokes in a car, there's a problem. One of them wants to show off, if there's four, two want to show off, so they get mouthy and they do this, that and the other. And it's the same with a lot of these immigrants ... I'm afraid because they're all coming in

and we're taking a lot of asylum seekers and God knows what. I think I'd be a bit afraid then, yeah, I think so.

Q   Of what?

A   As I said, three or four together, could be a problem, one or two on its own wouldn't be a problem because they could be prepared to learn and listen, but three or four together, they just want to do it their way. They just want to bring their culture to this country and exclude you. They don't want you to know about their culture, personally.

Q   What are your feelings about immigration into the country?

A   Too many.

Q   Have your thoughts changed over time?

A   Put it this way, be blunt, I've never liked coloureds, all my life, I don't know why. I've never liked them.

This respondent was quite clearly projecting his own fears and phantasies about immigrants onto them; later in the interview he admitted that he knew very little about immigration and other cultures and what he did know came from the popular press and not his own practical experience, an issue we will discuss in the next chapter. This was an issue that another respondent highlighted:

You start to sort of paint everybody the same, don't you, and they're not. But I think that like again, I said, the media I think. I mean, my husband was there [city centre] the other week and he said to me there was a car stopped by a policeman, and he said, I bet it's bloody illegal immigrants, but because there was about four or five dark-skinned Arab-looking people, and I said, you're just painting everybody with the same brush now, but it probably was true, but I think it don't help you reading the paper and that.

In constructing their white identities respondents often attributed problems to welfare and housing policy, blaming Europe and central government, and not being recognised, as the Welsh or Scottish are, as having a distinct ethnic culture. Strong emotional identifications were made at a more local than national level, which we discuss in chapter 8, and people thought that they were losing their sense of English or British identity:

> From an identity of being British, I think we have probably lost a lot because a lot of traditional things we used to do, I can remember doing at school as a child, we don't do anymore because well, you know, we can't upset the Muslims, and we can't upset the Sikhs if we do this, and we can't upset, you know, the Jews might not like this if we don't, and the people from Africa might not like this. Because in a way, rather than trying to include people from other cultures and other religions, rather than sort of being inclusive, it's oh, we don't know how we're going to include these people, so we won't do it at all.

So, we can theorise psycho-socially about the emotional attachment people have to ideas around home, community and identity, which we do in the following chapters to a certain degree. But we feel the most important aspect of the emerging psycho-social tradition is the research methodologies that generate the rich interview material we use in this book. In allowing people to use the psychoanalytic idea of free association we were able to learn about people's life histories and then understand the way they feel about certain things, ideas and thoughts that developed in the later semi-structured interviews.[1]

Conclusion

In this chapter we have introduced some of what we feel are the most important ideas around identity and identity construction. We feel that none of them are right or wrong, but used in tandem in what we term a psycho-social approach we can gain a better understanding of identity and how it is both socially and psychologically constructed in relation to others. Goffman's approach is important because it shows us how we present ourselves in everyday life, in other words the performances through which we manage to convince others that we are who we are. Thus, we have seen for Goffman, performances are not only realised but idealised, shown in the best possible light to conform to cultural and societal norms, in other words cultural identities are often an idealisation set in opposition to stigmatised identities – they are made distinctive. So, as we have noted this is not about our inner essence, how we feel we are and exist in the world, it's about a complex and continuous profiling about who we are in relation to society that marks us as an individual. We have questioned the status that the role of emotion holds in Goffman's model of self and identity. The emphasis placed on social and personal identity draws away from the feeling self and in some sense negates identity as a felt state of being, it ignores our inner world, our unconscious feelings and desires. We have argued that it is largely affirming Mead's (1934) work that the idea of a sense of cultural identity from the position of the subject is rather overwhelmed by the normalisation of self by society.

In looking at Foucault's work we have seen how sense of self is constructed through discourse that may be largely out of the subject's control. Expert discourses on madness, delinquency and sexuality lead to the creation of the modern self. Thus, the social construction of identity is tied in with notions of rationality, discourse and power. With the help of experts we can work on our self, change our identity or even discover who we actually are. But this analysis is strongly centred on the construction of identity within a given culture and lacks any referent to passion or emotion. We go on to introduce some psychoanalytically informed perspectives on the construction of self and other through the work of the Frankfurt School and Fanon as a basis for a psycho-social perspective on the construction of white identities. A psycho-social perspective, we argue, combines both an analysis of the social construction of reality together with an acknowledge-ment that we are passionate beings and the notion of both outer reality and our inner world work together to form who we are, or perhaps more precisely who we are not. In the next chapter of this book we examine the issue of asylum and immigration in contemporary Britain in the context of media representations using both psycho-social and sociological ideas. In it we argue that there is a worrying trend towards the conflation of asylum issues with terrorism. Using examples from the media and politics we argue that there is a new politics of fear emerging which more than ever concentrates on difference and the demonisation of the Other. In particular, this othering process constructs 'not white' in an atmosphere of global insecurity. This politics uses emotional and psychological methods to play on our social fears and anxieties around community. This goes hand-in-hand with the mainstreaming of anti-immigration policy as a political value: a process that has drawn Left and Right into the battle to appear toughest on defending the nation against external threats. Finally we ask why these policies are becoming acceptable, and indeed ask in the following chapter why the notion of 'community' has become so important.

7

MEDIA REPRESENTATIONS: CONSTRUCTING THE 'NOT WHITE' OTHER

In this chapter we address the issue of asylum and asylum seekers in contemporary Britain. In it we argue that there is a worrying trend towards the conflation of asylum issues with terrorism. Using examples from the media and politics we argue that there is a new politics of fear emerging, which more than ever concentrates on difference and the demonisation of the Other. This politics uses emotional and psychological methods to play on our social fears and anxieties around community. This goes hand-in-hand with a mainstreaming of anti-immigration policy as a political value: a process that has drawn Left and Right into the battle to appear toughest on defending the nation. We ask why these policies are becoming acceptable and we theorise this through the notion of the asylum seeker as 'stranger' in a political sociology of the human imagination.

It's difficult to know where to start when talking of the issue of asylum and asylum seekers in contemporary Britain. There is no doubt that the asylum seeker has become a folk demon in the popular press and also a political pawn in the run up to the 2005 British general election. The weight placed on asylum and the conflation of this issue with labour migration and terrorism is reminiscent of Powell's 'rivers of blood' speech. The most worrying aspect is the way in which the asylum seeker has become equated with the terrorist. So, we not only have people who are going to flood the country moving from outside to inside, but also these people may destroy us from within. Since we first began to think about writing this book, the worst-case scenario has taken place: British-born terrorists have started to use the tactics of suicide bombing. This, we feel, creates an even greater impetus to make sure that those seeking asylum are not pathologised in the wake of the bombings in London. We feel that politicians and the press have themselves been using psychological mechanisms to spread fear into the social body of society by targeting the inner world of the British psyche, terrorising the population to justify immigration policy and to make political gains. We no longer know what is fact or fiction, imagination or reality, emotional or rational thinking. This, we believe, is the state that both the politically motivated press and politicians want us to be in, a state that led to the collusion of the Labour government in the war on Iraq and the spiralling ethnocentric, Islamophobic, anti-asylum seeker prejudice that is enveloping Britain. This, then, is the problem as we see it – the conflation of a set of issues into a kind of otherness that may well destroy us from within, and which has been used for social and political means, not just in Britain, but on the global political stage.

In the first part of this chapter, we look at the relationship between politics, the popular press and issues of asylum. We argue that our fears of invasion by others is very much based in phantasy and a distorted perception of the nature of asylum and immigration. We show how various newspapers try to compete with each other, some providing rational answers to the irrational fears that are evoked by one reading of a newspaper contra to the other. So, for example, the *Daily Mail* might carry pictures one day of asylum seekers flooding the country, the following day the *Observer* will refute those claims with some quite rational explanation of why the *Daily Mail* was wrong. We argue that this process unwittingly colludes with the anti-asylum agenda, ensuring that asylum remains an issue. We then go on to give an example of how asylum seeker issues get translated into what we call a 'socio-politics of fear' and how this political rhetoric is acted out in everyday life.

The second part of this chapter looks at the idea that anti-immigration has been mainstreamed as a political value. We argue that focusing on the UK Independence Party (UKIP) or the BNP to demonstrate anti-immigration policy would be misleading when the manifesto of both the Labour and Conservative parties place a huge emphasis on the removal of bodies from national space. While protecting the rights of genuine (the few) refugees, anti-immigration has been mainstreamed in the name of defending the nation against infiltration and national defence. Something that in the wake of the London bombings is likely to become even more controversial.

In the final sections of this chapter we ask ourselves why it is so easy for these policies to be accepted, and explore popular misconceptions of asylum seekers through the lens of sociology of the imagination. Primarily using the work of Bauman (1990) and Žižek (1993), we address the way in which the refugee as 'stranger' represents all our own fears of displacement, of chaos, of the ambiguity of living in the modern world.

The Press and Politics

In this section of the chapter, we shall give some examples of how political issues around asylum are both conflated by and influenced by the popular press, using examples drawn from the period of our fieldwork. The first example is that of the press criticising the press, in this case a report by the *Observer* newspaper on 17 April 2005, responding to pictures in the previous week's *Daily Mail*, of huge queues of asylum seekers waiting to enter the country at Calais. The *Observer* reporters visited Calais two days later and found a completely different story:

> There was a lone jogger, then a mother dragging her two screaming children. Five minutes passed before a British couple ambled by, lugging crates of lager. But that was about it. The sweeping square bordering the verdant Parc Richelieu in Calais was remarkably quiet on Friday.
>
> Where had all the asylum seekers gone? After all, photographs taken at precisely the same location had appeared 24 hours earlier offering a quite dissimilar scene. In them, a queue of immigrants 'destined for England' had

been pictured snaking alongside the entire length of the park's neat flower beds. (Townsend and Hinsliff, 2005)

So, rather than an 'open door' to the UK and 'hundreds' of young men 'hoping to reach the shores of England' in 'the next few days', the *Observer* reporters found a handful of asylum seekers and refugees from various parts of the globe. In their concern to report how difficult it is to actually gain entry into the UK, the *Observer* highlighted the plight of various people who had injured themselves in different ways – falling from trains and walls.[1] 'All agreed security measures were formidable, borders were not out of control'. So, this piece in the *Observer* seeks to dispel some of the myths surrounding asylum and immigration: for example there are as few as five asylum seekers coming through Dover per day by spring 2005 (as opposed to 60 in 2003):

Groups of European tourists are routinely mistaken for illegal immigrants, according to the Home Office-funded charity Migrant Helpline, yards from Dover's bustling ferry port. Fantasy thrives in a climate of distrust. One tale involves a resident who reported asylum seekers in Argos buying 'expensive goods'. They turned out to be the crew of a cruise ship. (Townsend and Hinsliff, 2005)

It seems from this that our fears of invasion are very much based in phantasy and a distorted perception of asylum and immigration. What we need to do is question why this story was ever run at all. The damage has been done, and it seems that if we use the premise that the asylum issue is tapping into our unconscious fears and anxieties, then a rational argument from one newspaper is not going to temper the irrational fears fuelled by another. It is of course a political duel between left- and right-wing press (if this dichotomy still exists); the *Observer* is unwittingly or unconsciously colluding with the psychodynamic: it ensures that asylum remains a headline issue by replying and reporting it. In some sense the fact that it is a reasonably well-respected newspaper adds weight to the idea that asylum is an issue. As Michael Rustin (1991) has noted, beliefs in difference and in particular racial difference 'are among the most irrational that men and women hold' (Rustin, 1991: 61). Difference is the basis of the construction of cultural identities and often, meaning ascribed to it is primitive in nature, that is, it taps into our unconscious and archaic side. This is why rational argumentation cuts very little ice in the asylum debate in the national papers.

Our second example is even more disturbing and chilling. Michael Howard in the run up to the 2005 general election placed a strong emphasis on issues of immigration and asylum, most notably in the case of the failed asylum seeker Kamel Bourgass, convicted of the murder of Detective Constable Stephen Oake, and of plotting to spread poisons. Not withstanding the personal tragedy involved in this affair, a deep vein of political terrorism, or at least the spread of terror, could be mined. The two issues that are central to fear – phantasy and the provocation of anxiety – in the political agenda are found in one object, terror and asylum, or should we say the terrorist as asylum seeker. According to Howard:

> The tragedy of what happened is that Kamel Bourgass, an al-Qaeda operative, should not have been in Britain at all. He was one of the quarter of a million failed asylum-seekers living in Britain. If Mr Blair had delivered the firm but fair immigration controls promised eight years ago, Bourgass wouldn't have been in Britain. He wouldn't have been here free to plot a ricin attack. (BBC News, 2005)

So we start to see a real politics of fear develop where what some have described as a small attempt by an individual (the case against the other four men returned a not guilty verdict) is conflated into a case of global terrorism. Not only have we got to deal with the internal anxiety of being invaded and flooded by Others (asylum seekers) but we are also in danger of being destroyed from within by the Other (the terrorist). Worse still, the asylum seeker is a terrorist; our worst fears are realised. So we start to see yet another spiral of ethnocentrism, racism, Islamophobia and the idea, to return to where we started, of Powellism, in which 'genuine fears' and now 'bogus refugees' raise their ugly heads. Worse still, the politics of fear seems to use the same psychological mechanisms as terrorism itself, it instils a sense of anxiety in people so that you are never certain of your own safety, whether something might happen, whether your next door neighbour might turn against you, etc. You don't know whether it's safe to get on a train or a plane – and we all live under the anxiety of an imminent threat.

How does the rhetoric of the politics of fear translate into everyday life? The final example we want to give is from the research project that this book is based on. We met Mr N in a pub during our initial attempts to find gatekeepers to help locate respondents for the project. It was a chance meeting and we were in no way consciously looking for people to talk about issues around asylum. We had asked Mr N to give an opinion on organisations that might be gatekeepers in that ward. There was an associated conversation going on at another table about an asylum seekers' hostel and its whereabouts. The local Licensed Victuallers Association man (seated on the next table) was asked if he knew of a bed and breakfast where asylum seekers were housed in the city centre. He responded that the local council wouldn't use bed and breakfasts any more because they were too expensive. Any such housing would be Home Office responsibility with a private contractor like 'Adolphi' [sic]. Mr N quickly joined the other discussion.[2] He floated the figure of 40,000 asylum seekers in Plymouth (i.e. 100 times higher than the actual number).

A lot of asylum seekers were in Mr N's mind, 'economic migrants', and he singled out the Iraqis as particularly undeserving: an Iraqi regiment should be formed out of the asylum seekers in Britain, he argued, so they can go and fight for their country's freedom. A few other stories were narrated to demonstrate unspoken injustices in the system. He gave the example of grocery shopping. Many asylum seekers shop collectively at Lidl, going round with one trolley, paying with one cheque and finally putting the shopping in one 'newish' car. In the context of Mr N's interpretation, this ostensibly normal behaviour at a supermarket emerges as concealing an unnamed scam, whose source or nature can only be implied.

When it was put to him that asylum seekers 'do not get access to the same levels of benefit as nationals, or social housing', which he must be aware of as a postmaster, he responded by drawing an imaginary line on the table with his finger. 'Where is the line', he asked, 'between an asylum seeker, a refugee and a citizen?' The evening ended on a splendidly contradictory note. After castigating asylum seekers and other immigrants for claiming benefits and not working for their money, he asked a cabbie, who had come into the pub to call for his client, where he was from. 'The Czech Republic', came the reply. Mr. N looked resigned and triumphant, his case rested: 'This is typical of what you get here now'.

This example may seem rather anecdotal: a chance meeting at the very start of the research programme, which could portray the far end of a spectrum of views. Yet it offers a glimpse of the associations and assumptions in people's minds. These may appear as the views of a right-wing member of the white working class, but I think we have to think long and hard about who we are demonising if we use this label. Another, middle-class and church-going, respondent seemed to share similar phantasies. While on the one hand he was prepared to raise money and provide blankets for 'genuine' refugees, he certainly didn't want them over here and felt we had let too many people come here in the past. He told us he would be voting for UKIP in the 2005 election.

The project has shown that there are very clear links between people's perception of asylum and otherness and what the respondents gleaned from the media. Three snippets from various interviewees follow:

I don't like the fear that's going on and the seeming escalation of fear, whether that is media-fuelled, and I think that has something to do with it, but the perception that most people have and they start being afraid of other people and other cultures and other coloured skins and other people's religions, I don't like how that's evolving and it's not heading in the right direction. I don't like that way it's heading, that's quite uncomfortable for me.

I think the trouble is with the media they portray them sometimes as something awful, something we've all got to be frightened of and worried about. And it's like, no, it's not like that. It shouldn't be like that. And as far as I'm concerned you should just be able to cross between countries,

> it should be a case of, you have your passport to show who you are, for identity obviously, but why shouldn't you just go in and out? ... The trouble is with terrorism and that you can't these days, but in an ideal world you should be able to just say, right, go there and get a job if I want one, do whatever I've got to do.

> All I know is what I read and hear, which is third hand really, isn't it. It might be a load of old tosh.

These are paradoxical, as on the one hand people seem to realise that the media often exaggerate things to get a good story, but on the other hand, for many people, the media is their only source of information about asylum and immigration. We now turn to the way in which anti-immigration has been mainstreamed as a political value.

Mainstreaming Anti-Immigration as a Political Value

The situation referred to here has not emerged from nowhere, nor is it anchored exclusively in British political and social culture. There are international material contexts in which asylum seekers occupy a specific status (cf. Garner and Moran (2006) on Australia and the Republic of Ireland's recent experiences). In this section we will explore the idea that while they may occupy a slightly different imaginary space to the self and the Other, as Bauman suggests, this might also be seen not as an intermediate zone between the two, but as a special case of otherness, and that they are constituted differently by particular groups.

Generally asylum seekers' forced unproductiveness, in a culture where economic output is so prized, stigmatises them. It also places further distance between them and vectors of integration such as the unions and informal work-based networks. While legally excluded from the workforce, asylum seekers come to constitute a symbolic threat to resources, having not fulfilled the implicit (and sometimes explicit) contract requiring input, in terms of tax, before benefits can be awarded. This explains the coalescence of narratives of unfairness around consumption (asylum seekers buying groceries, cars, etc.). Trapped outside the workforce, often segregated physically in detention centres or hostels, asylum seekers are marked out for different forms of attack by at least three groups: working-class putative competitors for benefits; middle-class NIMBYs seeking to retain spatial purity (Hubbard, 2005b), and a political class that both regulates asylum seekers' freedoms and increasingly uses them as objects that enable the state to demonstrate it is more clearly defending 'us'.

Examples of this are placing asylum seekers in detention centres and prisons, and even locating them outside national jurisdiction. Australia's pioneering 'Pacific Solution' and the construction of detention centres in the outback have served as models for the UK and other EU countries. In March 2003, the then Home Secretary David Blunkett tabled a plan to site asylum seeker processing centres in 'Third Countries' outside the EU's border. Years later this is still being debated, and a pilot scheme run by the Dutch government (astonishingly backed by the UNHCR) and the EU, is training Libyan civil servants to run a camp for asylum seekers seeking asylum in the Netherlands (given the green light in autumn 2004). Additionally, 'Regional Protection Plans' involving the administration of asylum in situ in the Great Lakes region and the Ukraine are also at a pilot stage (Waterfield, 2005).[3]

Both strands of this strategy of locating asylum seekers where they are increasingly remote from a) our hearts, and b) our homes, are mutually reinforcing and perform a security rather than an economic function. All of this costs money, but money well spent. It confirms the asylum seekers as unsettled, out of place, chaotic, abnormal and requiring special treatment, and us as necessarily settled, in place, ordered and normal.

Indeed, tempting though it is to focus solely on UKIP and the BNP as bearers of such tidings in Britain, this would be grossly misleading (Garner, 2005). Authoritarian responses to immigration, based on a dwindling grasp of the complexities of the issues among policy-makers and public, have been both causes and effects of the political mainstreaming of anti-immigration. From the 2005 manifestoes of the Conservative and Labour parties (who together have won at least 65 per cent of the vote at every general election since the 1930s) emerge an emphasis on the control of bodies and their removal from national space, justified by the values of order and national defence, in which the UK is constructed as a business, with 'a proud tradition of offering a safe haven to those genuinely fleeing persecution'.[4]

Evidently, to use contemporary equal opportunities terminology, defending the nation against infiltration in this form has now been successfully 'mainstreamed'.[5] The degree of difference between the BNP, UKIP, centre-right and centre-left parties in the treatment given to the issues is relative rather than absolute: they might be more fully understood as points on a continuum. Moreover, only Labour and the Conservatives have held power nationally in the post-war period, characterised by both increasingly exclusive nationality and immigration legislation, and the rebirth and reconfiguration of debates about immigration.[6] There was no serious far-right challenge in the UK in the immediate post-war period, yet scrutiny of Cabinet Papers demonstrates that 'coloured immigration' was problematised by both the Attlee and Churchill administrations (Miles, 1993; Carter et al., 1993; Carter, 2000). This predated the Union of British Fascists' unsuccessful attempt to capitalise on the Notting Hill riots at the 1958 Kensington by-election. Brown (1999) traces Powell's themes back to the late 1950s and a Birmingham-based Conservative lobby group of MPs. Moreover, it was a Conservative candidate who dislodged Labour cabinet member Patrick Gordon-Walker in 1964 with the notorious 'If you want a nigger neighbour, vote Labour' slogan. Based on this admittedly brief summary, can we really conclude that far-right parties overly influenced mainstream politicians?

The arguments deployed to problematise 'coloured immigration' in the post-war period[7] were based on assumptions about people that link the natural to the social, i.e. irredeemable and unbridgeable cultural difference making social problems inevitable and unmanageable. Ensuing policy models procured racist outcomes: the use of the concept of 'patriality' for example (in the 1968 and 1971 Acts), broke the imperial tie of common allegiance to the British Crown by prioritising bloodlines over membership of empire. Previously, birth in the empire had been on an equal par with birth in the UK in terms of access to nationality.

From the late 1960s, priority was accorded to those with at least one grandparent born in the UK. Recent immigrants from the Caribbean and Asia and their British-born children were thus disadvantaged in relation to white Commonwealth nationals and longer standing white British nationals. Although some white Commonwealth nationals also suffered as a consequence, we would argue that shifting membership criteria in this way de facto constructs a racialised border aimed at excluding a large proportion of non-white immigrants from British nationality.

Indeed, most intentions frequently generate negative outcomes in this field. The obsession with appearing 'tough' on immigration over the last decade appears to have generated a downward spiral into hostility among all sections of the public. The outsourcing of immigration controls to private companies, carriers, social security officials, employers, etc. (Lahav and Guiraudon, 2000) has spawned a political subculture of informal and frequently unnecessary checks carried out by untrained and unmonitored staff. The example of the Asylum and Immigration Act 1996, aimed ostensibly at eliminating benefit fraud, demonstrates the kind of slippage that can be generated.[8] Research on the Act in practice (CRE, 1998) turned up cases where non-white British nationals were being asked to prove their entitlement to employment, refugees were being given reduced benefit options and, in some cases, migrant workers with entitlement to particular benefits were refused:

> some people, in particular those from ethnic minority, immigrant and refugee communities, are wrongly being denied benefits, services or employment opportunities, and often face unfair treatment at the hands of officials and employers. Many face long delays before it is acknowledged that they are legally entitled to benefits or to be employed. (CRE, 1998: 5)

So when decision-making about entitlement suddenly becomes the domain of individuals, a picture of the imagined nation comes into focus. The kinds of 'administrative incivility' referred to here are mundane realities for many people, as their official status is conflated with Others in the morass of signifiers – 'asylum seeker', 'immigrant', 'refugee' – that are deployed to function as what Back and Solomos (1996) call 'coded signifiers', to refer to people seen as not belonging in some way, regardless of their actual rights and entitlements.

Moreover, New Labour in power has been responsible for the Immigration and Asylum Act 1999, and the Nationality, Asylum and Immigration Act 2002, plus its 2004 amendments (as well as the Equality Acts and visa schemes to have been established since 1997). A focus on immigration as a policy area at all may well be counter-productive if the objective is to soften attitudes: a recent survey in the UK has demonstrated that traditionally conservative values on immigration have spread to the liberal middle classes (Carvel, 2004; Park et al., 2004). Over the 1995–2003 period, the proportion of graduates wanting curbs on immigration rose from 33 per cent to 56 per cent, while the overall figure remained virtually stable (81 per cent, down from 82 per cent). The proportion of Labour supporters in favour of reducing immigration increased from 58 per cent to 71 per cent (cf. Conservative voters, 71 per cent up to 84 per cent). New Labour's constituency has either been dragged rightwards with the party, or the party has correctly pre-empted such a shift by its progressively stricter policies (especially on asylum) since 1997. We are in uncharted territory: the centre has not held. Michael Howard on *Question Time*'s Election Special[9] admitted the Conservative party would actually like to withdraw from the 'out of date' Geneva Convention, but wanted to 'take more genuine refugees, who can't afford to pay the people traffickers and aren't strong enough to cross Europe in a container lorry … the women and the children'. In this enactment of power relations, Howard posited a future in which he could opt in and out of international treaties in order to convey to the electorate that he was taking the defence of borders so seriously that the UK's interest trumps international obligations. He also asserted the power to authenticate, sort the wheat from the chaff, and in doing so, evoke the required emotional responses. 'Genuine' asylum seekers are weak and pitiful (thankfully small in number and generally far, far away); while 'bogus' asylum seekers are hateful monsters come to drain our resources.

Each month seems to bring ever tougher measures sending out contradictory messages to migrants: come and work here, or study and pay large fees in the UK but get the hell out as soon as we have finished with you. In the wake of 7/7, a new Bill was introduced into parliament that seeks to deter people from overstaying visas by withholding a proportion of income earned while resident with legal status and placing it in an account in the migrant worker's country of origin (Travis, 2005). Normally such measures are allowable only for non-payment of outstanding taxes or fines. Once again the placing of Others who have committed no offence in the same legal category as people who have (cf. asylum seekers in detention) becomes a norm. Repeatedly making non-nationals a category of people to whom the law de facto applies differently can only be interpreted as criminalising them. Against such a context how can we expect most people, uninterested in the definitions of asylum seeker, immigrant or refugee, to arrive at any conclusion other than the one presented: these people are a genuine threat to us.

Yet the very values promulgated by those so keen on controlling immigration do not pass unchallenged outside the pages of particular newspapers, think tanks and focus groups. Such discourse always entails a counter-discourse, in which the idea of community values is contested. Ralph Grillo's (2005) study of Saltdean, near Brighton, where a plan was floated to house 20 asylum seekers in a hotel, shows that 'community values' are actually the basis of intra-communal fault-lines. The anti-hostel group in Saltdean proclaimed it was seeking to protect resources, space, safety and low levels of crime, while the pro-group focused on seeking to question the accuracy of the negative links made between asylum seekers, crime, violence and resource absorption. It constructed the imminent arrival of asylum seekers in a positive light. A similar split is evidenced in the Channel 4 documentary, *Keep Them Out* (Modell, 2004) filmed in Lee-on-Solent in Hampshire. A local group was formed to protest against a former naval base being turned into an asylum seeker holding centre. In this configuration, the state is depicted as pro-asylum seeker and anti-local, ignoring the democratic wishes of the community,[10] but it is clear also that asylum polarises rather than simply unites communities behind common values. Asylum seekers thus act as catalysts for debate on the values of a given community. While the Lee-on-Solent group campaigned on the basis of asylum seekers representing a range of threats to culture, resources and morals, as well as being potential terrorists, there was also a response, in the form of a pro-asylum seeker group and individual acts of anti-racist resistance.

In light of this, and more generally in the apparent mainstreaming of asylum issues, we want to start theorising asylum, and more specifically ask why people are responding to this mainstreaming in the way that they are. We have already alluded to a politics of fear in which both politicians and the press reach into our emotional selves, and we feel that the work of Zygmunt Bauman is particularly helpful in exploring what we find strange in Others. First though, we will briefly explore the work of Slajov Žižek, whose writing has an uncanny resonance with the asylum seeker issue in the UK.

Theorising Asylum and the Inner World

If we think about British identity and the question of asylum and immigration then it would be easy to get drawn into Žižek's (1993) ideas around ethno-national conflict and the notion of the 'Theft of Enjoyment' in the former Yugoslavia. Žižek argues that the bond holding a given community together is some form of shared relationship to a Thing – 'to our enjoyment incarnate'. The relationship we have to our Thing is structured more by fantasy than reality and is what people talk of when they refer to a threat to 'our' way of life. This nation Thing is not a clear set of values to which we can refer, argues Žižek, but a set of properties that are often contradictory and appear as 'our' Thing. This Thing, this quasi way of life, is only accessible to us, but tirelessly sought after by the Other. Žižek argues that Others are unable grasp it, but it is constantly menaced by 'them'. So, this Thing is present, or is in some way to do with what we refer to as our 'way of life'; the way we organise our rituals, ceremonies, feasts, 'in short, all the details by which is made visible the unique way a community organises its enjoyment' (Žižek, 1993: 201). Žižek warns us, however, that this Thing is more complex than a simple set of features that comprise a way of life: there is something present in it, people believe in it, or more importantly, 'I believe that other members of the community believe in this thing'. The Thing exists because people believe in it; it is an effect of belief itself. Thus Žižek argues that:

> We always impute to the 'other' an excessive enjoyment: he wants to steal our enjoyment (by ruining our way of life) and/or he has access to some secret, perverse enjoyment. In short, what really bothers us about the 'other' is the peculiar way he organises his enjoyment, precisely the surplus, the 'excess' that pertains to this way: the smell of 'their' food, 'their' noisy songs and dances, 'their' strange manners, 'their' attitude to work. (Žižek, 1993: 203)

We are therefore faced with the paradoxical nature of this Thing; on the one hand the Other is a workaholic who steals our jobs and labour, on the other an idler, a lazy person relying on the state for benefits. Our Thing is therefore something that cannot be accessed by the Other but is constantly threatened by otherness. In some sense we can place this parallel to the idea that the asylum seeker is taking our jobs and welfare benefits, something to which they have no, or should not have access. What Žižek's work highlights is the role of myth and phantasy in the construction of cultural and national identity, and more importantly, the way in which this identity is wholly imagined rather than grounded in some reality, i.e. it is at some level resistant to argument – the irrational cannot be overruled by the rational.

In our empirical fieldwork, threats to both community and identity were seen as a central issue in contemporary Britain. The theme of disintegrating networks is also reflected in nostalgia, particularly among older respondents, for the perceived reliability and stability of past communities reminiscent of Les Back's 'Golden Era' (1996) in which there were tighter family and community structures. As Tony Blair argued in Bristol on 23 June 2006, when talking of 'our' nation's future, there was something both comforting and suffocating in past communities, a sense of fairness and honour which has gone (*Guardian*, 2006). Picking up on the putative fairness and honour inherent in past communities, there is a strong focus, particularly among the narratives of the less well-off respondents in our research, on the perceived lack of fairness in contemporary Britain. This is reflected in the way resources, such as benefits and social housing, are seen as being allocated to those who know how to 'work the system' or who have come from another country and not previously contributed and have therefore unfairly jumped the queue. Anxiety was expressed about the numbers of immigrants perceived as being allowed to come into the country as correspondingly fewer resources were seen as available for the 'native' population who, it was felt, had more entitlement, having contributed to and invested in the system.

Cultural diversity was, however, seen positively within itself by many respondents, and welcomed as such, although usually with the contradictory proviso that incomers should adapt to British culture and values and integrate, learning the language and accepting British customs. Nevertheless, some did feel that Britain has lost, or is losing some of its identity. Most of those who expressed this view did so in the context of multiculturalism and 'political correctness', particularly with regard to traditional British customs such as those surrounding Christmas. There was real resentment, again whether real or imagined, particularly from the more working-class respondents, that 'Christmas' has in some instances been replaced by 'winter-time', and that carols, nativity plays and Christmas decorations have been banned in several places in the name of not offending other cultures and other faiths. Again we have tones of Žižek: what we most fear is the theft of that enjoyment by others. Christmas is noted for being a time of celebration, and limitations on traditional forms of enjoyment are especially likely to stimulate resentment:

> You can't call them Christmas lights; they're winter lights because you might upset the Muslim community. Why? We are a Christian country at the end of the day, a Christian nation. Great Britain is Christian, predominantly. So why should we have to bury our faith if you like, to please the Muslims,

the Hindus, the Buddhas, whatever, in our country? And that is political correctness gone mad.

I think that, you know, we should allow for different religions, but not when their religion takes precedence over ours, because we certainly can't go to a Muslim country and have the same rights.

In the same way that some perceive the 'native' population as potentially having to compete with immigrants to access the resources of the welfare system, here we see resentment that there is somehow competition for spiritual resources and that the 'outsiders' (invariably Muslim) are receiving undue favouritism.

So, we fear the theft of our way of life and our imaginary notions of home by some other, while simultaneously projecting our fear and loathing onto some other group – here 'asylum seekers'. This is then justified in terms of something stolen – our entitlement, our welfare benefits – thus we have the circular motion or cycle, of decantations of the theft of enjoyment, classical Freudian projection really. We think this is far more complex though. The problem as we see it is that many of the new groups of immigrants to the UK are very similar, not only in skin colour, which we know is a major symbolic referent, but also in social (but often not economic) background to those that feel threatened. Many of them are young white people seeking shelter and asylum. They are more akin to Bauman's (1989, 1990) 'stranger'.

The 'stranger' throws identity construction into the land of ambiguity and if we are to believe Zygmunt Bauman (1990), we now all live under the condition of universal 'strangerhood'. The concept of the 'stranger' has a psycho-social quality, partly fictive, partly real, partly a figment of our own imagination. Whereas identity often feels clear cut, we know who 'we' are and we know who 'they' are, the 'stranger' blurs these definitions and literally defies all contemporary rules that ascribe who we are. Although rooted in Simmel's (1950 [1905]) concept of stranger, Bauman's 'stranger' represents a far more complex and often sinister identity, and Bauman has used it at length to describe and analyse the position of Jewish peoples in Europe. Quite simply for Bauman, the 'universal stranger' is the Jew, in this post-'race', post-Holocaust world. In Bauman's words, 'There are friends and enemies. And there are "strangers"' (Bauman, 1991: 53). 'Strangers' are not unfamiliar people, but they cross or break the dividing line of dualism, they are neither 'us' nor 'them'. There is a clear definition of the social and physical boundaries between 'us' and 'them', 'friends' and 'enemies', both are subject to the same structures and ideas. They define good and bad, true and false, and they stand in polarity, creating an illusion of order and symmetry. The 'stranger' violates this structure and order, to paraphrase Bauman: they (the 'strangers') bring the 'outside' 'inside' and poison the comfort of order with the suspicion of chaos.

Unlike the nomad or wanderer of past times, who comes today and leaves tomorrow, the 'stranger' comes today and stays. The 'stranger' in modernity has been persecuted as Jew, as Gypsy, as Muslim, as victim and as potential victimiser. This is also the case when we start to think of indigenous peoples. The Aborigine as uncanny 'strangers' have had their basic rights stripped from them by colonial powers and settlers, including their right to their own land, sacred places and their own sense of history (Clarke and Moran, 2003). More recently the notion and actuality of a fortress Europe has created a rift between the 'west' and the 'rest' and we have argued (Clarke, 2002b) that this is nowhere better demonstrated than the way in which refugees have been perceived in the UK and demonised in the popular press as outsiders who have penetrated the inside. This then feeds into distinctions made by the public about what discourses are legitimate: neutrality over 'equal opportunities', but no holds barred over immigration, for example (Statham, 2003; Lewis, 2005). The dispersal of refugees from Kosovo and Somalia, North Africa and the Middle East around the country has, if we were to believe the media, planted a 'stranger' within our community who lives off us, while returning nothing. If cultural identities are essentially defined by difference then the concept of 'stranger' brings a whole new set of rules and ambiguities into the equation. We feel that it is particularly helpful in the analysis of the position of the asylum seeker in contemporary Britain and Europe because it allows us to see how the human imagination often runs riot, in particular when dealing with the ambiguous subject. Farhad Dalal (2005) vividly captures this incursion into our inner world:

> Contempt, disgust, hate, fear, rage, dread, anxiety and panic: these are some of the common reactions to the creatures we call 'asylum-seekers'. I say 'creatures' because to some they are hardly human, inhabiting as they do such dark and dirty places as tunnels, crates, containers. They continually test and probe our boundaries to exploit the slightest weakness and slip into our land under cover of night. Once in, like parasites they leech off the state and bring havoc to our civilised way of life with their large families, foul smells and work-shy and violent ways. (Dalal, 2005: 21)

For Dalal, these sentiments are not new and have been common through history, often in relation to the poorer classes in general. The entry of asylum seekers into the UK sparks off anxieties around dilution and contamination of identity, identity that is often constructed through the practice of social exclusion. The problem is, we are literally no longer sure who 'we' are, and in some sense we have to learn to live with ambiguity.

Conclusion

The socio-politics of fear has added a new psychodynamic dimension to asylum. Not only does the asylum seeker represent our own fears of chaos and displacement, but also the possibility of being destroyed from within by both our own phantasies of terror and the terrorist in our midst. The terrorist in our midst is now a concrete reality and it is even more important that ideas of asylum and anti-immigration are not conflated and confused with terrorism. Our argument is quite straightforward: the asylum seeker represents all our own fears of displacement, of potential chaos and living with ambiguity in the modern world. The asylum seeker is the contemporary version of this. The Jew, the gypsy, the migrant, etc., can also serve this purpose, but the actual contemporary of it focuses on specific circumstance such as the decline of the welfare state, 'mass migration on the march', increased awareness of these things as global phenomena. The press and politicians tap into our inner world of anxiety and imagination, placing a stress on difference that is irreconcilable and incompatible with 'our' ways of life, which threatens our ethnicity, our whiteness. In some sense, it is a more sophisticated version of Barker's (1981) 'New Racism' thesis, in which ideas about cultural difference, identity and attachments to 'our way of life' come to the fore. We start to see yet another spiral of racism, ethnocentrism and Islamophobia, but this is not coming from right-wing individuals, but from the centre, as anti-immigration policy becomes mainstreamed. We have attempted to theorise why people are reacting to this mainstreaming in the way that they are, in other words generally embracing what appears to be an anti-immigration stance. We feel, as we have suggested, that the socio-politics of fear has a lot to do with the acceptance of these policies through the way in which both the press and politicians reach into our emotional 'selves', reaching a place impervious to rational argument.

8

WHITENESS, HOME AND COMMUNITY

The idea of community has always been central to the construction of group and individual identity. It has been the site of moral panics about the disintegration of traditional community and values as well as concerns around racism and segregation (see chapter 5). The notion of community is of central importance in contemporary policy and political thinking. So, for example, as Anna Marie Smith (1992) argues in the 1980s and early 1990s new right Thatcherite policy concentrated on creating a hegemonic project that aimed at defining social space through the construction of outsider figures. Smith argues that the construction of demonised groups, what we could call communities, allowed for a political bartering for power in which politicians claimed that the only way they could protect British families (the British family) was to have more control over local government. In other words, strengthen the authoritarian hold of central government. More recently David Miliband (2006), then Minister for Communities and Local Government, has talked of the opposite in what he calls 'double devolution'. That is, not just devolving power to local government, but to local communities and people. In 2006 a new Commission on Integration and Cohesion was announced 'to make practical recommendations to help develop capacity to build cohesive and integrated communities'. In this chapter we set out to explore how people today construct their identities in relation to community and whether traditional forms of identity construction still hold. As most of us are essentially sociable people, much, although not all, of this identity construction takes place against the background of the communities that people live in. We therefore look at what people mean when they talk of a 'community' and the factors that increase or decrease community cohesion between groups. Based on the authors' empirical research, this chapter examines the construction of 'white' community within the context of an increasing political interest in the notion of community. As we noted in the previous chapter, Tony Blair stated in Bristol on 23 June 2006, when talking about the changing nature of community and crime:

> There was, at the same time, something both comforting and suffocating about these communities. But they were very effective at reproducing informal codes of conduct and order. They contained a sense of fairness and honour, what Orwell habitually referred to as 'decency.' Now, this fixed order of community has gone ... In reality, what is happening is simply another facet of globalisation and a changing world. Fixed communities go. The nuclear family changes. Mass migration is on the march. (*Guardian*, 2006).

Our research has found conflicting views, some may disagree with Blair but others reinforced his views. What we did find, however, was an overwhelming stress on the importance of community and the link this has with white identity construction at a very local rather than national level. In the next section we want to discuss some of the existing literature on the notion of community, a notion that is contested in itself, before going on to examine some of the empirical data we have collected in a psycho-social analysis of community and identity construction.

Contested Communities

In much the same way that the notion of identity can take on multiple meanings the same could be said for the concept of community. So, we can have community as geographical location, as a set of ideas and values, as something real and concrete or even imagined. We even now have the idea of virtual communities. We have community schools, community centres, community buses and in terms of policy, community regeneration, ideas around community cohesion and disintegration. Communities may be very local, or even global. The sense or idea of community can be very different in rural areas to that of inner cities and again may differ between social housing estates and areas made up of owner occupiers. This is why we report in the next section of this chapter what the notion of community actually meant to the people we interviewed and how they thought this related to their identity. This is problematic in itself, as many people have never thought of themselves as having some form of white identity or ethnicity.

The very idea of community is contested, as Paul Hoggett (1997) argues in his book of the same name:

> It is not even clear that community means much to the ordinary man or woman in the street these days. Certainly in many urban areas the idea of community in its traditional sense, as referring to a place or neighbourhood with which one feels some sense of identification may be waning. (Hoggett, 1997: 1)

But Hoggett also points out that new social groups have begun to appropriate the term, he gives examples of the 'gay community' and 'communities of faith' to describe Christians. He goes on to argue that if the concept of community has any value today it is very different from the idea of community that existed over a hundred years ago. Many of the people we interviewed would disagree with this, which we discuss in the next section, but Hoggett does offer some very clear insights into both the history and development of the notion of community. He notes that the origin of the sociological term community can be found in the work of Tönnies (1988 [1887]) and the differentiation between the idea of *Gemeinschaft* (community) and *Gesellschaft* (society). Gerard Delanty in his book *Community* (2003) elaborates:

> Community as Gemeinschaft is expressed, to follow Tönnies's terms, in family life in concord, in rural village life in folkways, and in town life in religion. Society as Gesellschaft is expressed in city life in convention, in national life in legislation, and in cosmopolitan life in public opinion ... These are the words Tönnies uses, and which indicate that community and society, while being very different, express different kinds of associative life. (Delanty, 2003: 33)

He argues that Tönnies's view of community was very much rooted in tradition while society was expressed in terms of social relations. Hoggett (1997) expresses this slightly differently by arguing that for Tönnies, community is based on similarity while society is based on interdependence and exchange. Both Delanty (2003) and Hoggett (1997) point to the work of another sociologist writing around the same period of time, Emile Durkheim, who proposed a very different view of community and society in his book *The Division of Labour* (1893) where he talks of organic and mechanical forms of solidarity as forms of social bonding. Put simply, mechanical solidarity is small scale, based in tradition, cooperation, shared values, beliefs and emotions, the division of labour is based in a shared feeling of cooperation and individualism is underdeveloped. Whereas organic solidarity involves a far more complex division of labour, individuals are interdependent economically on others to perform tasks they cannot do themselves, solidarity is no longer based in tradition, belief, religion or ties of kinship, the individual in modern society has more freedom and rights, but this is still a collective activity (see Giddens, 1972 for discussion). In fact, Delanty argues that Durkheim effectively reversed Tönnies's ideas. The emphasis in Durkheim's work is on the division of labour in modernity and the changing relationship people have to industrialisation. Durkheim effectively argues that in modernity we actually see the growth of organic solidarity. Again, Delanty notes that in a review of Tönnies's *Community and Society*, Durkheim fundamentally disagreed with Tönnies's notion of society:

Accepting Tönnies's argument that society derives from community, he argued that society is not primarily characteristic of utilitarian individualism and mechanical social relations. In Durkheim's view, life in large groups is as natural as in small ones, claiming 'there is a collective activity in our contemporary societies which is just as natural as that of smaller societies of previous ages' (Durkheim, 1964 [1893]: 146–7). Durkheim rejected the assumption that lay behind Tönnies's argument of community as organic and society as mechanical (Delanty, 2003: 36–7).

As Delanty notes, Durkheim's sociology was precisely about what forms of social integration can exist in modern society, regarding his view of community as post traditional with the emphasis on community as a moral force rather than a traditional myth. Hoggett (1997) argues that despite the romanticism in Tönnies's work he provides us with a far better critique than Durkheim of exchange relations: 'The target of Tönnies's critique is unequal exchange, a concept almost entirely absent in Durkheim's description of the division of labour' (Hoggett, 1997: 5). Thus we have two earlier sociological models of community, traditional and post-traditional. The traditional form of community has been replaced but it is interesting to note that many of the people we talked to in our study imagined community or even yearned for community to be more in the vein of Tönnies's concept of *Gemeinschaft*.

As Hoggett (1997) notes a tradition of community studies emerged in the 1950s and 1960s. These studies used social anthropological methods where the researchers went 'native' in towns and villages in the UK. Hoggett gives examples of work in Gosforth (Williams, 1956), Glyceirog (Frankenberg, 1957) and Swansea (Rosser and Harris, 1965). He argues that these studies 'were immensely rich in detail but often also deeply flawed' (Hoggett, 1997: 5). For Hoggett, the studies revealed communities that were strangely undifferentiated and non-conflictual, particularly in the context of wider social change and inequality. Delanty (2003) also highlights the growth of urban studies in relation to community with an emphasis on locality and belonging. Although not a new area (Weber, 1958 [1905]; Simmel, 1950 [1905]) the place of community in modern urban city areas has been a site of research in modern sociology. Delanty points to the work of the Chicago School, arguing that despite many problems the city, for the Chicago School, was the natural base of community and in some sense represented 'the human order of society'. This is seen in the work of Robert Park (1915) and later William Foote Whyte's *Street Corner Society* (1943) and Herbert Gans's *The Urban Villagers* (1962). Delanty argues that these later works tended to see 'community as something preserved in locality, while being under threat in the wider city' (Delanty, 2003: 54). These works see community as a place of attachment at a very local level, in neighbourhoods for example. Indeed, Graham Crow (1997) argues that sociological traditions sit in an uneasy position within the empirical analysis of community with a few exceptions: Crow cites Rex and Moore's *Race, Community and Conflict* (1967) and Pahl's *Divisions of Labour* (1984). Instead, Crow highlights the importance of the study of neighbours and neighbourhoods. For Crow, without theoretically informed research it is impossible to analyse whether neighbouring is emotive or rational, forced or chosen, or on the decline or being reinforced. This has specific implications for the study of community as 'it has the potential to contribute to the explanation of why community can be understood and experienced in so many different ways' (Crow, 1997: 30).

Thus these arguments focus on the changing nature of the idea of community in relation to the city, to urban life, and to changes in social stratification and social relations; these now have to be considered against a backdrop of multiculturalism, global society, virtual communities and communication communities. There are almost an infinite number of ideas about what the word community means and its place in modern, or if you are to believe in it, post-modern society. If we look at the work of Anthony Giddens (1990) then we can see an illustration of how modern technology and globalisation change the nature of community. For Giddens, in the late modern age it is not sufficient to talk about, or invent new terms such as post-modernity, rather we need to look at the nature of modernity itself, where the actual consequences of modernity have become more radicalised and universal. The dynamism of modernity for Giddens lies in the separation of time and space. If we look at pre-modern or traditional societies, or communities, then social relations are embedded in time and space. For the peasant, time is based in the agricultural calendar – the seasons. In terms of identity, status is ascribed at birth and there is little social mobility. In some sense there is little idea of space beyond boundaries, beyond a series of villages for example, this is the community. Day to day life is always linked to time and space. Although in pre-modern times we have the agrarian calendar, the calculation of time and space is variable and imprecise. In other words, nobody could precisely tell the time of day, but instead made reference to time through 'where', or natural occurrences (Giddens, 1990: 17). Something happens though to change this way of life:

> The invention of the mechanical clock and its diffusion to virtually all members of the population (a phenomenon which dates at its earliest from the late eighteenth century) were of key significance in the separation of time from space. The clock expressed a uniform dimension of 'empty' time, quantified in such a way as to permit the precise designation of 'zones' of the day e.g., the 'working day'. (Giddens, 1990: 17)

So, with the invention of the mechanical clock time is no longer seasonal and intimately connected with 'where', with community, but becomes universal. Giddens argues that the emptying of time is the precondition for the emptying of space. Think of place as a locale, as a physical setting, a geography of the social. In pre-modern time space and place more or less coincide, as we said earlier there was little recognition of space beyond the boundaries of the locale. In modernity, however, space is removed from place in that there is a reduction in the social distance between communities on one hand, on another a given community can be influenced by a distant locale. Thus, again, the idea of community and its relationship to one's own identity change.

John Urry (2000) has argued that one theoretical issue has concerned the concept of community, pointing to the work of Bell and Newby (1976) who distinguish between three different senses of the idea of community:

> First, there is its use in a topographical sense, to refer to boundaries of a particular settlement; second, there is the sense of community as a local system implying a degree of social inter-connection of local people and institutions; and third, there is 'communion', a particular kind of human association that implies personal ties, belongingness, and warmth. Bell and Newby point out that the third of these uses is not necessarily by any particular settlement type. (Urry, 2000: 423–4)

Urry goes on to say that there is a fourth sense, community as ideology, where efforts are made to attach conceptions of communion to buildings and estates in ways that conceal the non-communion relations that are actually found. He goes on to mention that most of the existing literature is based in the work of Tönnies's *Gemeinschaft* and *Gesellschaft*. A critique of Tönnies's work, argues Urry, can be found in the writings of Schmalenbach (1977) who adds a third sense to the idea of community, the *bund*: this is a community that is conscious and freely chosen on the basis of mutual sentiment, emotion and feeling. This, asserts Urry, is contra to the work of Weber, who argues that the affective basis of such a *bund* is not irrational and unconscious. Affective commitment to the *bund* is conscious, rational and non-traditional. Unlike *Gemeinschaft* communities, the *bund*-type communities are not permanent or stable. Urry notes the work of Hetherington (1994: 16) who argues that the *bund* is maintained symbolically through active monitoring of group solidarity, is self referential, enclosed, producing codes of practices and symbols, blurring the public and private spheres of the members.

In *Postmodern Ethics*, Zygmunt Bauman (1993) argues that the very idea of community borders is difficult to draw in relation to that of nation-states. Indeed for Bauman, 'If the identity of a community is to be defined by the grip in which it holds the selves it "situates" and hence by the extent of the moral consensus it is capable of generating in them, then the very idea of community borders ... becomes ever so difficult, nay impossible, to uphold' (Bauman, 1993: 44). Bauman is sceptical of the idea of community, of social spacing and identity building, which he describes as the contrived and made up community that masquerades as *Gemeinschaft*, but is more akin to Kant's aesthetic communities, which he argues are brought into being and kept in existence almost solely by the members' dedication. Indeed, for Bauman, 'such community lives under the condition of constant anxiety and thus shows a sinister and but thinly masked tendency to aggression and intolerance' (Bauman, 1993: 235). This is because community constantly lives with built-in uncertainty. Delanty (2003) notes Bauman's scepticism, arguing that for Bauman, community is merely a word that conveys a feeling of security in uncertain times, making the world feel like a warm and cosy place. Quoting Bauman from his 2001 book on community: 'We miss community because we miss security, a quality crucial to a happy life, but one which the world we inhabit is ever less able to offer and ever more reluctant to promise' (Bauman, 2001b: 144). Thus, community promises security but only delivers illusion and nostalgia. Delanty argues that for Bauman, community should be a place where nobody is a stranger, where we share understanding and meanings, but this type of community does not exist:

> The really existing community is a besieged fortress defending itself from the outside world. Bauman sees the contemporary world as one obsessed with digging cultural trenches. In fact community is being resurrected today as the problem of identity becomes more acute. As real communities decline, identity replaces it around a new understanding of community. (Delanty, 2003: 118)

So, the idea of community has become a myth, an illusion, indeed community is impossible because it cannot address the problems it is faced with, for example, the notion of certainty where it does not exist. This is reinforced by Blackshaw (2005) in his analysis of Bauman's work. Paraphrasing Bauman he says that the liquid modern version of community consolidated into reality is nothing but second best, we embrace the idea of community because in reality it no longer exists. Blackshaw argues that what Bauman is saying is that if sociologists are really interested in community then we should look at how it is lived and experienced today (Blackshaw, 2005: 102). This is something we attempt to do in the next section of this chapter where we asked people what community meant to them and how it related to their sense of identity. For Blackshaw, Bauman's understanding of 'liquid modern' community is that it is just a metaphor about the kind of relationship between the highly individualised modern person and the world that exists outside their own selves. Blackshaw argues that what we can conclude from Bauman's work is that what he terms liquid modern communities are not communities as we have known them, just distant cousins. Communities are imagined and in this sense Blackshaw argues that Bauman would agree with Benedict Anderson's (1991) work:

> liquid modern community can be conceived as a deep felt mutuality, albeit temporarily. He also agrees with Anderson that community is imagined in the sense that it is limited by its strictly demarcated, though elastic boundaries; beyond which lie ways of being and living that take the form of various threats, anxieties and uncertainties. (Blackshaw, 2005: 110)

Thus we have a range of ideas and theories about the notion of community and as Hoggett (1997) argues it is a continually contested term; indeed for Hoggett, community is a fundamentally political concept, which he does not mean in the sense of political parties *per se*, but community is saturated with power: 'meanings of community are fought over by different groups – the rough and respectable, cosmopolitans and locals, the state and the people, old and young, men and women' (Hoggett, 1997: 14). In the next section of this chapter we want to discuss some of the findings from our fieldwork which we feel express what ordinary people, not theorists, feel about the relationship that identity has to community, what community means to them and how they situate themselves in wider society, in other words what it means to be British, English or even European.

Community and White Identities: A Case Study

As we saw in chapter 6, identity has been theorised at a number of levels and it is commonplace now to talk about multiple identities or cultural identity. As we argued, the very real locus of these factors, however, is the notion of difference. The question of difference is emotive, and we start to hear ideas about 'us' and 'them', friend and foe, belonging and not belonging, familiarity and the unknown, in-groups and out-groups, which define 'us' in relation to others, or the Other. A central question in this debate, we have argued, is who ascribes identity and for what reason. Do we choose our identity or is it beyond our control? We have also argued in chapter 6 that identity is a social construction and part of a psychodynamic process. Indeed, the importance of emotions in human relations has long been acknowledged along with the recognition that humans' behaviour is not just driven by rationality and reason (Tönnies, 1988 [1887]: 7).

From the notion of difference and the Other, we get ideas about communities, even 'imagined communities', in which all the members never get to see each other face-to-face, and ethno-national boundaries, which we touched on briefly in the previous section. According to Anderson (1991):

> [A]ll communities larger than primordial villages of face-to-face contact (and perhaps even these) are imagined. Communities are to be distinguished, not by their falsity/genuineness, but by the style in which they are imagined ... The nation is limited because even the largest of them ... has finite, if elastic boundaries, beyond which lie other nations ... Finally it is imagined as a community, because, regardless of the actual inequality and exploitation that may prevail in each, the nation is always conceived as a deep, horizontal comradeship. Ultimately it is this fraternity that makes it possible, over the past two centuries, for so many millions of people, not so much to kill, as willingly to die for such limited imaginings. (Anderson, 1991: 6–7)

Anderson shows the strength of that community feeling and of the 'comradeship' that people can experience in what is, essentially, a concept, an imagining, which makes that concept something infinitely desirable and something longed for. The idea of community is something very positive for people; not one of the people we talked to in the project had anything negative to say about the actual idea. Their positive views were generally focused on something more localised than the nation. Very few felt that they belonged to 'the British community' and most questioned whether such a thing existed any longer. As one respondent noted, in phrases very reminiscent of Tönnies's concept of the larger-scale, more distant society (*Gesellschaft*), rather than the more familiar community (*Gemeinschaft*):

> I probably wouldn't stick British and community together. They wouldn't be two words that I would attach because probably British I see it as a kind of nation-wide whole country kind of governmental thing, and I probably wouldn't use community to describe something that size. So I'd

use community on a smaller scale level where I think there is meaningful relationship and interaction between people. And I think on that level, I don't think British wouldn't be a term I would use to describe things on that level, even though probably the majority of people in that community would be British, or those communities would be British. It wouldn't be the thing that defines it to me.

When asked about Europe most people were clear that it offered them very little in terms of either a community identification or identity, indeed the vast majority of people interviewed had very little to say about Europe. Instead, there was a clear focus on what was closer to home, to the local. As noted in chapter 4, people often stressed their Englishness rather than their Britishness and there was an almost nostalgic desire to have this recognised. People also expressed resentment that the Scottish and Welsh could celebrate both their heritage and individuality but the white English person could not:

> Q   How do you feel about being British?
>
> A   Quite happy about being British, but more so English. It's just one of those things. The Scots are patriotic about being Scots, the Welsh are patriotic about being Welsh, the Irish are patriotic about being Irish, and if you're patriotic about being English, there's something wrong with you. This is the sort of attitude I feel that in this country we don't stand up for it, for who we are, the distinction of being English as opposed to being British as the Scots or whatever would say they're Scots and British second, so that's where I stand on that one.

This was expressed in the way people told us that they wanted to write 'English' as their nationality and ethnic origin on forms but were not given the opportunity to do so. Sport was identified by several people as having a strong bond with Englishness, while others felt Englishness to have a strong link with their ethnic roots or ethnicity. Britishness was perceived to be more connected with the global and political and became more important when visiting other countries:

> British has come to mean something to do with being part of Europe, being part of a wider almost global society, and English is something you might

find in country villages if we had any country villages anymore. And to do with people who are humble and rooted in this country, actually rooted in the soil, in the place.

Some people preferred their Englishness to Britishness for less positive reasons. While some were proud to be British, talking of the royal family, the history, freedom of speech, democracy, others saw it as something much more negative and talked of British people behaving badly abroad and of terrorists and expressed the view that Britishness was now 'diluted': 'British has ceased to mean something that stands for honour, courtesy, good government, integrity. It doesn't have any integrity in it any longer, so if somebody asks me what I am now I say I'm English'.

As we explained in chapter 7, cultural diversity was seen positively by many respondents; others, however, felt that Britain has lost or is losing at least some of its identity, with most talking about this in the context of multiculturalism and 'political correctness' with regard to old British customs such as those surrounding Christmas.

Some people blamed other cultures for the change in British customs, others projected their anger at those in power, in politics, to being too sensitive to political correctness and the needs of ethnic minorities. Many of the people we talked to on lower incomes expressed both concern and resentment about the numbers of people coming into the country. Britain was perceived as a 'soft touch' in comparison with other countries and some expressed the negative effect this has on the native population:

> I would definitely say that we're an easier country than a lot of other countries. I would say we're just too easy. We're just a country that is just being taken advantage of, and yet ... it's neglecting people that already exist in this country and they're sort of not looking at people that are British citizen, you know, people that are already here, looking at people that come to the country.

In the case of many people, their potential confidence in their larger, national identity, if they felt it existed, thus seemed seriously threatened and many seemed much more at ease with a more local white identity that is situated in the notion of community. Identity is rooted in community.

If we think about Anderson's concept of imagined communities, people clearly had nostalgic phantasies, probably conscious and unconscious, about what community meant to them and what community should be. But often these were limited to what they could see and experience in a very local setting, in other words community is small and experienced first hand and not through any notions of a larger national community presented in the media and politics. There was a strong need to link these imaginings to concrete reality and in some sense create community, thus the people we spoke to emphasised local institutions such as youth clubs, schools and the church and without these community starts to disintegrate. This was particularly the case with schools where friendships, networks and relationships develop between families, children and parents. The closing of a school takes away a sense of ownership from the local community and causes extreme resentment. Two of the areas we looked at had lost their secondary schools:

> You feel 'us against the world', that sort of attitude develops, when you attack a school, you attack its community as well.

> I can't think of anyone I've met who's had an involvement with the school in the past who's not felt a real sense of loss from it closing. And obviously especially the kids that were going there until a year or so ago, they've not got anything good to say about the change at all, but are very negative about it ... The expression I keep hearing from a number of people is that it seemed to sort of rip the soul out of the area for a lot of people.

As the local schools close down there is a disintegration of community networks as students have to attend schools in other areas or indeed families move away to get children in a school of their choice. We argue that this instils a sense in people that community cannot offer them what they want so they themselves are less willing to contribute to something that seems to be disintegrating. This has far reaching consequences for some people who talked of an increase in crime and territorial infighting, a split community as children no longer attend the same schools and youth clubs but still live in the same area (Brent, 1997). Both in Bristol and Plymouth where a local school had been closed there was a brooding resentment towards the local authorities who people felt had taken action without consulting the community, and therefore a sense that a part of the community identity had been changed and this impacted on individual identities, which in some way had to be reclaimed within another context. There was a sense that identity was no longer stable and influenced by powers that were beyond the individual's control. There are therefore tangible psychological and structural factors that influence the construction of 'white' identity. This sense of lost identity was visible in an increase in tribal and territorial divisions in both areas. Again we see a splitting of good and bad between groups. Among teenagers attending a youth club in Bristol one group tried to provoke another by calling them names associated with the residential area. One person commented that going to a new school in the other area was really difficult for that group because of the territorial rivalry: 'They went to their sworn enemies if you like. It was the same when we were at school, there was fighting amongst the schools'.

In Plymouth parents tried to avoid such overt conflict in a similar situation by bussing their children to a different area that had not traditionally had any hostile relations with their area. So the boundary drawn around an area can sometimes be more important than those drawn within that area. The reinforcement of this tribal or territorial area and rivalry was evident within the adult population too. Adults 'inter-marry' [sic] within their own residential area and thus reinforce their local white identity:

> You never saw, hardly ever saw foreigners here, so there was a very insular, and even if you came from, I mean, if you lived in Devonport and you moved to some parts of Plymouth, what's regarded, it's all Plymouth, but Devonports regard themselves as separate, there's rivalry there. There's rivalry between Efford and Eggbuckland, they don't inter-marry. One of the things I've noted with the work I do is that families don't marry outside their estate, it's almost like they're a village, like Efford. They'll marry within

Efford and ... Swilly will marry in Swilly, you don't marry from St Budeaux if you live in Swilly.

Q   It's all tribal stuff.

A   Very, very tribal.

There's a lot of tribal relationships, I can only put it like that, in these areas, where everybody knows everybody else and is inter-married and inter-related. I think it is not only at a local level, but at a global level, people ignore these tribal structures and try and impose very, very foreign unworkable structures on them. The people who they're imposed on don't understand. They don't understand how it works. They quickly revert to what they do understand which is their tribal affinities and loyalties and so on.

In the second quote, we again see a reinforcement of the idea that outsiders with power are perceived to interfere with local identity construction and impose inappropriate ideas on communities, which the communities themselves reject. Thus we have split communities trying to re-build identities in tandem with a strong mistrust of 'outsiders' with power. At a more subtle level one person, talking about why there were so few ethnic minority people in the area, argued that no one would be against it, but doubted whether they would share the local values. There then seems to be a perception that particular communities are repositories of distinct sets of values and identity construction.

Why Community?

We found that some people identify so closely with the idea of community that it actually becomes their identity. One couple interviewed had actually set up a community centre in their own living room and held regular children's clubs in it. This was in one of the estates in Plymouth and although such commitment seems rare, the couple were seen as role models by other residents: 'Community is what you make of it'. Some people 'bury themselves in their family life, which is great'. Others are different – like Jack and Kathy. He'd like to be like them in his 60s/70s. 'It's like having a second Mum and Dad really with them two'.

There was a general admiration for people who actively tried to create a sense of community and also an acknowledgement that women often take the lead in this, in particular within the context of schooling. Community, then, seems to be something you actually have to create, it does not just happen. It was striking that community groups are often maintained and kept alive by older generations:

> The problem is that no one is coming through the ranks as a youth who'd like to keep the community spirit going. They're all thinking of each other now instead of thinking of others, they're all ... what they can get out of life, not what they can get out for other people or what they can do for other people ... It's all one vision now, it's what can I do for me?

Community, for the majority of people we spoke to, is about a shared vision, values and responsibility, which fosters a sense of belonging and trust, a feeling that you are not on your own and others are there for you, something Bauman (1993) articulates when he mentions that sense of security and is echoed below in some of the comments from the people we spoke to:

> It's just knowing your neighbours, it's having people around you, it's working with them, just working, shopping, interfacing, you just meet with them and bump into them occasionally, getting to know the people around you, that gives you a sense not just of security, but belonging, and things like that, ownership, those sort of words.

> I think it is having contact with people who live near you who have got similar ideas and values to you, a feeling that you're not alone, that you're not cut off, that if you had a problem, you could ring up a neighbour and they would come and help you or you could knock on someone's door and they would help you and also vice versa as well, and being able to walk down the street and talk to people. I think that is an important thing about community. It's just generally including everybody and that you do feel as if you're not in a little box and that you don't speak to anyone else around you.

> You can't think you belong to anything really until you do something for the community, can you?

Thus a key element of community is about the familiar, or familiarity, not just with other members of community, but a sense of ownership of an area, which created feelings of safety that in turn comforted people from all age groups:

> Just in the sense of knowing people from school because I wouldn't feel intimidated at going anywhere in my area because I knew people rather than if, you know, if you went into an area you didn't know, you would feel intimidated and you know, people's perception, you think, 'Well what are you doing here? Why are you here?'

People were also aware of things that were detrimental to community cohesion, factors such as social mobility, changing work patterns, school closures mean that people are less likely to invest in what for them may be a temporary community. While some of the people we spoke to had lived in the same city or even area all their lives, others had travelled, lived and worked in different places. This mobility was far more marked as you would expect among the more middle-class people we spoke to, whereas those who lived on estates tended to stay there all their lives and in some cases if they had moved away they often moved back. It was thought that changing work patterns had contributed to a lack of community spirit, people work longer hours, commute more and thus have little desire to join in with community projects, although many said they would in later life when they had more time. Even cars were cited as a detriment to community life, people no longer had a chat in the street but jumped straight in their car, driveways were seen as a boundary to communication in relation to older forms of terraced housing where people had a 'chat' on the doorstep. Consumerism and a new materialistic form of life was perceived as corroding community spirit in the sense that it was felt that younger people tended to be more interested in staying at home with a takeaway and video than participating in community activities. Older respondents stressed that when they were younger they were more content and that younger people were more interested in material things: 'As you get more of the things in life, it seems there's less caring for other people. People seem to close their door, and they don't want to know others, they want their barriers like'.

Identity, Community, Nostalgia and Loss

Earlier in this book we talked about Les Back's (1996) work on nostalgia and loss and the way in which a 'golden age of community' was created in the post-war reconstruction of an estate where crime was low and children could play safely in the streets. As things changed and new families moved in who were perceived as a 'problem' there developed a hostility towards these incomers, many from minority backgrounds. This hostility was predictably accompanied by a longing to return to the stability of the 'golden age'. This is the paradoxical nature of community. People make communities, they are ever evolving and changing yet there is a deeply psycho-social element to this construction. We start to imagine how community was and how it might be in tandem with a series of projections as to why and who is taking this away from us, our fear and loss is projected onto families who are perceived as a problem, whether real or imagined. So, for example, Colin Webster (2008) notes how remarkable it is that white ethnicity and class remain largely anonymous in discussions of ethnicity and crime: 'especially as self report studies suggest that "whites" disproportionately offend compared to other ethnic groups and obviously commit the vast bulk of crimes' (Webster, 2008: 294). Indeed for Webster, white ethnicity at a community or neighbourhood level is not produced at a visible level, rather it sets itself against any marginalised group including poor white people: 'It is this proximity to the poor rather than visible ethnicity per se that so unsettles locals, leading to anxiety and fear – fear of crime and fear of "falling" through downward mobility into the ranks of the poor' (Webster, 2008: 303).

In one of the areas in Plymouth people attributed many of the problems on the estate to incomers, to 'problem families', and both in Bristol and Plymouth burglaries, drugs, stolen cars and problems with harassment were seen as relatively new phenomena and again attributed to 'problem' families. This again sparked off a nostalgia and sense of loss for earlier times of the community, to a history where such problems did not arise:

> You could go just anywhere when I was small and not worry about it but you wouldn't let kids do it nowadays because of what is happening now, you know.

> Looking back, it was nice because everybody was always there for you, but you never felt they lived in your houses.

There seemed almost a sense of mourning among the more elderly people we spoke to for a time when people did not lock their doors, when the milkman collected his money from the kitchen table and an affection for a time of much greater neighbourliness, when people looked after each other and went on community trips, a time of intimate relations that no longer seemed to exist. Of course, this is also the contrast between the city, the urban and the rural where some of these traditions actually do exist. As we argued, people actively create community and we found this in one of our Plymouth areas where a range of things had been done to create a more traditional community 'spirit'. These included welcome packs for new residents, the establishment of a local festival and classes for adults and children. It was explicitly acknowledged by the people driving these activities that they were trying to recreate for younger generations the sense of community they had experienced as children and young adults. In one of the areas in Bristol, people were trying to create an emphasis on community rather than individuals, holding events in the village hall and negotiating as a group with the local council. We have seen this in the re-emergence of weekly farmers markets, with their traditional foods and an emphasis on locally grown produce.

If we examine the notion of community psycho-socially then there is no 'golden age' of community, rather we have different generations expressing a loss for different ideas that psychologically they associate with identity and community. But, we feel that although we could term this as nostalgia, it is really an identification with a particular lifestyle or way of life and our evidence suggests that people are active in trying to create a sense of community and community identity. We feel that in times of anxiety and uncertainty this becomes particularly strong. Both fear and loss are projected into those that are seen as a threat to community. This is the second paradox in the notion of community, that the stronger feeling that we have of community cohesion then the more likely we are to have community exclusion, closed communities where outsiders are not welcome; strong attachments and identifications bring about exclusionary practices. We have seen this in the work of Barker (1981) in which he describes what he calls the 'new racism' based in ways of life rather than notions of inferiority. Smith (1992) has also highlighted the way in which outsider figures have been used in political projects to define both social space and community, in other words, to draw boundaries around 'ways of life'. In chapters 4 and 7, we discussed the work of Žižek (1993) and noted that for him, what we fear most is the 'theft of our enjoyment' by others. Again, the way we imagine community is based on a nostalgic identification with a way of life that may have never existed in the first place or has been lost. This has been exemplified in several studies (Seabrook, 1973; Rustin, 1991; Hoggett, 1992). Rustin (1991) highlights Seabrook's work in Blackburn in the 1960s whereby the Asian community started to take on some of the characteristics of the white working class while simultaneously, through economic decline and disintegration, the white working class suffered a loss of these qualities. The white community projected into the Asian community the demoralised and disintegrated state they were experiencing in the form of hostility towards the Asian community. Similarly, as we discussed earlier in this book, Paul Hoggett's (1992) study of Tower Hamlets shows that tension between communities corresponds to a period of sustained uncertainty for groups and individuals where both group and collective identity is challenged and undermined.

There is, therefore, a 'sting in the tail' of community and identity construction. You could ask whether this is mere nostalgia or people wanting to create the sense of community feeling and spirit that they experienced for their children and grandchildren and at what cost, and therefore what does community cohesion actually mean, is it detrimental or positive or both, or even possible? As all the people we spoke to were white, we feel the views expressed by them very much point to the construction of 'whiteness' in modern Britain. But at the same time, we acknowledge that we have to think, after Stuart Hall (1992), not of white ethnicity, but 'ethnicities' (plural), as we all speak from a particular place, history and experience of life, and therefore white identities are constructed from community attachments, multiple ethnicities, experiences and geographical locations.

Conclusion

In this chapter we have examined the way in which community is linked to identity, and particularly white identity in Britain today. We have provided an overview of some of the important debates around the notion of community before going on to look at the empirical research findings that formed part of our project on whiteness in Britain. Some very strong key themes emerged. Community is seen as an overwhelmingly positive and powerful idea. Key institutions are vitally important to a successful sense of community such as schools, churches, youth clubs, etc. Many of those interviewed said that community disintegrates without them. Community is about people, knowing your neighbours, working and shopping with them. This gives both a sense of security, but more importantly belonging. Community is about a shared vision and shared values. This enables trust. A key element of community is also the familiarity that goes with it, not just with the people, but also with the local geography, affording a certain sense of ownership of the terrain and creating a feeling of safety. We found that the familiarity was a very comforting concept for many of the people we spoke to. Community is generational. A striking finding from our work is the way in which community groups are kept active by older generations, many of whom are concerned about who will 'pick up the baton' when they stop being so active.

Community for some people is about duty – people ought to get involved. Identity, who we are, is linked to a sense of belonging to a community. This tends to be the smaller local community rather than a national or international one. Identity is formed within the family and then the wider community. Social class is still an important part of identity construction, in particular your job, trade or former job give you a sense of who you are and where you have come from. Many people were keen to mention where their own parents came from in terms of class. In relation to community and identity there were clear distinctions made between insiders and outsiders. This was not necessarily always about class or ethnicity but in many cases simply how long someone had lived there and whether they were 'born and bred' there. There was very little talk of what we might term fluid post-modern consuming selves, narratives in which the individual is sovereign and the community is of little importance. Rather there is an emphasis on the family, class and geographical locations, which were in turn linked to ideas about outsiders and defining your self by who you are not. Interestingly, there was a strong emphasis on the notion of a shared identity that linked in with the notion of community. There is also a deeply psycho-social element where people often create their perceptions of others in their own imagination, which helps them create who they are. This was exemplified in the discussions of what it is to be 'Bristolian' or 'Plymouthian', where we started to see the emotional dynamics involved in notions of contempt, acceptance and tribalism between geographical areas and groups of people.

In the next chapter of this book we look at different ways in which we can research 'whiteness'. With a growing emphasis on research methodology and knowledge transfer at both undergraduate and postgraduate level teaching we provide an outline of a psycho-social method and how we put it into practice. Drawing on cutting edge research in sociology and the social sciences and the authors' own experience, we guide the reader with examples of the methodological application of theory.

9

RESEARCHING WHITENESS: PSYCHO-SOCIAL METHODOLOGIES

Psycho-social studies is an emerging tradition that very much focuses on emotion and affect to illuminate some of the core issues in the social sciences. Issues such as identity construction, dilemmas in public service sectors and the experience of rapid social change. It recognises that the split between individual and society, sociology and psychology is now unhelpful if we are to understand social and psychological phenomena. It therefore seeks to research beneath the surface using both psychoanalytic and sociological ideas using innovative new methodologies including the use of free association, biographical life history interviews and the development of psychoanalytic fieldwork. It is quite distinct in its approach: it is more an attitude or position towards the subjects of our study rather than just another methodology. It is a cluster of methodologies that might entail the study of group dynamics, infant observation and the co-construction of the research environment by both researcher and researched. From this comes the notion of the reflexive researcher, that is sustained self reflection on our practice and method which involves an acknowledgement of our emotional involvement and attachment to our area of study and the relationship between ourselves and those we research (see Clarke and Hoggett, 2009). In our research we use what we might term a 'light' psycho-social approach, that is, we acknowledge that there are often unconscious forces and motivations at work behind certain situations, that we co-construct research environments, but we also avoid using complex psychoanalytic language in order to make the work more accessible to the reader.

We start this chapter by outlining some of the background to the research, in other words how we went about it, before going on to discuss the aims and origins of psycho-social research, innovations in research methodology and describing a method. We then explore the research encounter – the idea that this encounter may be full of different types of affect, for example, anxiety, fear and identifications. Uncomfortable material can often arise during an interview, producing a 'defended' subject and/or interviewer. There are also specific implications for the generation and analysis of the data as the level of subjectivity applied by the researcher is much greater than in other forms of social science methods, and thus the question of ethics arises. Finally, we offer a case study to illustrate our method and practice, its qualities as well as limitations.

The Background

The aims of the research project, which we mention in the introductory chapter, were very clear but at the same time we approached the project with an open mind in order that we could unravel and represent the 'lived' lives of the people that we interviewed. The main aim was to explore the construction of identity in contemporary Britain by analysing psychological and social elements together. This enabled us to highlight the emotional aspects of attachment (Clarke, Gilmour and Garner, 2007) as well as individuals' location within broader social change (e.g. mobility from working class into middle class; home-ownership). We carefully selected areas that are not multicultural in which to do fieldwork. Simpson (2005) shows that despite the trend towards less ethnically segregated residence, the vast majority of the British live in wards with fewer than 10 per cent ethnic minorities. The absence of explicit local multicultures is therefore the majority experience for white British people. From this we aimed to explore the idea of 'whiteness' or white ethnicity. In asking questions about Britishness, Europe, welfare and immigration in the broadest terms, we hoped to identify some common themes in the ways people discursively constructed communities, and allowed the complexity of the associations to emerge in a way that focusing purely on 'race' would not have allowed, because of the sensitivity of this topic in public debate. For example, when answering a question about Britishness with talk of how conditions had worsened, many people identified a process of being taken advantage of culturally by immigrant-descended groups in particular ways, thus drawing a line between 'them' and 'us'. As we have shown in chapter 8, the idea of community is central to the construction of group and individual identity and we looked at what people mean when they talk of 'community'. There are also important configurations in the way identity is constructed relationally in varying conditions. We looked at this in the context of asylum seekers (Clarke and Garner, 2005; Clarke, Gilmour and Garner, 2007), arguing that they have become 'folk devils' (Cohen, 1972) onto whom an array of fears about loss, order and respectability are projected. Interestingly, there was an emphasis on the notion of a shared identity that linked with the notion of community. There is also a deeply psycho-social element where people often create their perceptions of others in their own imagination, which helps them create who they are.

We also sought to examine the ways in which people perceive access to welfare and social housing and hypothesised that a 'hierarchy of entitlement' to welfare would appear in the told narratives, and indeed this was the case. We asked people about their views on immigration and this became tied in with perceptions of access to welfare, housing and even the right to a certain identity. Finally, we sought to build on and develop a psycho-social method for the social sciences, which we describe in the next sections of this chapter, and combine it with more traditional qualitative data analysis and collection techniques.

Two rounds of interviews were conducted with 64 respondents in Bristol and Plymouth and two electoral wards in each city (128 interviews were conducted in total). The interviews were followed up by sending all respondents a detailed preliminary report on the findings. We asked respondents to comment on both the results of the research and their experience of taking part in the project. To contextualise the project we also interviewed local councillors, community and youth workers, religious practitioners and local NGO representatives. This did not form part of the data set. The interviews that formed the first round of the research are biographical in nature, very unstructured and allowed the respondent to tell us what they thought was important about their life and history. We also had three very broad questions that we asked all the people we spoke to: what their views were on the notion of identity, what it meant to them, what the idea of community meant to them and the notion of home. We wanted people to use as much of their own voice as possible, and therefore produce unprompted responses from the first round of interviews.

In the second round of interviews we tried to pick up on some issues from the first round and to ask people more specific questions. We formulated a semi-structured interview schedule in which we specifically asked people about what it meant to be British, whether this was closely tied in with Englishness and whether they thought that there was a British identity that we could talk about. We also asked questions about Europe, what it meant to be European and how Europe had affected their life. We then went on to talk about entitlement to welfare and social housing, and whether ownership of property had changed the way in which people thought of themselves. (Several of the respondents live in rented social accommodation.) Our final set of questions surrounded immigration into the UK and whether it had affected the respondents' lives at all.

While the first round of interviews had been very successful in producing some rich life history data and had provided some very real insights into the notions of home and community, the second round interviews proved more difficult. We found ourselves as a team feeling uncomfortable with the questions and uneasy with the respondents. Some subjects, particularly around immigration and welfare benefits, felt as if they were too 'hot' to talk about. Some of the respondents were uneasy and gave stunted or short answers to very difficult questions (see chapter 4). In some sense, this was the crux of the problem: the questions were very difficult to answer. Many people had never thought about what it meant to be British or even how immigration had affected their lives. Whereas they had generally been quite relaxed talking about their own histories, there was occasionally a feeling that they were being in some way 'tested' in the second interview and that they were not necessarily up to the mark. There was the feeling in some instances that the experience was no longer so personal and was more like a real interview with ourselves in the position of interviewer rather than listener.

After several team meetings and re-wording of questions, we decided that our semi-structured interview had to become less structured if we wanted to elicit real responses, emotions and feelings. So, for example, a question about British identity was rephrased in a positive manner: 'What pleases you about being British?' Most of the questions on Europe were dropped as they seemed to have little relevance to most of our respondents and we were getting nowhere with the area. We also had to be careful about the order and phrasing of the questions, for example we could not talk about immigration then ask about entitlement to welfare.

We believe that the most important point which emerged from the second round of interviews is that the team need to constantly reflect on their practice, the response from the respondents and the data collected. In particular, we need to be aware of the agenda that we are bringing to the research environment. Our original interview schedule wasn't working because we were asking questions that we thought were important to the way in which people construct their identities instead of listening to what was/ is important to the respondents. There has to be some starting point, but you also have to constantly adapt, reframe and listen to respondents in order to gain some insight into their emotions and feelings around identity and community. Thus, with later interviews we were left with four key themes to discuss rather than an interview schedule, and this has led to richer and more representative data. The key themes were: what it means to be British, or English, in relation to identity; the impact of this on community cohesion, in other words the difference between local and national communities; how do people feel about provision of welfare (respondent stipulated what welfare meant to them, i.e., social housing, benefits, health) in the United Kingdom. Finally, we looked at the nature of immigration in the United Kingdom. In the next section of this chapter we look in more detail at the development of psycho-social research methodologies before going on to present a case study from one of the interviews.

Psycho-Social Methodology

Psycho-social research methods have emerged fairly recently. Previously, there had been little fieldwork that used psychoanalysis as a tool for understanding social phenomena. One exception was Jennifer Hunt (1989) who argues that fieldworkers shared an assumption that 'there was one reality that existed independently of the researcher's conscious mental activity' (Hunt, 1989: 17). In other words there existed an objective separation between observer and observed. Researcher subjectivity, emotional and participatory involvement in the world of the researched, was seen as a hindrance to scientific study. Hunt (1989) refers to the Chicago School as a particularly good example of this type of ethnography, as Hammersley (1990: 3) notes: 'Chicago sociologists came to see the city as a kind of natural laboratory in which the diversity and processes of change characteristic of human behaviour could be studied'. Fieldwork was somewhat paradoxical in that researchers were encouraged to immerse themselves in the 'natural' setting of the research subject but not to the extent where they would lose their objective focus – in other words not succumbing to, or recognising the emotional and affectual dynamics at play in the research encounter.

Hunt (1989), however, argues that subjectivity and self understanding are critical to well executed fieldwork, suggesting a synthesis of ethnographic methods which incorporate psychoanalytic tools of interpretation. Psychoanalytic practice in fieldwork is important in that it contributes to our understanding of how sociological data is both structured and constructed. There are two main areas in which psychoanalytic ethnography differs from conventional fieldwork. First, there is the notion that the unconscious plays a role in the construction of our reality and the way in which we perceive others. This is the theoretical framework on which we base the analysis of our research findings. Second, the unconscious plays a significant part in both the generation of research data and the construction of the research environment, thus recognising and using ethnography as a social activity. Hunt (1989) argues that the psychoanalytic analysis of fieldwork is crucial as it helps us understand the structuring of social science data: 'For example the unconscious communications which are negotiated in the research encounter affect empathy and rapport. They therefore play a role in the materials that subjects reveal and researchers grasp' (Hunt, 1989: 27).

Hunt points to a number of areas where unconscious forces may affect research. For example, the choice of research subject and setting may reflect an 'inner dynamic'. A deep interest in racism may arise from certain incidents or events in a researcher's past, the impacts of which become disguised as curiosity and professional interest. Once the research is taking place unconscious forces may mediate encounters between researcher and researched: 'the subject's behaviour and unconscious transferences toward the researcher may generate the development of reciprocal reactions and transferences' (Hunt, 1989: 33). We feel that an important point that Hunt highlights, which is rarely discussed in methodological literature, is the discomfort and guilt that may accompany the collection of data, the feeling of being a 'spy' or 'voyeur'. This is certainly something that we experienced in our fieldwork as we gained people's trust and openness. Hunt discusses at length the psychoanalytic concepts of transference and counter-transference within the fieldwork environment. This is where most of the unconscious interplay between researcher and respondent takes place:

> The term transference will be used to refer to researchers' unconscious reactions to subjects and some aspects of their world. Transference will also be used to describe the unconscious archaic images that the subject imposes onto the person of the researcher. Counter-transference, in contrast, will

be used to refer to the researcher's unconscious reaction to the subject's transference. (Hunt, 1989: 58)

While both psychoanalysis and hermeneutics assume an 'internal' world, hermeneutics assumes that much of this world is accessible to the 'confessor' of it. In psychoanalytic ethnography this world is often hidden and the transference and counter-transference between respondent and researcher thus becomes a way in which the hidden inner world reveals itself. The nature of ethnographic fieldwork is described not in terms of one or many pictures, but rather, in terms of a voyage, in which researcher and researched are engaged. Rae Sherwood, in *The Psycho-dynamics of Race* (1980), uses a series of unstructured life history interviews to explore the 'inner' and 'outer' worlds of multiracial areas. The subjects, all from different ethnic backgrounds, are researched in a cultural, social and historical context, yielding information on a conscious surface level to provide insights into unconscious 'motivations and defences' (Sherwood, 1980: 13). This methodology considers psychological, sociological and cultural aspects of our lives as interdependent and, as such, each has an influence on the other in the way in which we construct social life through relationships, feelings and action. Innes (1998) also comments on the usefulness of psychoanalytic concepts as a social worker involved in a mental health after-care hostel: 'These accounts enable me to think of racist and other responses to the experience of difference as originating not only in historical, political and social reality but also in the unconscious internal conflicts of the individual' (1998: 187).

Thus we have a threefold argument for the synthesis of methodologies. First, structural explanation is able to explain how, but not why, certain social phenomena occur. Psycho-analysis addresses this deficiency by recognising the role of the unconscious mind in the construction of social realities; with its suggestion that feelings and emotions shape our perception and motivation, constructing the way in which we perceive others. Second, the psychoanalytic method recognises the role of the researcher in the interpretation of realities and the way in which unconscious forces shape the research environment. Finally, there is an integration of social, cultural and historical factors at a conscious level, which yields information about unconscious motivations and defences.

The importance or recognition of the interplay between internal and external worlds has been developed substantially over the past ten years into the discipline we now call psycho-social studies. This can be seen by example in some of the authors we mentioned in chapter 6: in Hollway and Jefferson's (2000) work on fear of crime, in the work of Stephen Frosh et al. (2002, 2003) on young masculinities and the work of Valerie Walkerdine et al. on young femininities (Walkerdine et al., 2001; Lucey et al., 2003). Chamberlayne, Bornat and Wengraf (2000) have used biographical narrative methods and applied these to social policies and professional practice (Chamberlayne, Rustin and Wengraf, 2002); also Hinshelwood and Skogstad (2000) use psychoanalytically informed observation techniques to study anxiety within institutions. More recently, Hoggett and his colleagues (2006) have used a psycho-social narrative method to understand the nature of personal identifications, for example class and gender, that underpin the commitment of welfare workers to their jobs. If we look at the different disciplines involved in the psycho-social project – sociology, psychology, critical psychology, political studies and social policy – then we can see a truly interdisciplinary tradition emerging, which uses psychoanalytic concepts in varying degrees to deepen existing qualitative research in the social sciences.

If we look at the aims of psycho-social research then at the heart of the project is the reflexive practitioner or researcher. As we mentioned in the introduction to this chapter, the idea of the reflexive researcher involves sustained and critical self reflection on our methods and practice, to recognise our emotional involvement in the project whether conscious or unconscious. So, for example, we could ask ourselves a set of questions. Why are we interested in our research project, why choose this area and not some other? What is our investment in it and how will this affect the way we go about the research? Importantly, how will the above affect us and our relationship to the subject(s) of our study? To answer such questions requires an exploration of the intersections between personal biography and discourse, in other words, to examine 'lived' lives. This enables the researcher to do two things: first, to deepen our understanding of social relations and second, to restore the focus on human motivation (both conscious and unconscious) that is often lost in discourse.

A psycho-social approach to research has brought about some ground-breaking innovations in the way that we generate data. The starting point here is the psycho-social approaches to biographical narrative interviews developed by Wendy Hollway and Tony Jefferson (2000) and Tom Wengraf (2001) and Prue Chamberlayne (Wengraf and Chamberlayne, 2006). Hollway and Jefferson argue that using a psycho-social perspective in research practice necessarily involves conceptualising both researcher and respondent as co-producers of meanings. There is an emphasis in their work on the unconscious dynamics between researcher and researched and the use of free association through narrative interviews. Hollway and Jefferson (2000) use the free association narrative interview (FANI), which can be summarised in terms of four principles, each designed to facilitate the production of the interviewee's 'meaning frame' (Hollway and Jefferson, 2000: 34). The first is to use open-ended questions. So, for example, in this research project to try and dig deeper into people's perceptions of home, identity and the construction of 'whiteness' in contemporary Britain we would simply ask the person what the notion of 'home' meant to them rather than use a closed or leading question that may have evoked either a yes/no answer or made the respondent feel that they had to think of a particular incident. This question was designed to get the respondent to talk about the meaning and quality of experience of notions of home, identity and community, in other words, how it related to their life. The second principle of the free association narrative method is that of eliciting a story. Again, a question such as 'tell me something about your background' is more likely to elicit a story, a narrative, than, for example, 'where were you born?'. As Hollway and Jefferson note, story telling shares many things in common with the psychoanalytic method of free association. This principle also allows the researcher to look at various forms of unconscious communication, of transference, countertransference and projective identifications that are present in the interview relationship. Why do people tell certain parts of certain stories? Why are they telling them? What form of response are they trying to elicit from the interviewer? It's often the case that the respondent will say at the end of an interview, 'did I give you the "right" answers?'.

The third principle is to try and avoid using 'why' questions. Hollway and Jefferson note that this may seem counter intuitive as people's own explanations of their actions are useful in understanding them. The problem with a 'why' question, however, is that you often get a sociological or clichéd answer. This is a more difficult area in fieldwork because the 'why' question tempts an explanation, something we are all looking for. If we ask why someone moved to a particular community, then a respondent will often couch answers in terms of school availability, transport links or proximity to shops and services. These are all very important, but do not necessarily help us to understand what community means to the respondent. If instead we couch the question in terms 'how do you feel about living in this particular area?', then the response is more likely to be in the form of a story or narrative, where the respondent attaches meaning to experience.

The final principle is that of using respondents' ordering and phrasing. This involves careful listening in order to be able to ask follow up questions using the respondents' own words and phrases without offering our own interpretations. As Hollway and Jefferson note, although appearing a relatively simple task 'it required discipline and practice to transform ourselves from a highly visible "asker" of questions, to the almost invisible, facilitating catalyst to their stories' (Hollway and Jefferson, 2000: 36). This does not imply the stance of an objective observer; rather it means trying not to impose a structure on the narrative. The importance of the psychoanalytic technique of free association cannot be overstressed in this method. By allowing the respondent to structure the interview and talk of what they 'feel' like talking about, we are able to gain some indication of unconscious feelings and motivation, something that is not possible with traditional research methods. As Hollway and Jefferson argue: 'By eliciting a narrative structured according to the principles of free association, therefore, we secure access to a person's concerns which would probably not be visible using a more traditional method' (Hollway and Jefferson, 2000: 37).

This method then uses biography and life history interviews (Chamberlayne, Bornat and Wengraf, 2000; Hollway and Jefferson, 2000) to situate processes of identification within the subject's life history. In the case of our own recent research, these identifications include affective attachments to notions of community, nation and belonging. Tracing such identifications will uncover the more subtle psychological dynamics behind identity formation within the context of the in-depth interview. This method is both biographical and systematic, and crucially addresses the construction of the research environment and data by both researcher and respondent.

Another contribution to biographical interviewing has been made by Tom Wengraf and Prue Chamberlayne. In very much the same vein as Hollway and Jefferson's model, the biographic narrative-interpretive method (BNIM) places an emphasis on eliciting narratives about people's biographies in a way that is not interrupted, but at the same time it offers a slightly different approach to interviewing and data analysis advocating the use of a research panel to create a greater degree of objectivity in the process of data analysis. Wengraf and Chamberlayne make a distinction between what they call the 'told story' and the 'lived life', something we have placed a real emphasis on in this research project. They argue that a 'Real Author' exists which is not always presented or obvious in the interview, an author that can be revealed through analysis of the told story. They also make a distinction between psychodynamics and socio-dynamics and in some of their later research on organisations they combine narrative interview with observational methods to explore the way in which the 'unsaid' of the organisation may find expression both in the narratives of organisational actors and in the dialogues of the research team (Chamberlayne, 2005).

Social science research has always been aware of the nature of the relationship between the researcher and the researched but these dynamics have been presented in sociological terms such as Goffman's Dramaturgical Model, which we examined in chapter 6. A psycho-social method seeks to deepen our understanding of this relationship, which has several aspects. There is a recognition that the research environment or encounter involves many different kinds of affect, these could be fear, anxiety or even boredom, and these may be co-produced or induced in the relationship by either the researcher or researched. The inexperienced researcher may be anxious about his or her status, whether they are doing it right, in much the same way that interviewees often ask if they have given the right answers. It is important that these feelings are dealt with because as Wendy Hollway and Tony Jefferson (2000) have noted, the research interview may stir up uncomfortable material for both those being interviewed and those doing the interview, producing both the 'defended subject' and the 'defended researcher'. This means that very little useful or representable data is produced. This is why it is so important to explore the psychodynamic processes at work in such an encounter.

This method then, has specific implications for data analysis. Psycho-social methods place a considerable emphasis upon creating the conditions for the emergence of the subject, by revealing the 'lived' life of an individual. This means imposing very little structure on biographical interviews, by the use of 'free association'. But where does analysis come in? Hollway and Jefferson (2000: 77) originally argued that the analysis comes later and we must not interpret into the interview. This view is now starting to be challenged; as humans, we constantly interpret even when we are not aware of it, as researchers, we constantly make interpretations during encounters with the subjects of our research, not matter how hard we try not to (Miller, Hoggett and Mayo, 2008). Not all psycho-social research adheres strictly to the FANI and BNIM, indeed as we mentioned earlier in this chapter we used a combination of unstructured and semi-structured interviews, which we constantly revised as we went along and learnt from experience of the encounters, what made people feel uncomfortable and made us feel the same way. This represents a paradox in psycho-social research because on the one hand there is an emphasis on minimal structure, on the other a stress on the researchers' subjectivity, which many traditional social science researchers would find unacceptable. These same issues are faced in data analysis. If we do not take our subjects' narrative on face value then surely we are just imposing our preconceptions on the data, our 'findings' could just be wild analysis, which the researcher needs to be aware of. One way to guard against this is team work and analysis, another is to share our data with the respondents. We preferred in the context of our research project to send out a preliminary report of our findings to all the people we interviewed and ask for their feedback. Others take a dialogic approach, for example Miller, Hoggett and Mayo (2008) shared the material generated through procedures such as engaging participants in dialogue around emerging findings, sharing written drafts that feature respondents' case material or running inquiry groups and conferences for research participants during the later stages of the research. The psycho-social method is a labour-intensive activity with multiple sources of data ranging from reflective fieldnotes, through live recordings to transcription of the interview, where the transcription is only one source of data and often key themes get lost in transcription. In terms of the research that this book is based in, a member of the research team carried out transcription to become immersed in the data. We combined individual in-depth analysis of transcripts with a cross sectional analysis. Transcripts were coded by hand. We were going to employ Nvivo software but decided that the manual coding of data would enable a greater immersion. While this was very time-consuming, we think it yielded more fruitful results and enabled us to represent the views of respondents more accurately. We also performed a team analysis of some of the data sets, both reading the transcript and listening to the original recording of the interview. This enabled us to check for representativeness in the transcription and also to perform an analysis of what 'gets lost in transcription' (Clarke, 2008a). Team members also shared data with other project teams in the 'Identities' programme and formed part of both the psycho-social and 'ethnicities' sub-groupings within the programme. We now want to present a case study of one of the people we interviewed to demonstrate some of the key themes in psycho-social method and analysis that we have discussed thus far.

Case Study: Two Sides of Billy[1]

Billy is one of the respondents that we interviewed several times for the project. It would not be difficult to portray Billy as not a very nice person, but there are many sides to Billy and many reasons that he holds the views he does. Our concern here is about the selective use of interview transcripts, about falling into the trap of not listening to our respondents and making our data fit our preconceived ideas and research questions. We need to know why Billy is the way he is, not just literally say that he is what we want him to appear as. What follows then, is what we term the two sides of Billy, in other words two readings of the interview and material collected, and is written in the first person of the interviewer.

Literal Billy

On the face of things it would seem that Billy hasn't got a lot going for him. He has a violent past and used to be a semi-professional wrestler, an amateur boxer and worked as a heavy lifter in industry for many years. He is now retired through ill health and in his 60s. His way of dealing with things tended to involve force or violence. He gave me several examples of this over the course of the interviews, which usually involved taking someone outside for a chat. He had problems with his neighbour for several years. The neighbour's dog had killed Billy's dog and the man mocked him about it (being mocked or called stupid was usually a catalyst for the violence which I'll talk about later). So Billy took out his 'teeth, took off my glasses and bang bang, I went in … I made him squeal like a pig in front of the kids who all heard him… I just let him go then. For months and months the kids were saying hello piggy'.

I was confused as to why Billy wanted to convey this impression of toughness to me, I felt both welcomed and intimidated by his presence. I had spent a lot of time with him, going through a rich life history interview using a free association method. I felt quite close to Billy and when I read the second set of interview transcriptions a few months later I was shocked. The second set of interviews was comprised of more specific structured questions, but this did not seem to be the Billy I knew or the interview I conducted. I remembered the emotional feeling around the interview, the anxiety and difficulty, but none of the substantive content. There are two points to bear in mind here before I discuss some of Billy's responses to the structured interview. First, he felt very uncomfortable, found it difficult to answer the questions and felt like he was being tested. Second, I think some of these examples show how we can misrepresent the data and research subject. We started the interview by talking about the previous interview, which Billy had enjoyed; he told me about some of his achievements since I'd last seen him and talked about his brother. When I asked some specific questions Billy started to wander away from the point, but of course he was talking about what was important to him. I asked him 'What does being British mean to you?' His reply:

> A lot actually … To me, as a, I call meself, a learned historian. The British flag means a lot to me because as you know I study military things, but there again, I study German U-Boats, you see, so when you see a British flag, you look at it and feel a bit proud, I must admit.

Billy continued to tell me how proud he was about being British. I asked him if he thought there was something about the British character. Yes, he replied, it's about the history 'it did, it's about British history'. We continued to talk about what pleased Billy about being British; we couched the questions in terms of positive experiences. Billy liked the food, didn't like the food in other countries, he couldn't buy fish and chips abroad, he would rather stay in England. We went on to talk about things that Billy felt more comfortable with – his childhood, his job, these were in relation to a question around whether he had ever felt like an outsider in his own community. Reading the transcript literally Billy seemed not to answer questions and frequently went off at a tangent. This was interspersed with very opinionated statements around questions that he found difficult to answer. Billy was a tough guy who had an interest in German U-Boats and didn't particularly like anything foreign. It's hardly surprising that when I asked him about his thoughts on immigration and whether he was afraid of anything in British society he said the following:

> I can go into the question you're going to ask me later ... I'm not prejudiced, I'm not prejudiced, I wouldn't say it, but I fear at what's coming on this country at the moment. Too many immigrants, they're letting them in, there's far too many, far too many, and obviously the more people you've got, the more quarrelling (?) you've got. I'm not blaming everything on them. Don't get me wrong.

> I'm afraid because they're all coming in and we're taking a lot of asylum seekers and God knows what. The British people, I'm just speaking for British now, have lost a lot of things .... because they're like some people, and always, what do you call, got a social security number or social service number, and they get away with murder. That's what I'm afraid of. Society is going to beat itself.

Billy's feelings on immigration seem to be based on some fear of the Other or the unknown and they are certainly forthright. Billy seems to slip between issues of immigration and ethnicity. He also seems unaware that when he talks of British people, 'speaking for the British now', that British people include many different ethnicities and white identities. He went on to tell me that he had never liked 'coloureds' but he didn't know why.

So, if we read the transcript literally and selectively we get one view of Billy that portrays him as a tough man, who doesn't like anything foreign, who could be viewed as a violent racist who has a fairly uncaring approach to others and life. In the next section of this case study I want to discuss the Billy I knew from the first interview, the Billy that was presented in the free association interview, the Billy that was open and honest with his feelings and entrusted the researcher with them.

The Other Billy

I feel that with a psycho-social approach we can get behind the reasons, the 'why', of why people say what they do in interviews. There has to be some continuity to enable a holistic view of the research material and to be able to recognise the co-construction of the data by researcher and researched. There also has to be a certain toleration of uncertainty, to let things go the way the respondent wants to take them. The Billy presented in the previous section was not the Billy I knew, I was shocked when I saw the transcripts even though I'd conducted both interviews. I was shocked because I could see how someone could be portrayed in a very different light on paper if one is not careful and reflexive about methodological practice. There was also something very likeable about Billy. The other side of Billy is that of a resilient person, someone who can overcome personal tragedy, who is willing to learn and try new things, and of someone who cares deeply about those close to him. Billy seemed to represent something about hope. The life history free association interview reveals many of the dynamics behind Billy's seemingly opinionated and uncaring statements in the structured interview. As I noted earlier, Billy had real problems with the questions in the structured interview and felt uneasy about answering. He was far more at home in the first interview where he talked lucidly about his life history for the first time. Indeed, he constantly tried to steer the structured interview back to the subjects he talked about in the first interview. I had to stop talking about immigration with him; he really didn't want to talk about it.

Billy's life history revealed that he was brought up in care, 'in homes and boarding schools and God knows what' from the age of six. His father had hung himself after being torpedoed several times by German U-Boats and losing a lung. Billy had no formal education and was illiterate when he left school. He didn't learn to read and write until he got married – his wife taught him and he also taught himself. He only saw his mother once when he was in care and wasn't really sure it was his mother, but his brother said it was so he accepted it. He moved back in with his mother when he was fifteen and a half and stayed with her until he got married. His working life mainly revolved around heavy labouring. He did the same job for 28 years then took voluntary retirement. Billy was proud of his job and got a lot of his sense of self-esteem from it. He became a leading person in it and worked his way up despite not being able to read and write. Illiteracy and tests have always been a source of anxiety for Billy and he also found out recently he is dyslexic – 'I do struggle sometimes, but I'm not afraid of it now'. Billy found another job after taking voluntary retirement but suffered a terrible accident while driving to work. He lost the use of one of his arms and suffered serious neurological injuries. He lost his memory and as a result of the accident he has been unable to work again. Today Billy cares for his disabled wife, is an active member of a community group, has completed a City and Guilds in computing and now helps teach new students. He is constantly learning and open to new ideas.

If we go back to some of the issues raised in the first part of this vignette then we can speculate about some of the reasons behind Billy's ideas and behaviours. It was noticeable that every time Billy talked about something violent, an incident or a feeling, it was always around the issue of his illiteracy, around feeling stupid, around being called stupid or mocked as he put it. Billy's obsession (his term) with U-Boats, which developed after his accident, seemed not just an extension of his propensity for violence, but more to do with his father who he still mourns and still wants to get to know. Billy's childhood in turmoil and uncertainty not only left him incredibly good at adapting to change and resilient in the face of redundancy and ill health, but also on the other hand resistant and fearful of change. I think this is reflected in his comments about immigrants. His comments about immigration were constantly peppered with comments like, 'I'm talking blind because I don't know whether they do it or not', 'I don't know, I'm talking blind you see', 'I wouldn't know. We don't have nothing to do with that. We can only go on what we are told or hearsay'. Billy almost admitted that he didn't really know anything about immigration:

> You know, if you lived with them, then fine, you can put your rights and wrongs, but I'm only going on hearsay, people that's lived with them and whatever. There's a difference in that, isn't there.

I think these statements are telling. I think by using the structured interview we pushed Billy into a corner, to talk about things he knew nothing about. I think he felt compelled to comment lest he appear ignorant, something he had been battling all his life. I feel this is a classic example of the researcher co-producing the data. I didn't feel comfortable and nor did Billy and I often colluded with him. Of course, rather than just a typed transcript of the interview I had the experience of the interview in mind, the emotion, the body language and the tensions. This has been lost in transcription, part of Billy has been lost in transcription, the identifications and projection do not appear and the very great trust that Billy offered me by inviting me into his life is unwritten.

Thus far I have tried to illustrate two different readings of the same material. The first, a literal reading of the transcripts, the second, a subjective reading of the interpretation of the interview and the co-construction of the data by myself and the respondent. The more I think about it, the more I'm alarmed. What would happen if I didn't like Billy? I could have portrayed him as a racist bigot without trying to understand some of the underlying dynamics at play. The paradoxical nature of the semi-structured interview is also a problem. On the one hand we need to ask questions, on the other we are in danger of pushing people into corners. Billy constantly moved away from questions and talked about things that were important him.

In trying to theorise the dynamics of these interviews I think it's useful to use a Kleinian framework, in particular to think about paranoid schizoid and depressive functioning (Klein, 1946; Clarke, 2003), processes of identification, projection, and the idealisation of good objects. I think this holds both for researcher and researched because in some sense this type of interview makes the researcher confront his or her own racism(s) through identification and countertransference. Why, for example, did I admire Billy and enjoy his company so much? Why did he want to convey this image of toughness to me?

If we think about the two sides of Billy, then the literal Billy lives in the world of the paranoid schizoid position. Things are either really good or really bad. Violence pervades this position and bad things are disposed of both metaphorically and often physically in Billy's case. Billy is proud to be British, British is good and we don't want anything alien contaminating our goodness, whether that be people, immigrants or that foreign food – 'fish and chips' is best. A lot of this is based in phantasy, by his own admission Billy knew little about immigration or different ethnic groups and his prejudice stems from a fear of difference and of the unknown. I wonder to what extent Billy's inability to deal with difference and uncertainty – the unknown – is to do with the loss of his parents, the death of his father and not being sure that his mother was really his mother. So, we keep it clear cut. Yes/no, black/white, them/us – good and bad. In the second interview where we asked difficult questions about immigration Billy felt cornered and resorted to the paranoid schizoid defences I have detailed above. The other side of Billy, however, has much more of an air of the depressive position, seeing both good and bad in a whole person. It's possible to identify with a person who may have some distasteful views and violent ways, but is basically a good person who cares for his family. Billy actually gives us hope as he has struggled through life and made the most of it, indeed, this is classic depressive functioning: 'as good as it gets'.

This is only half of the story though. What gets 'lost in transcription' with the account of literal Billy is the relationality between researcher and researched. I too bring my own paranoid schizoid and depressive functioning to the research environment, in particular my class position(s) that forms a strong identification with Billy's world (see Layton, 2004; Stopford, 2004). A further layer constrains the interview in which I'm aware of the original aims of the research project and feel a great deal of anxiety around 'delivering the goods'. This makes it difficult to be able to tolerate the uncertainty that a psycho-social method requires. I felt uncomfortable asking certain questions that Billy then felt uncomfortable answering – we made each other uncomfortable. My own background as a bricklayer who went back to school and became 'literate' again has very strong similarities to Billy's story. I found myself identifying with him, seeing myself in him and liking him, indeed I became fascinated with Billy's story. Billy identified with the 'learned' bricklayer: 'I call myself a learned historian', he says. There is also an element of the gendered macho world of heavy work. Billy portrayed the impression of toughness to me as a form of identification because he knew that I would unconsciously understand. I said at the start of this vignette that I was confused about why Billy conveyed this impression of toughness to me, but of course on reflection it was a basic point of identification between us. It was in fact where we both used to be, and in Billy's case violent feelings return when anyone challenges who he is – he is not stupid!

On the one hand I'm identifying with Billy and projecting things into him, a feeling of a good, almost idealised object who I strongly identify with, someone who symbolises hope. Someone I want to protect from misinterpretation and mis-re-presentation. On the other hand, however, I see a reparative Billy, someone who has learned by experience and changed for the better, someone who contains both good and bad: the ambivalent Billy in me. The problem is, however, that these positions often become confused. Because Billy offers hope there is a danger that he becomes an idealised good object and that his blatantly racist views are just whitewashed to preserve him in this state. Billy doesn't really initiate conversation or communication with other ethnic groups and indeed is fearful of Others. He seems unaware of his own white ethnicity, at least at a conscious level, which is very localised. While we can gain great insights through psycho-social interpretation we also have to be mindful of the strong countertransference reaction that happens within certain situations.

Conclusion

In this chapter we have talked about some of the practical issues around the research project that has informed the content of this book, our aims, methods and practices. We then charted the early use of psychoanalytic concepts in ethnographic research before going on to discuss the emergence of the tradition that we call psycho-social studies. In describing a method we argue that at the heart of a psycho-social approach to empirical qualitative research is the idea of the reflexive practitioner, a practitioner who recognises his or her emotional involvement in the research and maintains a critical and sustained self reflective attitude to the project in hand. We have stressed the importance of the free association life history interview that not only reveals the 'lived' lives of the people we talked to, but also helped us understand some of the motivations and reasons behind the responses to the second round of more structured questions. In using the case study of Billy we have highlighted how a psycho-social approach adds to more traditional forms of qualitative research by going beneath the surface, looking at often unconscious communications and collusions between researcher and researched and revealing unconscious motivations, in other words trying to understand why people hold the views they do, and why they choose to tell us a particular story.

There are very strong ethical implications in the practice of psycho-social research. Indeed ethical issues are present throughout the whole research process from the commencement of the research design through to the analysis and presentation of the data. What frames the primary ethical challenge in psycho-social research is care for the subject. These ethical issues can be seen in the case study of Billy. They centre around concern and care for the subject of our research, on not taking transcripts at face value, and around the role of projections, collusions and fear. These concerns are about the need to avoid mis-re-presentation of the respondent, about the need to ensure that the research does present what is really important to the respondent; these concerns are also about guilt, a duty of care and the fact that our respondents have trusted us with their thoughts on some very contentious issues. It would be easy to portray Billy as not a very nice person, but there are many sides to Billy and many reasons that he holds the views he does. Our concern here is about the selective use of interview transcripts, about falling into the trap of not listening to our respondents and making our data fit our preconceived ideas and research questions. Ethically then, a psycho-social approach must guard against these mistakes, and really this needs to be reinforced with team work.

We have to recognise that ethical issues are present throughout the whole research process. This means that informed consent, for example, really does mean informed consent, in other words, making sure that people know what they are participating in. It entails being aware of the ethical demands of the actual research encounter, recognising countertransference, identifications and projective identifications. It involves an ethical approach to data analysis, one that is able to recognise what gets left in and what gets left out, in talk, transcription and presentation. It also means that we need to think very carefully about how we present our data as we have an ethical obligation of care for the subject and avoidance of any harm. Ethically this is about relationality. We have to recognise that we bring our own unconscious feelings around class or ethnicity, for example; that we identify with people; indeed we have to in order to understand their affective states, meanings and experiences. But on the other hand we have to be careful that we do not merge parts of our 'selves' with the Other.

10
CONCLUSION

Our exploration of the themes of community and identity in provincial England is necessarily qualified. Our sample was relatively small and restricted to two cities. However, we suggest, in the light of further research, which admittedly focused on working-class respondents (Hoggett et al., 2008; Garner et al., 2009), that the discourses on community, Britishness and whiteness are generally applicable outside of some large metropolitan areas where Gilroy's model of conviviality might be the dominant mode. The temptation for researcher and reader alike is to become absorbed into the details and start to lose track of the bigger picture. There are structural parameters on the talk of identity. This work was undertaken at a specific moment in specific places. The very framework we used, socio-economic categories, suggests that there are inequalities in the distribution of resources that are collective and long-term. The state and the media play different but complementary roles in constructing the limits within which national and ethnic identities are formed, and the assumptions underlying these processes. The whiteness of our respondents is virtually never expressed in direct terms of them claiming superiority, but rather through sets of assumptions about who is entitled to what and why. Moreover, our claims that these identities are 'white' neither exhausts the field of identity formation, nor forecloses the possibility of change. We would argue that social identities are multifaceted, and that some elements become more salient at a given moment or within a particular process. Being 'white' and English does not say that your identity is not also inflected by class, gender, age, education, etc., it merely draws the attention to the configuration that draws your identity into line with the other people who fall into that category in relation to specific contexts. Moreover, to draw on the distinction between whiteness as a set of oppressive practices, and people who are racialised as white (Frye, 1992; Yancy, 2008), people can identify the former and choose not to engage in them. There are, of course, also long-term processes that cannot be opted out of merely by choice, as Charles Mills notes in his conclusion that not all white people are signatories to the 'racial contract', but all benefit from it (1997: 6).

The choice of the psycho-social method does not preclude consideration of these issues: it is not an either/or equation. While we demonstrate how different methodologies can enable links to be made between individual experiences and the way people engage with collective ideas and practices, the key point is that we are looking at an interface between the individual and collective, rather than imagining them as distinct spheres. People draw on the culture surrounding them to make sense of social relationships, and when that culture is saturated with hierarchical understandings of social relationships it is to be expected that these will inform people's interpretations.

Whiteness has been explored as a source of privilege in the American context and conceptualised as a multifaceted object of study. It is a dominant racialised social location, whose effects can be read as long-term structural processes fundamentally impacting the distribution of life chances and resources. Systematic acts of terror and the establishment of a system of white supremacy in the United States have heavily inflected the ways in which African-American writers describe whiteness. However, it also manifests itself in a variety of forms, as cultural capital, values and norms, in which particular understandings of behaviour are attributed to 'race'. In the 1990s and 2000s especially, with social censorship of explicit race talk, this type of culture-based expression of racialisation has become the norm in public discourse on both sides of the Atlantic. Finally, while the most important social border has always been between those designated 'white' and those designated 'not white' at a particular moment in a particular context, there is another, internal border of whiteness. This separates the white from the less white, and encompasses a variety of groups: the undeserving white poor, gypsy-travellers, Jews, Eastern and Southern European migrants at different times, for example. As we have referred to the contingency of time and place in determining these hierarchies, it is clear there is nothing fixed about where the borders actually lie. Moreover, as demonstrated in the British fieldwork, the various white actors can include or exclude different groups of people from the 'honorary white' club depending on the circumstances.

There is a lot of overlap between the American and British fieldwork on white identities despite the different historical development of the societies, patterns of migration and contact between white and non-white people. We can observe similar deployments of whiteness: as cultural capitals, as values and norms, and as contingent hierarchies. One of the things thrown up in the British fieldwork is the importance of local dynamics. This can be to do with an area's demographic mix in terms of class and ethnicity, but also to do with the history of settlement. A historical transition point for incoming migrants such as the East End of London, which is investigated by a number of researchers, is not the same social space as the semi-urban 'village' and small white town where Katherine Tyler does her fieldwork, for example. Indeed, the rural/urban split is an interesting development in British studies, revealing an implicit understanding on the part of the actors that minorities do not belong outside urban space (even though they may also face a similar discourse in those very spaces).

As with the US studies (Ferber, 2007) there is a gap in terms of female subjects in the research agenda, which is overwhelmingly male and working class. Our work was in part an attempt to fill in the space from which the middle class evaporate in such studies in Britain. There is also a role played by the legacy of empire, in the way that hierarchies are constructed and distance is measured from a point when Britishness was globally dominant. That is examined in chapter 5.

Our exploration of what Britishness means to white English people shows that they are increasingly withdrawing from

Britishness as a serious identification, and retreating into a defensive and 'defended' space of Englishness. Britishness generates a range of responses, from indifference through to frustration at its lack of specificity. Anyone can be British, seems to be the critique, therefore it does not say anything specific about the English. This is in direct contrast to the other constituent nationalities of the UK, whose identities are enviously viewed as rich and above all 'celebrate-able' without guilt. There is a parallel between the way in which English identity is constructed as one of victims in the post-war changes vis-à-vis other identities, just as the white working class are often portrayed as victims of the same process. The stories of diminishing capacity and respect and participation focus on cultural difference rather than economics. Immigrants are thus seen as agents of capital rather than fellow objects upon whom capitalist social relations inscribe themselves. Britishness is a conundrum. On one hand the people tend to associate 'immigration-asylum' as posing threats to Britishness, but there is no consensus about what Britishness consists of, and the white UK group appears to have less interest in defining itself in terms of Britishness than some of the minority groups. This disinterest in Britishness represents a nostalgic quest for a purer space that is not under attack from pc central and local government or minorities, but nevertheless one that is haunted by the imperial legacy.

Empire provides an awareness of hierarchy, which might be denied by some as a justifiable way to organise society, but is nonetheless understood as having been the dominant model within living memory. Our interviewees are aware of that hierarchy even in the attempts of some of them to interrogate and think past it. The socio-geographical terrain of segregated communities that provides the national commentary to the discussions we had inflects the way people tie groups to places. Minorities are fixed in segregated spaces, which seem to be the result of 'trying to be different', or not joining in (culturally and linguistically). The logics applied to the various groups are hierarchical and differential. Minorities self-segregate, whites engage in 'flight', whereas the wealthiest, segregated by price of property in their class enclaves and sometimes gated communities, do not even register in the discussion. Like all dominant locations of power, that of the white upper-middle class is rendered so unremarkable and natural that discourse on segregation and integration omits it. However, with more evidence available to say that segregation in the UK is along the lines of class rather than ethnicity, the national conversation on ethnic segregation still flourishes. At some level then, this public discourse is missing the point. Indeed, against such a backdrop, the debate about 'integration' is actually being conducted about 'assimilation'. What people are understood to be assimilating into is a hazy sketch of culture defined by what it is not (banning Christmas, pc, Muslim dress codes, etc.), fractured by the need for productivity and by both migrants and lazy local white people who are viewed as not putting into the system and only taking out. By detaching themselves from such a space, white English people in provincial post-colonial UK are striving to imagine a smaller, more immediate and distinctive space: one in which class seems absent and only immigrants (even if they are not immigrants) who assimilate fully are tolerated members. Empire provides a racialised framework for weighing up how far Britain has come or fallen since it held a dominant position in the world economy.

In chapter 6 we introduced a number of ways of theorising white identity construction. In particular we have stressed that identity is formed in a number of multifaceted ways that range from the social construction of being to the psychological imagining of Others. We have argued that a psycho-social approach, a new emergent discipline that is slowly being embedded in the academy, adds a further layer of understanding in the exploration of the social, cultural and political world. It uses both sociological and psychological ideas to examine the factors that influence human behaviour and the construction of white identity. Using psycho-analytic ideas to breech the gaps between disciplines it places an emphasis on the inner world of the subject while recognising that the split between individual and society is not helpful if we are to make sense of phenomena such as racism and fear of the Other. We are firmly behind Frantz Fanon's (1967) ideas where the construction of colonial black identity and white identity is the product of both a political economy of hatred and a psychodynamic of racism. A psycho-social perspective on the construction of white identity recognises that there is both a social construction of our realities and that we are passionate beings, full of emotion. Both our outer reality and inner world work together to form who we are, or more precisely who we are not.

We then went on to argue that in relation to issues of asylum and immigration in contemporary Britain a new politics of fear is emerging which now more than ever before concentrates on difference and demonisation of the Other. This can be seen by example in both politics and media representations where emotional and psychological methods are used to play on our social fears and anxieties. This has happened in tandem with the mainstreaming of anti-immigration policy as a political value in which getting tough on 'defending' the nation is seen as a priority. Using the work of Žižek (1993) we have argued that we fear the theft of our own identity, our ways of life and our imaginary notions of home by some Other. This is conflated by media representations in which groups of immigrants become akin to what Bauman (1989, 1991) would describe as 'strangers' in our midst. Identity becomes confusing rather than clear cut. We used to know who 'we' are and who 'they' are, but the concept of the 'stranger' blurs these definitions and defies all contemporary rules that describe who we are. We have argued that the socio-politics of fear has added a new dimension to asylum, where the asylum seeker represents our fears of chaos and displacement on one hand and on the other threatens us with the possibility of being destroyed within by our own fear of terror and terrorists in our midst. Terrorism is now a concrete reality and we argue that it is more important than ever that ideas of asylum and anti-immigration are not conflated and confused with terrorism. The press and politics tap into our inner world of anxiety and imagination placing a stress on difference, which is incompatible with our 'ways of life', threatening our identity, our whiteness.

We have argued that in much the same way that the concept of 'identity' can have multiple meanings, so does the concept of 'community'. The concept of community has always been central to the construction of group and individual identity; it can be a source of cohesion on one hand and exclusion on the other hand. We found conflicting views of the notion of community but there was an overwhelming stress on its importance and the link it has with white identity construction at a very local rather than national level. We argue that there is a 'sting in the tail' in the link between community and identity construction in that we could ask whether this yearning for a better community is just nostalgia, or is it more the case that people want to create a sense of community or community spirit so their children can experience a better and safer environment to grow up in. We have therefore questioned what community cohesion actually means, is it detrimental or positive or indeed possible? As all the people we spoke to were white, we feel the views expressed by them very much point to the construction of 'whiteness' in modern Britain. But at the same time we acknowledge that we have to think, after Stuart Hall (1992), not of white ethnicity, but ethnicities, as we all speak from a particular place, history and experience of life, and therefore white identities are constructed from community attachments, multiple ethnicities, experiences and geographical locations.

As we have indicated, there was very little talk of what we might term fluid post-modern consuming selves, narratives in which the individual is sovereign and the community is of little importance. Rather there is an emphasis on the family, class and geographical locations, which were in turn linked to ideas about outsiders and defining your self by who you are not. There was a strong emphasis on the notion of a shared identity that linked in with the notion of community. A deeply psycho-social element also appears where people often create their perceptions of others in their own imagination, which helps them create who *they* are. This was exemplified in the discussions of what it is to be 'Bristolian' or 'Plymouthian', where we started to see the emotional dynamics involved in notions of contempt, acceptance and tribalism between geographical areas and groups of people.

Although it is becoming less usual to incorporate a methodological chapter in a book we felt compelled to do so as it represents a new way of thinking and, more importantly, practice. The psychosocial method we have used we describe as a 'light' psycho-social approach where we acknowledge that there are often unconscious motivations at work in the research encounter as indeed both researcher and researched co-construct the data within the research environment. We feel that without highlighting both the sociological and psychological aspects of identity construction we would not be able to represent the 'lived' lives of the people we spoke to. As the notion of white identity largely remains hidden and unspoken the biographical free association life history interviews enabled us to 'research beneath the surface' (Clarke and Hoggett, 2009). This method also helped us understand some of the motivations and reasons behind the responses in the second round of more structured interviews. It is a method for trying to understand why people hold the views that they do, and why they choose to tell us a particular story and present a certain identity to us, their lived life. It also recognises, as we have argued, that the polar split between individual and society is no longer useful, there are strong links between individual experiences and the way people engage as a collective and vice versa. We also recognise this method has its limitations, not least the amount of time and in-depth analysis involved, which was fairly manageable with our relatively small sample. This method enabled us to understand the affective meanings and experiences of people that constructed their white identity, notions of community and belonging. Now we want to turn to some of the public policy ramifications that this research throws up.

Public Policy Ramifications

These are as much to do with how policy is conceptualised than how it is implemented.

On the question of integration/assimilation, it is clear that people's understanding of integration is not that of the policy-makers. This has a knock-on effect in all talk of engaging in community cohesion and Britishness. This limits the space for action, particularly given that the other workings of the state (immigration regulations and asylum policy) and the media militate against cohesion in a number of ways.

The idea of 'community' should be understood as something that is actively created, not just passively experienced. Communities do not just 'happen': people make them. A government department of communities and local government ought to reflect on this and develop ways to listen and respond, as much as impose ideas of what communities should look like.

Identities are complex and multidimensional: policy often seeks to reduce this to a single source (whether it be ethnic, geographical, religious, etc.). This should not mean, however, going to the other extreme, which would mean becoming so caught up in the intricacies that the bigger picture of discrimination and patterns of poverty get neglected. There are good reasons to collect ethnic monitoring data, and use some kind of categorisation system for description. The problem comes when these are used as the basis for predictive and analytical procedures, assuming that members of an ethnic group are homogeneous, when on a range of issues they are almost certainly not.

Lastly, there is clearly an 'information deficit' issue that is affecting the construction of white identities in the UK relative to non-white Others. Understandings of policy regarding immigration, asylum and, especially, associated resource allocation are very weak indeed. Contact with minorities on an equal footing is infrequent, which enables the development of negative ideas unchecked by personal experience.

The period in which we undertook our study is one in which multiculturalism has come under fire from all sides. When seeking examples of what was not British to illustrate various points about Britishness, frequently the first group used to demonstrate this was Muslims. We wonder whether, if this work had been carried out a decade earlier (the mid-1990s), this pattern would have been observed.

The new project of Britishness alluded to in chapter 4 is justified by its advocates as an alternative to fragmentation by drawing people together around a shared set of values. Let's put to one side for a moment the idea that this is based on the assumption that people do not share a set of values already, and whatever the 60 million of us in the UK do every day is not already 'being British' enough. The Commission on Integration and Cohesion (CIC) was set up to investigate how communities were integrating and what problems remained. Ruth Kelly MP, the minister responsible for the CIC, urged people to engage in a 'new and honest debate' so that the concerns of white Britons 'detached from the benefits' of multiculturalism enter into the equation.[1] This rather odd formulation deserves its own analysis, but serves adequately to capture the direction of public discourse, in which a significant proportion of the population are held up to be suffering from the outcomes of too much multiculturalism rather than from the traditional material sources of disadvantage, such as a dwindling social housing stock linked to a housing market that was still booming while the fieldwork for this project was completed, and increasing disparities in the distribution of wealth.

A challenge for sociologists interested in analysing and combating racism is that part of our endeavour is to try and account for the way in which the concerns of those white Britons coalesce around the embodied difference of their non-white compatriots and new migrants. Additionally, we have to find out how strategies posited as means of managing such issues actually impact upon white Britons' understanding of the dynamics of change.

Among the list of areas noted by Ruth Kelly as worthy of the CIC's attention is the 'challenge to win hearts and minds across all our communities. Across white communities that are adjusting to rapid change in their local area'.[2] One of the outcomes of this period of change is the discursive attachment of the asylum and immigration issues to the shortage of social housing, as identified as long ago as the mid-1990s in the fieldwork of Dench et al. (2006), so that it is now presented as a direct competition between longstanding locals and immigrant newcomers. Perceived manipulation of such perceptions has prompted responses such as that of the then Minister Margaret Hodge (2007), Labour MP for Barking (in the East End of London), where the far-right

British National Party has a number of local councillors. Hodge stated in May 2007 that British nationals should be prioritised in the allocation of social housing. Such presentations of problems that could be formulated in other ways, such as a shortage of social housing *per se*, rather than simply a competition between two disempowered and heterogeneous groups (immigrants and working-class locals), thus forms part of what there is to explore in the British vernacular arena of 'whiteness' (Sveinsson, 2009).

In addition to qualitative fieldwork, the current moment necessitates some theoretical analysis of the variety of ways in which whiteness is surreptitiously invoked as the norm in state actions. This occurs by consistently prioritising European over non-European immigration (BBC News, 2006; Home Office, 2006: 1) thus jeopardising black British and Asian people's tenuous claims on employment (Wills, 2008); increasing immigration controls on non-EU nationals while anti-immigration discourse of all shades continually posits that there is 'uncontrolled' immigration (N. Watt, 2007b); treating immigration primarily as a threat; treating asylum as a crisis even though numbers dropped sharply between 2002 and 2008, before levelling off; and continuously adjusting regulations governing the status of migrants in a way that suggests that they are universally unwilling to integrate.

Indeed, the so-called asylum 'crisis' (Buchanan and Grillo, 2004; Lea and Lynn, 2004; Modell, 2004; Grillo, 2005; Hubbard, 2005a, 2005b) is perhaps the key contemporary vector of British whiteness, expressing vulnerability, beleagueredness under invasion, and national pride. If, as American radical Randolph Bourne (1918) argued, 'War is the health of the State', then perhaps in a perverse way, the threat of invasion – Britain's finest hour, 1939–45 (Gilroy, 2004; Dench et al., 2006) – is the health of the white British people: it invokes the psychosis that binds them ethnically to one another. As the political centre of gravity slides rightwards, and racialised permutations of Britishness compete in many places, such as those where we have carried out fieldwork, the task of analysing whiteness in Britain has never been so urgent or so potentially laden with risks.

A research agenda on the issue of white identities should now be prepared to develop a strand aimed at actively resolving some of the issues thrown up in the work done so far. We know there is a combination of local, contingent process and long-term structural ones at play, and that people appear to be shrinking their identities. We also suggest that in terms of what people find useful and reassuring in a community (chapter 8), this provides an opportunity for bringing together those racialised as white, black, Asian, etc. around some common purpose. There are economic factors that seem to place such communities closer to each other than might be imagined, and there is scope for people to act together around transforming a range of institutions into something more participative and which reflects the requirements of the people they are serving. People are not as different from each other as they might think, as Billy admits in chapter 9, after he spends time with what he calls 'coloureds'. What we have found above all in our fieldwork, however, is that the existing discourse channels the resentment and frustration of most of the white British people sideways, towards people who are either level with or below them on the socio-economic scale. The voices of people who reflect critically on this process are few, and they have often arrived at their critical and reflective space because of first-hand experiences of intimacy and or/exposure to discrimination or discomfort that has triggered their empathy, and now see social relationships differently from how they did before.

NOTES

Chapter 1

1. See the special issue of *International Labor and Working Class History*, 60, Fall 2001, 'Scholarly Controversy: Whiteness and the Historians' Imagination'.
2. As we put the final touches to this book, Polish migration to Britain peaked (Morris, 2008) and subsided (Harrison, 2009) as the economy shrinks.
3. Source: BBC Online (2004) 'A Short History of Immigration': http://news.bbc.co.uk/hi/english/static/in_depth/uk/2002/race/short_history_of_immigration.stm.

Chapter 2

1. For an example of each, respectively, see Frye (1992); Barrett and Roediger (1997); Hartigan (1997); Segrest (1994) and Harris (1993).
2. See also Ireland, Garner (2003).
3. cf. Dee Brown's (1972) work on the use of violence to clear Native Americans out of the Mid-West.
4. Although the examples of Tulsa in 1921, and Rosewood, Florida in January 1923 show that even when African-Americans set up their own areas they were not beyond the reach of racial punishment: www.displaysforschools.com/rosewoodrp.html.
5. The creation by financial institutions of areas – outlined on maps with red lines – within which the cost of services is higher than elsewhere, or, in the case of mortgages, impossible to obtain. Typically these are poor and/or minority areas. The practice began in 1935 when the Federal Housing Authority commissioned the Home Owners Loan Corporation to survey 239 American cities in terms of lending security risks. The term 'redlining' itself emerged in the 1960s.
6. Fuller treatment is given in Garner (2007), chapter 1. Harris argues that whiteness as property survived the civil rights era, to resurface in the form of successful legal challenges to affirmative action programmes. She ends by explaining how affirmative action can best be conceptualised as combining both reparative and distributive

justice, thus avoiding the impasse of individuals competing for employment, university places, etc.

7. The six dimensions are: juridico-political; economic; cultural; cognitive-evaluative; somatic; and metaphysical. The explanations of these dimensions can be found in Mills (2004: 46–8).

8. Goldberg (2005) suggests that racialisation should be understood as the Americanisation of race. Scholarship in dialogue with Barrett and Roediger has debated the extent to which various ethnic groups such as Jewish (Brodkin, 1994, 1998) and Italian-Americans (Guglielmo and Salerno, 2003) can be considered 'white'. These arguments suggest some parallels between the Irish, Italians and Jews in America in that over time they 'became' white as the result of a transitional process.

Chapter 3

1. 'Whiteness and Terror/(Post)Empire', Institute for Social Psychology, London School of Economics, 19 May 2006.

2. Both cities are in the English Midlands. Coalville is a small former mining town near the city of Leicester, while Stoke-on-Trent is a city north west of Birmingham.

3. The abbreviations mc (middle class) and wc (working class) will be used throughout.

4. See Paynter (2001), Jacobson (1998), Morrison (1993), and for the latter, see Frye (1992).

5. The principally working-class districts of the East End of London have traditionally been areas of primary settlement for migrants, especially those from Eastern Europe in the late nineteenth and early twentieth centuries, and most recently, since the 1970s, Bengalis. It is also an area where the organised far-right has sporadically found support.

6. Oldham, a town near Manchester in the north west of England, was the scene of rioting in 2001. A similar set of resentments is expressed in Lesley White's long *Sunday Times* article on post 2001-riots Oldham (White, 2002), where local Pakistani Muslims are seen as 'taking over' particular estates and council funding largely by means of operationalising the values of previous generations of white working-class Oldhamites.

7. The British National Party is a far-right, anti-immigration party which has had sporadic success in local elections in Britain in recent years. Its best ever result in parliamentary elections was in the Oldham West constituency in 2001. In the UK, 'Asian' refers to

people from the Indian sub-continent and their descendants rather than China and South East Asia, like the North American usage.

8. The city of Newcastle-upon-Tyne in the north east of England was a centre of mining and shipbuilding until the 1980s. The term Geordie is used to describe a native of the city. Newcastle United FC is the local soccer team, which enjoys fanatical support in an area of the country that has produced a number of the most popular players at national level over the past 50 years.

9. This point recalls Hartigan's emphasis on inter-personal relationships frequently over-riding 'race' in his studies of inner-city Detroit. Knowledge of family and place make some spaces much safer for people to travel through. When he tells them he is interested in 'race relations', his white Detroit respondents direct him across the highway to a mainly African-American housing project. 'In this [their own] neighbourhood', he writes, 'they were one family among many, white and black, who held elaborate and lengthy knowledge of each other reaching back over the tumultuous past three decades. But across the intersection [i.e. in that particular project] they were simply "whites", partly for their skin color and partly in terms of location and being out of place' (1997: 191). On (multi)cultural capital in the UK, see Reay et al. (2007).

10. See Bourne, J. (2006) 'Labour's Love Lost?', *IRR News*, 22 February; Bunting, M. (2006) 'Ignored, Angry and Anxious: The World of the White Working Class', *The Guardian*, 13 February: www.guardian.co.uk/print/0,,5397882-103390,00.html; Dench, G. and Gavron, K. (2006) 'Lost Horizons', *The Guardian*, 8 February: www.guardian.co.uk/society/2006/feb/08/socialexclusion. guardiansocietysupplement; Moore, R. (2008) '"Careless Talk": A Critique of Dench, Gavron and Young's *The New East End*', *Critical Social Policy*, 28 (3): 349–60; Keith, M. (2008) 'Between Being and Becoming? Rights, Responsibilities and the Politics of Multiculture in the New East End', *Sociological Research Online*: www.socresonline.org.uk/13/5/11.html. The book also prompted the formation of a panel at the 2007 British Sociological Association and the papers from that were developed into a special issue of *Sociological Research Online* (2008): www.socresonline.org. uk/13/5/contents.html.

11. It is not clear why the findings were not published until 2006. In the time since that fieldwork, Eastern European migration has further complicated the picture.

12. Paul Watt's (2007) research in such places finds people glad to escape from inner-city London, to some extent because the former space was 'polluted' with migrants and their descendants, but finding

traces of that pollution still tangible in the areas now surrounding them.

13. Wemyss (2008) argues that in fact this relationship is expressed in glaring absences.

14. See also Rogaly and Taylor's (2010) analysis of interviews with former British servicemen and their wives, who had been stationed overseas since 1945.

Chapter 4

1. See Calhoun (2003) or Hearn (2006) for good introductions to literature on nationalism. The journal *Nations and Nationalism* is a good place to start.

2. This is one of the most frequent critiques of the content of Britishness put forward, but to be fair, Brown (2004) does acknowledge this. However he goes on to say there is a specifically British combination of them.

3. David and Goliath is an Old Testament story from the Book of Genesis, and David later became the King of the Jews, so in a way the knowledge being imparted is not as different as Les might think. The inclusion of religious studies at primary level requires knowledge of the major world religions, which is why young children's books would have pictures of Hindu gods (which we suppose is what Les is referring to).

4. Integration and critical interpretations of immigration discourse are examined in the following chapter.

5. In one of our seminars at UWE-Bristol in 2008, on the topic of national identity, a black Londoner claimed she felt British but could not identify with Englishness. A Welsh student contested this logic, arguing that Britain is comprised of the constituent nations, so Britishness merely reflected membership of one of them. You couldn't be British without simultaneously being Scottish, Welsh, Northern Irish or English. The other student resisted this logic. The space for being British *as an alternative* to being English clearly appealed to her.

Chapter 5

1. During the period between completing the fieldwork and writing this manuscript, there have been changes in the terminology on ethnicity in the UK. The term 'Afro-Caribbean' has been jettisoned in favour of 'African-Caribbean', and the Black and Minority Ethnic

acronym, BME, is now being displaced by Black and Asian Minority Ethnic (BAME).

2. As the actual paper given is not available, we cannot suppose that the reports actually represent what Poulsen argued, hence the construction of this sentence.

3. Simpson has also produced a shorter guide to 'race' and migration (Simpson and Finney, 2009).

4. One of the referees commented on a paper written on this that if we wanted to gauge opinions on integration, we should have chosen more multicultural places to do our fieldwork in the first place. After a talk one of us gave on our findings in Bristol in 2008, a Muslim member of the audience remarked that going by the comments made about Islam, the people we spoke to seemed to know nothing about it, and that we should have done our research in London with some interviewees who knew what they were talking about. These types of response are interesting reflections on the way that messages are received. The way that our interviewees' responses to these topics are discounted as invalid seems to encapsulate a view that the national conversation on integration can only be engaged in with people who have a certain level of knowledge about the various cultural groups in Britain and in places that are already mixed.

Chapter 6

1. For an in-depth discussion of the nature of psycho-social studies as a discipline see the special edition of *Psychoanalysis, Culture & Society*, 13 (4), 2008, which is entirely dedicated to a discussion of 'British Psycho(-)social Studies'.

Chapter 7

1. Back's (2003) article talks about people falling from aeroplanes, and articles such as Lewis (2006) report the deaths of immigrants falling from lorries onto British roads.

2. Adelphi and Clearwater are the two largest companies contracted by the National Asylum Support Service (NASS) to provide temporary accommodation for asylum seekers in the UK.

3. For more on the EU dimension see Garner (2005), and the Statewatch Observatory on Asylum and Immigration, accessible at: www.statewatch.org/asylum/obserasylum.htm.

4. Quote from the first paragraph of Labour's policy outline: www.labour.org.uk/asylumandimmigration04/. The Conservative 2005

manifesto is downloadable from: www.conservatives.com/tile. do?def=policy.listing.page.

5. This announcement, however, might be argued old news. Paul Gilroy (1987, 1990) claimed that racism united Left and Right in the UK more than 15 years ago.

6. Clearly, migration and anxiety around it did not begin in 1945. Debates around Irish immigration in the mid-nineteenth century and the first immigration act in UK law, the 1905 Aliens Act, predate the narrative presented here. The point is that the stakes in the post-war period were different in that an era of mass migration from outside Europe had begun.

7. This, in the context of the 1950s, meant immigration from the recently independent African colonies, the British West Indies, India and Pakistan.

8. The 1996 Act made all employers and some public bodies responsible for carrying out checks on the immigration status of clients and/or prospective employees.

9. *Question Time*, BBC1, 28 April 2005.

10. As Wells and Watson argue in their study of shopkeepers' resentment of Others in London, the state is identified as an 'agent' of the 'destruction of the social and/or economic fabric of the neighbourhood' (2005: 263).

Chapter 9

1. This case study was originally published as part of a book chapter in: Clarke, S., Hahn, H. and Hoggett, P. (eds) (2008) *Object Relations and Social Relations: The Implications of the Relational Turn in Psychoanalysis*, London: Karnac Books, and is reproduced with the kind permission of Karnac Books, London.

Conclusion

1. 'In full: Ruth Kelly speech', 24 August 2006: http://news.bbc. co.uk/2/hi/uk_news/politics/5281572.stm.

2. Kelly's speech at the launch of the CIC's Interim Report, 27 February 2007, is at: www.communities.gov.uk/speeches/corporate/integration-cohesion. The CIC report, *Our Shared Futures* was published in June 2007.

REFERENCES

Ahmed, S. (2004) 'Declarations of Whiteness: The Non-Performativity of Anti-Racism', *borderlands* ejournal, 3 (2): www.borderlandsejournal. adelaide.edu.au/issues/vol3no2.html.

Allen, T. (1994) *The Invention of the White Race (Vol. 2)*, New York: Verso.

Almaguer, T. (1994) *Racial Fault Lines: The Origins of White Supremacy in California*, Berkeley: University of California Press.

Alvesson, M. and Skoldberg, K. (2000) *Reflexive Methodology: New Vistas for Qualitative Research*, London: Sage.

Andersen, M. (2003) 'Whitewashing Race', in A. Doane and E. Bonilla-Silva (eds) *White Out: The Continuing Significance of Racism*, New York: Routledge, 22–34.

Anderson, B. (1991) *Imagined Communities*, London: Verso.

Back, L. (2003) 'Falling from the Sky', *Patterns of Prejudice*, 37 (3): 341–53.

—— (1996) *New Ethnicities and Urban Culture – Racisms and Multiculture in Young Lives*, London: UCL Press.

Back, L. and Solomos, J. (1996) *Racism and Society*, London: Macmillan.

Baldoz, R. (2008) 'The Racial Vectors of Empire', *Du Bois Review: Social Science Research on Race 5* (1): 69–94.

—— (2004) 'Valorizing Racial Boundaries: Hegemony and Conflict in the Racialization of Filipino Migrant Labor', *Ethnic and Racial Studies*, 27 (6): 969–86.

Baldwin, J. (1965) *Going to See the Man*, New York: Dial Press.

Balibar, E. (1991a) 'Racism and Nationalism', in E. Balibar and I. Wallerstein, *Race, Class, Nation: Ambiguous Identities*, New York: Verso, 37–68.

—— (1991b) 'Racism and Crisis', in E. Balibar and I. Wallerstein, *Race, Class, Nation: Ambiguous Identities*, New York: Verso, 217–27.

Banton, M. (1967) *The Idea of Race*, London: Tavistock.

Barker, M. (1981) *The New Racism*, London: Junction Books.

Barrett, J. and Roediger, D. (2005) 'The Irish and the "Americanization" of the "New Immigrants" in the Streets and in the Churches of the Urban United States, 1900–1930', *Journal of American Ethnic History*, 24 (4): 4–33.

—— (2004) 'Making New Immigrants Inbetween: Irish Hosts and White Pan-Ethnicity, 1890–1930', in N. Foner and G. Frederickson (eds) *Not*

Just Black and White: Immigration and Race, Then and Now, New York: Russell Sage Foundation Press, 167–96.

—— (1997) 'Inbetween Peoples: Race, Nationality and the "New Immigrant" Working Class', *Journal of American Ethnic History*, 16 (3): 3–44.

Bauman, Z. (2001a) *The Individualized Society*, London: Polity Press.

—— (2001b) *Community: Seeking Safety in an Insecure World*, London: Polity Press.

—— (1993) *Postmodern Ethics*, London: Blackwell.

—— (1991) *Modernity and Ambivalence*, Cambridge: Polity Press.

—— (1990) *Thinking Sociologically*, Oxford: Blackwell Publishers.

—— (1989) *Modernity and the Holocaust*, Cambridge: Polity Press.

BBC Online (2004) 'A Short History of Immigration': http://news.bbc.co.uk/hi/english/static/in_depth/uk/2002/race/short_history_of_immigration.stm.

BBC News (2006) 'UK Race Chief in Ghetto Apology', 30 August: http://news.bbc.co.uk/1/hi/uk/5297760.stm.

—— (2005): 'Ricin Case "Shows Asylum Chaos"', 14 April: http://news.bbc.co.uk/1/hi/uk_politics/vote_2005/frontpage/4442219.stm.

—— (2000) 'Blair Defines British Values', 28 March: http://news.bbc.co.uk/1/hi/uk_politics/693591.stm.

Bell, C. and Newby, H. (eds) (1976) *The Sociology of Community: A Selection of Readings*, London: Frank Cass.

Berger, P. and Luckmann, T. (1971) *The Social Construction of Reality: A Treatise in the Sociology of Knowledge*, London: Penguin.

Bernstein, I. (1990) *The New York Draft Riots of 1863: Their Significance for American Society in the Civil War Period*, New York: Oxford University Press.

Bhattacharyya, G. (2008) *Dangerous Brown Men: Exploiting Sex, Violence and Feminism in the War on Terror*, London: Zed.

—— (1997) *Tales of Dark-Skinned Women: Race, Gender and Global Culture*, London: UCL Press.

Billig, M. (1995) *Banal Nationalism*, London: Sage.

—— (1991) *Ideology, Rhetoric and Opinion*, London: Sage.

Blackshaw, T. (2005) *Zygmunt Bauman*, London: Routledge.

Bonilla-Silva, E. (2006) *Racism without Racists: Color-Blind Racism and the Persistence of Racial Inequality in the United States*, Lanham, MD: Rowman and Littlefield.

Bonilla-Silva, E. and Embrick, D. (2007) '"Every Place Has a Ghetto...": The Significance of Whites' Social and Residential Segregation', *Symbolic Interaction*, 30 (3): 323–45.

Bourne, R. (1918) 'The State', Bourne MSS, Columbia University Libraries.

Brent, J. (1997) 'Community Without Unity', in P. Hoggett (ed.) *Contested Communities: Experiences, Struggles, Policies*, Bristol: Policy Press, 8–83.

Bright, M. (2003) 'Refugees Find No Welcome in the City of Hate', *The Observer*, 29 June.

Brodkin, K. (1998) *How Jews Became White Folks: And What That Says About Race in America*, New Brunswick, NJ: Rutgers University Press.

—— (1994) 'How Did Jews Become White Folks?', in S. Gregory and R. Sanjck (eds) *Race*, New Brunswick, NJ: Rutgers University Press.

Brogan, B. (2005) 'It's Time to Celebrate the Empire, Says Brown', *Daily Mail*, 15 January: www.dailymail.co.uk/news/article-334208/Its-time-celebrate-Empire-says-Brown.html.

Brown, A. (1999) 'The Other Day I Met a Constituent of Mine: A Theory of Anecdotal Racism', *Ethnic and Racial Studies*, 22 (1): 23–55.

Brown, D. (1972) *Bury My Heart at Wounded Knee: An Indian History of the American West*, New York: Bantam.

Brown, G. (2004) 'Speech by the Rt Hon Gordon Brown MP, Chancellor of the Exchequer, at the British Council Annual Lecture, July 7 2004', *The Guardian*, 8 July.

Buchanan, S. and Grillo, B. (2004) 'What's the Story? Reporting on Asylum in the British Media', *Forced Migration Review*, 19 (1): 41–3.

Burkeman, O. (2006) 'The Phoney War on Christmas', *The Guardian*, 8 December: www.guardian.co.uk/world/2006/dec/08/religion.communities.

Burns, T. (1992) *Erving Goffman*, London: Routledge.

Burr, V. (2003) *Social Constructionism*, London: Routledge.

Butler, J. (1993) *Bodies that Matter: On the Discursive Limits of 'Sex'*, London: Routledge.

—— (1990) *Gender Trouble: Feminism and the Subversion of Identity*, London: Routledge.

Byrne, B. (2006) *White Lives: The Interplay of 'Race', Class and Gender in Everyday Life*, London: Routledge.

Calhoun, C. (2003) *Nationalism*, Oxford: Oxford University Press.

Cantle, T. (2001) *Community Cohesion: A Report of the Independent Review Team, Chaired by Ted Cantle*, London: Home Office.

Carby, H. (1982) 'White Woman Listen! Black Feminism and the Boundaries of Sisterhood', in Centre for Contemporary Cultural Studies, *The Empire Strikes Back*, London: Hutchinson, 212–31.

Carter, B. (2000) *Racism and Realism: Concepts in Sociological Research*, London: Routledge.

Carter, B., Harris, C. and Joshi, S. (1993) 'The 1951–55 Conservative Government and the Racialisation of Black Immigration', in W. James and C. Harris (eds) *Inside Babylon: The Caribbean Diaspora in Britain*, London: Verso, 55–71.

Carvel, J. (2004) 'Opposition to Immigrants Hardens Under Blair: Liberal Intelligentsia Want More Curbs', *The Guardian*, 7 December.

Chamberlayne, P. (2005) 'Inter-Subjectivity in Biographical Methods: Mirroring and Enactment in an Organisational Study', paper given to Biograhpieforschung im Sozialwissenschaftlichen Diskurs, Georg-August Universitaet Goettingen, 1–3 July.

Chamberlayne, P., Bornat, J. and Wengraf, T. (eds) (2000) *The Turn to Biographical Methods in Social Science*, London: Routledge.

Chamberlayne, P., Rustin, M. and Wengraf, M. (2002) *Biography and Social Exclusion in Europe: Experiences and Life Journeys*, Bristol: Policy Press.

Clarke, S. (2008a) 'Psycho-Social Research: Relating Self, Identity and Otherness', in S. Clarke, H. Hahn and P. Hoggett (eds) *Object Relations and Social Relations: The Implications of the Relational Turn in Psychoanalysis*, London: Karnac Books, 113–35.

—— (2008b) 'Culture and Identity', in T. Bennett and J. Frow (eds) *Handbook of Cultural Analysis*, London: Sage, 510–29.

—— (2006) 'Theory and Practice: Psychoanalytic Sociology as Psycho-Social Studies', *Sociology*, 40 (6): 1153–69.

—— (2005) *From Enlightenment to Risk: Social Theory and Contemporary Society*, London: Palgrave.

—— (2003) *Social Theory, Psychoanalysis and Racism*, London: Palgrave.

—— (2002a) 'Learning from Experience: Psycho-Social Research Methods in the Social Sciences', *Qualitative Research*, 2 (2): 173–94.

—— (2002b) 'On "Strangers": Phantasy, Terror and the Human Imagination', *Journal of Human Rights*, 1 (3): 1–11.

Clarke, S. and Garner, S. (2005) 'Psychoanalysis, Identity and Asylum', *Psychoanalysis, Culture & Society*, 10 (2): 197–206.

Clarke, S. and Hoggett, P. (2009) *Researching Beneath the Surface: Psycho-Social Research Methods in Practice*, London: Karnac Books.

Clarke, S. and Moran, A. (2003) 'The Uncanny "Stranger": Haunting the Australian Settler Imagination', *Free Associations*, 10 (2) 54: 165–89.

Clarke, S., Gilmour, R. and Garner, S. (2007) 'Home, Identity and Community Cohesion', in M. Wetherell, M. Laflèche and R. Berkeley (eds) *Identity, Ethnic Diversity and Community Cohesion*, London: The Runnymede Trust/ Sage, 87–101.

Clarke, S., Hahn, H. and Hoggett, P. (2008) *Object Relations and Social Relations: The Implications of the Relational Turn in Psychoanalysis*, London: Karnac Books.

Cohen, S. (1972) *Folk Devils and Moral Panics*, London: Routledge.

Colley, L. (1992) *Britons: Forging the Nation, 1707–1837*, New Haven, CT: Yale University Press.

Commission on Integration and Cohesion (2007) *Our Shared Futures*, Wetherby: HSMO.

Commission for Racial Equality (2007) *Race Relations 2006: A Research Study*, London: CRE: http://83.137.212.42/sitearchive/cre/downloads/racerelations2006final.pdf.

—— (2005) *Citizenship and Belonging: What Is Britishness?* London: CRE.

—— (1998) *A Culture of Suspicion: The Impact of Internal Immigration Controls*, London: CRE.

Condor, S. (2000) 'Pride and Prejudice: Identity Management in English People's Talk About "This Country"', *Discourse and Society*, 11: 163–93.

Craib, I. (1998) *Experiencing Identity*, London: Sage.

Crews, F. (1993) 'The Unknown Freud', *New York Review of Books*, 18 November.

Crow, G. (1997) 'What Do We Know About Neighbours? Sociological Perspectives on Neighbouring and Community', in P. Hoggett (ed.) *Contested Communities: Experiences, Struggles, Policies*, Bristol: Policy Press, 17–30.

Dalal, F. (2005) 'The Hatred of Asylum-Seekers', *Mediactive*, (4): 21–37.

—— (2002) *Race, Colour and the Processes of Racialization: New Perspectives from Group Analysis, Psychoanalysis and Sociology*, London: Brunner-Routledge.

Delanty, G. (2003) *Community*, London: Routledge.

Delphy, C. (2006) 'Antisexisme ou anti-racisme? Un faux dilemme', *Nouvelles questions féministes*, 25 (1): 59–83.

Dench, G., Gavron, K. and Young, M. (2006) *The New East End: Kinship, Race and Conflict*, London: Profile.

Dorling, D. (2005) 'Why Trevor Is Wrong About Race Ghettoes', *The Observer*, 25 September: www.guardian.co.uk/uk/2005/sep/25/communities.politics.

Dorling, D. and Thomas, B. (2004) *People and Places: A 2001 Census Atlas of the UK*, Bristol: Policy Press.

Douglas, M. (1966) *Purity and Danger: An Analysis of Concepts of Pollution and Taboo*, London: Routledge.

Douglass, F. (2003 [1845]) *The Narrative of the Life of Frederick Douglass, an American Slave*, New York: Barnes and Noble.

Dreyfus, H. and Rabinow, P. (1982) *Michel Foucault: Beyond Structuralism and Hermeneutics*, London: Harvester Wheatsheaf.

Du Bois, W.E.B. (1998 [1935]) *Black Reconstruction in America, 1860–1880*, New York: Free Press.

—— (1920) *Darkwater: Voices from Within the Veil*, New York: Harcourt, Brace & Co.

—— (1903) *The Souls of Back Folk*, Chicago: A.C. McClurg and Co.

Durkheim, E. (1964 [1893]) *The Division of Labour in Society*, Glencoe: Free Press.

Dwyer, C. (1999) 'Veiled Meanings: Young British Muslim Women and the Negotiation of Differences', *Gender, Place and Culture*, 6 (1): 5–26.

Dwyer, C. and Bressey, C. (2008) (eds) *New Geographies of Race and Racism*, Aldershot: Ashgate.

Dyer, R. (1997) *White*, London: Routledge.

—— (1988) 'White', *Screen*, 29 (4): 44–64.

Edwards, D. (2003) 'Analyzing Racial Discourse: The Discursive Psychology of Mind-World Relations', in H. Van den Berg, M. Wetherell and H. Houtkroop-Steenstra (eds) *Analyzing Race Talk: Multidisciplinary Perspectives on the Research Interview*, Cambridge: Cambridge University Press, 31–48.

Elliott, A. (2001) *Concepts of the Self*, London: Polity Press.

Ellison, R. (1952) *Invisible Man*, New York: Random House.

Evans, G. (2006) *Educational Failure and Working Class White Children in Britain*, London: Palgrave.

Eze, E. (1997) *Race and the Enlightenment: A Reader*, Boston: Blackwell.

Fanon, F. (1967) *Black Skin, White Masks*, London: MacGibbon & Kee.

Farough, S. (2004) 'The Social Geographies of White Masculinities', *Critical Sociology*, 30 (2): 241–64.

Feagin, J. (2006) *Systemic Racism: A Theory of Oppression*, New York: Routledge.

Fenton, S. (2007) 'Indifference Towards National Identity: What Young Adults Think About Being English and British', *Nations and Nationalism*, 13 (2): 321–39.

—— (2005) 'The Ethnic Majority in Britain: A Case of Banal Majoritarianism?', Inaugural professorial lecture, University of Bristol, 12 May: www.bristol.ac.uk/sociology/ethnicitycitizenship/sf_inaugural.pdf.

Ferber, A. (2007) 'Whiteness Studies and the Erasure of Gender', *Sociology Compass*, 1 (1): 265–82.

Field, B. (2001) 'Whiteness, Racism, and Identity', *International Labor and Working Class History*, 60: 48–56.

Forman, T. and Lewis, A. (2006) 'Racial Apathy and Hurricane Katrina: The Social Anatomy of Prejudice in the Post-Civil Rights Era', *Du Bois Review*, 3 (1): 175–202.

Foucault, M. (1995) *Madness and Civilization: A History of Insanity in the Age of Reason*, London: Routledge.

—— (1989) *The History of Sexuality Vol 3: The Care of the Self*, London: Penguin.

—— (1984) *The History of Sexuality Vol 2: The Use of Pleasure*, London: Penguin.

—— (1977) *Discipline and Punish: The Birth of the Prison*, London: Penguin.

—— (1976) *The History of Sexuality Vol 1: The Will to Knowledge*, London: Penguin.

Frankenberg, Ronnie (1957) *Village on the Border: A Social Study of Religion, Politics and Football in a North Wales Community*, London: Cohen and West.

Frankenberg, Ruth (1994) *White Women, Race Matters*, Madison: University of Wisconsin Press.

Freud, S. (1961 [1919]) 'The Uncanny', *The Standard Edition of the Complete Psychological Works of Sigmund Freud, Vol. XVII (1917–1919)*, London: Hogarth Press; 219–52.

Fromm, E. (1941) *Escape From Freedom*, London: Routledge.

Frosh, S., Phoenix, A. and Pattman, R. (2003) 'Taking a Stand: Using Psychoanalysis to Explore the Positioning of Subjects in Discourse', *British Journal of Social Psychology*, 42: 39–53.

—— (2002) *Young Masculinities: Understanding Boys in Contemporary Society*, London: Palgrave.

Frye, M. (1992) 'White Woman Feminist', in M. Frye, *Wilful Virgin: Essays in Feminism, 1976–1992*, Berkeley, CA: Crossing Press.

Fryer, P. (1984) *Staying Power: The History of Black People in Britain*, London: Pluto.

Gans, H. (1962) *The Urban Villagers*, New York: Free Press.

Garfinkel, H. (1967) *Studies in Ethnomethodology*, London: Prentice-Hall.

Garland, J. and Chakraborti, N. (2006) '"Race", Space and Place: Examining Identity and Cultures of Exclusion in Rural England', *Ethnicities*, 6 (2): 159–77.

Garner, S. (2007) *Whiteness: An Introduction*, London: Routledge.

—— (2006) 'The Uses of Whiteness: What Sociologists Studying Europe Can Draw from North American Work on Whiteness', *Sociology*, 40 (2): 257–75.

—— (2005) 'The Racialisation of Mainstream Politics in Europe', *Ethical Perspectives*, 14 (4): 123–40.

—— (2003) *Racism in the Irish Experience*, London: Pluto.

Garner, S. and Moran, A. (2006) 'Putting the "Order" Back into "Borders": State Strategies on Asylum in Australia and the Republic of Ireland', in R. Lentin and A. Lentin (eds) *Race and State*, Newcastle: Cambridge Scholar's Press, 103–20.

Garner, S., Cowles, J., Lung, B. and Stott, M. (2009) 'Sources of Resentment, and Perceptions of Ethnic Minorities Among Poor White People in England', National Community Forum/Department for Communities and Local Government: www.communities.gov.uk/documents/communities/pdf/1113921.pdf.

Gellner, E. (1985) *The Psychoanalytic Movement: The Cunning of Unreason*, London: Fontana.

Gergen, K.J. (2000) *An Invitation to Social Construction*, London: Sage.

Giddens, A. (1990) *The Consequences of Modernity*, London: Polity.

—— (1972) *Emile Durkheim: Selected Writings*, London: Cambridge University Press.

Gilroy, P. (2004) *After Empire: Multiculture or Postcolonial Melancholia*, London: Routledge.

—— (1990) 'The End of Anti-Racism', in W. Ball and J. Solomos (eds) *Race and Politics in the UK*, London: Macmillan, 192–209.

—— (1987) *Ain't No Black in the Union Jack*, London: Hutchinson.

Go, J. and Foster, A. (eds) (2003) *The American Colonial State in the Philippines: Global Perspectives*, Durham, NC: Duke University Press.

Goffman, E. (1969) *The Presentation of Self in Everyday Life*, London: Penguin.

—— (1968) *Stigma: Notes on the Management of Spoiled Identity*, London: Pelican.

Goldberg, D. (2005) 'On Racial Americanization', in K. Murji and J. Solomos (eds) *Racialization: Studies in Theory and Practice*, Oxford: Oxford University Press, 87–102.

—— (2000) *The Racial State*, Boston: Blackwell.

Gotham, K. (2000) 'Urban Space, Restrictive Covenants and the Origins of Racial Residential Segregation in a US City, 1900–50', *International Journal of Urban and Regional Research*, 24 (3): 616–33.

Grillo, R. (2005) '"Saltdean Can't Cope": Protests Against Asylum-Seekers in an English Seaside Suburb', *Ethnic and Racial Studies*, 28 (2): 235–60.

Grunbaum, A. (1984) *The Foundations of Psychoanalysis: A Philosophical Critique*, California: University of California Press.

Guardian (2006) 'Prime Minister's Speech on Criminal Justice Reform', speech given in Bristol, 23 June: www.guardian.co.uk/politics/2006/jun/23/immigrationpolicy.ukcrime1.

Guglielmo, T. (2004) *White on Arrival: Italians, Race, Color, and Power in Chicago, 1890–1945*, New York: Oxford University Press.

—— (2003) 'Rethinking Whiteness Historiography: The Case of Italians in Chicago, 1890–1945', in A. Doane and E. Bonilla-Silva (eds) *White Out: The Continuing Significance of Racism*, New York: Routledge, 49–61.

Guglielmo, J. and Salerno, S. (2003) *Are Italians White? How Race Is Made in America*, New York: Routledge.

Habermas, J. (1968) *Knowledge and Human Interests*, London: Heinemann.

Hall, S. (1992) 'The New Ethnicities', in J. Donald and A. Rattansi (eds) *Race, Culture and Difference*, London: Sage, 256–8.

Hall, S., Critcher, C., Clarke, J., Jefferson, A. and Robert, B. (1978) *Policing the Crisis: Mugging, the State and Law and Order*, London: Palgrave.

Hammersley, M. (1990) *Reading Ethnographic Research: A Critical Guide*, London: Longman.

Harris, C. (1993) 'Whiteness as Property', *Harvard Law Review*, 106 (8): 1707–93.

Harrison, D. (2009) 'UK Poles Return Home', *Daily Telegraph*, 21 February: www.telegraph.co.uk/news/worldnews/europe/poland/4742214/UK-Poles-return-home.html.

Hartigan, J. (2005) *Odd Tribes: Toward a Cultural Analysis of White People*, Durham, NC: Duke University Press.

—— (1999) *Racial Situations: Class Predicaments of Whiteness in Detroit*, Princeton NJ: Princeton University Press.

—— (1997) 'Locating White Detroit', in Ruth Frankenberg (ed.) *Displacing Whiteness: Essays in Social and Cultural Criticism*, Durham, NC: Duke University Press, 180–213.

Haywood, K. and Yar, M. (2005) 'The "Chav" Phenomenon: Consumption, Media and the Construction of a New Underclass', *Crime, Media, Culture*, 2 (1): 9–28.

Hearn, J. (2006) *Rethinking Nationalism: A Critical Introduction*, London: Palgrave.

Heath, A. (2005) *National Identity and Constitutional Change in England, Scotland, Wales and Northern Ireland, 2001 and 2003*, ESDS Dataset SN5249.

Held, D. (1980) *Introduction to Critical Theory: Horkheimer to Habermas*, London: Polity.

Herman, A. (1999) *The Better Angels of Capitalism*, Boulder, CO: Westview Press.

Hetherington, K. (1994) 'The Contemporary Significance of Schmalenbach's Concept of the Bund', *Sociological Review*, 42: 1–25.

Hewitt, R. (2005) *White Backlash: The Politics of Multiculturalism*, Cambridge: Cambridge University Press.

Hinshelwood, R. and Skogstad, W. (2000) *Observing Organisations: Anxiety, Defence and Culture in Health Care*, London: Routledge.

Hodge, Margaret (2007) 'A Message to My Fellow Immigrants', *The Observer*, 20 May: www.guardian.co.uk/commentisfree/story/0,,2083873,00.html.

Hoggett, P. (ed.) (1997) *Contested Communities: Experiences, Struggles, Policies*, Bristol: Policy Press.

—— (1992) 'A Place for Experience: A Psychoanalytic Perspective on Boundary, Identity, and Culture', *Environment and Planning D: Society and Space*, 10: 345–56.

Hoggett, P., Jeffers, S. and Harrison, L. (1996) 'Race, Ethnicity and Community in Three Localities', *New Community*, 22 (10): 111–25.

Hoggett, P., Beedell, P., Jimenez, L., Mayo, M. and Miller, C. (2006) 'Identity, Life History and Commitment to Welfare', *Journal of Social Policy*, 35 (4): 689–704.

Hoggett, P., Garner, S., Wilkinson, H., Cowles, J., Lung, B. and Beedell, P. (2008) *Race, Class and Cohesion: A Community Profile of Hillfields (Bristol)*, Bristol: Bristol City Council/UWE, Centre for Psychosocial Studies: www.uwe.ac.uk/hlss/research/cpss/research_reports/Hillfields.pdf.

Hollway, W. and Jefferson, T. (2000) *Doing Qualitative Research Differently: Free Association, Narrative and the Interview Method*, London: Sage.

Home Office (2006) *A Points-Based System: Making Migration Work for Britain*, Norwich: HMSO: www.homeoffice.gov.uk/documents/command-points-based-migration?view=Binary.

hooks, b. (2000) *Where We Stand: Class Matters*, New York: Routledge.

Horkheimer, M. and Adorno, T. (1994) *Dialectic of Enlightenment*, London: Continuum.

Horkheimer, M. and Flowerman, S. (1950) *Studies in Prejudice*, New York: Harper.

Horsman, R. (1981) *Race and Manifest Destiny: The Origins of American Anglo-Saxonism*, Cambridge: Cambridge University Press.

How, A. (2003) *Critical Theory*, London: Palgrave.

Howard, P. (2004) 'White Privilege: For or Against', *Race, Gender and Class*, 11 (4): 63–79.

Hubbard, P. (2005a) '"Inappropriate and Incongruous": Opposition to Asylum Centres in the English Countryside', *Journal of Rural Studies*, 21: 3–17.

—— (2005b) 'Accommodating Otherness: Anti-Asylum Centre Protest and the Maintenance of White Privilege', *Transactions*, 30: 52–65.

Hunt, J. (1989) *Psychoanalytic Aspects of Fieldwork*, London: Sage.

Hussain, Y. and Bagguley, P. (2005) 'Citizenship, Ethnicity and Identity: British Pakistanis after the 2001 "Riots"', *Sociology*, 39 (3): 407–25.

Innes, B. (1998) 'Experiences in Difference: An Exploration of the Usefulness and Relevance of Psychoanalytic Theory to Transcultural Mental Health Work', *Psychodynamic Counselling*, 4 (2): 171–89.

Institute for Public Policy Research (2005) *A New England: An English Identity Within Britain*: www.ippr.org.uk/publicationsandreports/publication.asp?id=255.

Irigaray, L. (1985) *The Sex Which Is Not One*, New York: Cornell University Press.

Jacobson, J. (1997) 'Perceptions of Britishness', *Nations and Nationalism*, 3 (2): 181–99.

Jacobson, M. (1998) *Whiteness of a Different Colour: European Immigrants and the Alchemy of Race*, Cambridge, MA: Harvard University Press.

Johnson, H.B. (2006) *The American Dream and the Power of Wealth*, New York: Routledge.

Johnson, H.B. and Shapiro, T. (2003) 'Good Neighborhoods, Good Schools: Race and the "Good Choices" of White Families', in A. Doane and E. Bonilla-Silva (eds) *White Out: The Continuing Significance of Racism*, New York: Routledge, 173–88.

Johnston, R. and Poulsen, M. (2006) 'Ethnic Residential Segregation in England: Getting the Right Message Across', *Environment and Planning A*, 38 (12): 2195–9.

Jones, D.M. (1997) 'Darkness Made Visible: Law, Metaphor and the Racial Self', in R. Delgado and J. Stefancic (eds) *Critical White Studies: Looking Behind the Mirror*, Philadelphia: Temple University Press, 66–78.

Jones, J. (2004) 'The Impairment of Empathy in Goodwill Whites for African Americans', in G. Yancy (ed.) *What White Looks Like: African-American Philosophers on the Whiteness Question*, New York: Routledge, 65–86.

Kaufman, E. (2006) 'The Dominant Ethnic Moment: Towards the Abolition of "Whiteness"?', *Ethnicities*, 6: 231–53.

Kaur, R. (2003) 'Westenders: Whiteness, Women and Sexuality in Southall', in J. Andall (ed.) *Gender and Migration in Contemporary Europe*, Oxford: Berg, 199–222.

Kearney, M. (2005) 'Brown Seeks Out "British Values"', BBC News, 14 March: http://news.bbc.co.uk/2/hi/programmes/newsnight/4347369.stm.

Keith, M. (2008) 'Between Being and Becoming? Rights, Responsibilities and the Politics of Multiculture in the New East End', *Sociological Research Online*, 13 (5): www.socresonline.org.uk/13/5/11.html.

Kiely, R., McCrone, D. and Bechhofer, F. (2005) 'Whither Britishness? English and Scottish People in Scotland', *Nations and Nationalism*, 11 (1): 65–82.

Klein, M. (1997) *Envy and Gratitude and Other Works 1946–1963*, London: Vintage.

—— (1975) *Love, Guilt and Reparation and Other Works 1921–1945*, London: Karnac Books.

—— (1946) 'Notes on Some Schizoid Mechanisms', *International Journal of Psycho-Analysis*, 26: 99–110.

Knowles, C. (2005) 'Making Whiteness: British Lifestyle Migrants in Hong Kong', in C. Alexander and C. Knowles (eds) *Making Race Matter*, Basingstoke: Palgrave, 90–110.

—— (2003) *Race and Social Analysis*, London: Sage.

Kolchin, P. (2002) 'Whiteness Studies: The New History of Race in America', *Journal of American History*, 89: 154–73.

Kristeva, J. (1991) *Strangers to Ourselves*, New York: Harvester.

—— (1989) *Black Sun: Depression and Melancholia*, New York: Columbia University Press.

Kushner, T. (2005) 'Racialization and "White European" Immigration to Britain', in K. Murji and J. Solomos (eds) *Racialization: Studies in Theory and Practice*, Oxford: Oxford University Press, 207–25.

Lahav, G. and Guiraudon, V. (2000) 'Comparative Perspectives on Border Control: Away from the Borders and Outside the State', in P. Andreas and T. Snyder, *The Wall Around the West: State Borders and Immigration Controls in North America and Europe*, Lanham, MD: Rowan and Littlefield, 55–77.

Lamont, M. (2000) *The Dignity of Working Men*, Cambridge, MA: Harvard University Press.

Lawler, S. (2005) 'Disgusted Subjects: The Making of Middle-class Identities', *Sociological Review*, 53 (3): 429–46.

Layton, L. (2004) 'A Fork in the Royal Road: On "Defining" the Unconscious and Its Stakes for Social Theory', *Psychoanalysis, Culture & Society*, 9 (1): 33–51.

Lea, S. and Lynn, N. (2004) 'A Phantom Menace and the New Apartheid: The Social Construction of Asylum-Seekers in the United Kingdom', *Discourse & Society*, 14 (4): 425–52.

Lewis, A. (2003) *Race in the Schoolyard: Negotiating the Color Line in Classrooms and Communities*, New Brunswick, NJ: Rutgers University Press.

Lewis, B. and Ramazanoglu, C. (1999) '"Not Guilty, Not Proud, Just White": Women's Accounts of Their Whiteness', in H. Brown, M. Gilkes and A. Kaloshi (eds) *White Women: Critical Perspectives on Race and Gender*, York: Raw Nerve, 23–62.

Lewis, M. (2005) *Asylum: Understanding Public Attitudes*, London: IPPR.

Lewis, P. (2006) 'Hanoi to Haddon Services – Life and Death of a Stowaway', *The Guardian*, 27 May.

Lipsitz, G. (1995) 'The Possessive Investment in Whiteness: Racialized Social Democracy and the "White" Problem in American Studies', *American Quarterly*, 47 (3): 369–87.

Loveman, M. (2007) 'The U.S. Census and the Contested Rules of Racial Classification in Early Twentieth-century Puerto Rico', *Caribbean Studies*, 35 (2): 79–113.

Loveman, M. and Muniz, J. (2008) 'How Puerto Rico Became White: Boundary Dynamics and Intercensus Racial Reclassification', *American Sociological Review*, 72: 919–39.

Lucey, H., Melody, J. and Walkerdine, V. (2003) 'Transitions to Womanhood: Developing a Psychosocial Perspective in One Longitudinal Study', *International Journal of Social Research Methodology*, 6 (3): 279–84.

MacDougall, A. (1982) *Racial Myth in English History, Trojans, Teutons, and Anglo-Saxons*, Hanover, NH: University Press of New England.

Macey, D. (2000) *Frantz Fanon: A Life*, London: Granta Books.

McIntosh, P. (1988) 'White Privilege and Male Privilege: A Personal Account of Coming to See Correspondences Through Work in Women's Studies', Working Paper 189, Wellesley College.

McKinney, K. (2005) *Being White: Stories of Race and Racism*, New York: Routledge.

Manning, P. (1992) *Erving Goffman and Modern Sociology*, London: Polity Press.

Marcuse, H. (1956) *Eros and Civilization*, London: Routledge.

Massey, D. and Denton, N. (1994) *American Apartheid: Segregation and the Making of the Underclass*, Cambridge, MA: Harvard University Press.

Mead, G.H. (1934) *Mind, Self and Society*, ed. C.W. Morris, Chicago: University of Chicago Press.

Miles, R. (1993) *Racism After Race Relations*, London: Routledge.

Miller, C., Hoggett, P. and Mayo, M. (2008) 'Psycho-Social Perspectives in Policy and Professional Practice Research', in P. Cox, T. Geisen and R. Green (eds) *Qualitative Research & Social Change: UK and Other European Contexts*, Basingstoke: Palgrave.

Miller, D. (1987) *Material Culture and Mass Consumption*, Oxford: Blackwell.

Miliband, D. (2006) 'More Power to the People': http://society.guardian.co.uk/localgovt/story/0,,1714613,00.html.

Mills, C.W. (2004) 'Racial Exploitation and the Wages of Whiteness', in G. Yancy (ed.) *What White Looks Like: African-American Philosophers on the Whiteness Question*, New York: Routledge, 25–54.

—— (2003) 'White Supremacy as a Sociopolitical System: A Philosophical Perspective', in A. Doane and E. Bonilla-Silva (eds) *White Out: The Continuing Significance of Racism*, New York: Routledge, 35–48.

—— (1998) *Blackness Visible: Essays on Philosophy and Race*, Ithaca, NY: Cornell University Press.

—— (1997) *The Racial Contract*, Ithaca, NY: Cornell University Press.

Mills, C.W. and Pateman, C. (2007) *Contract and Domination*, Cambridge: Polity Press.

Mirza, H.S., Bhavnani, R. and Meetoo, V. (2005) *Tackling the Roots of Racism: Lessons for Success*, Bristol: Policy Press.

Mitchell, J. (1974) *Psychoanalysis and Feminism*, London: Penguin.

Modell, D. (dir.) (2004) *Keep Them Out*, Channel 4, broadcast 6 May.

Modood, T. (2005) 'Remaking Multiculturalism After 7/7', *Open Democracy*, 29 September: www.opendemocracy.net/content/articles/PDF/2879.pdf.

MORI (2003) 'British Views on Immigration': www.ipsos-mori.com/polls/2003/migration.shtml.

Morris, N. (2008) 'Tide of Migration Turns as Polish Workers Return', *The Independent*, 27 February: www.independent.co.uk/news/uk/home-news/tide-of-migration-turns-as-polish-workers-return-787914.html.

Morrison, T. (1993) *Playing in the Dark: Whiteness and the Literary Imagination*, New York: Vintage.

—— (1987) *Beloved*, New York: Alfred Knopf.

Nairn, T. (2003 [1977]) *The Break-Up of Britain: Crisis and Nationalism*, Melbourne: Common Ground.

Nayak, A. (2003) 'Ivory Lives: Economic Restructuring and the Making of Whiteness in a Post-Industrial Youth Community', *European Journal of Cultural Studies*, 6 (3): 305–25.

Neal, S. and Agyemang, J. (2006) *The New Countryside: Ethnicity, Nation and Exclusion in Contemporary Rural Britain*, Bristol: Policy Press.

Oliver, M. and Shapiro, T. (1995) *Black Wealth/White Wealth: A New Perspective on Racial Inequality*, New York: Routledge.

Outhwaite, W. (1994) *Habermas: A Critical Introduction*, London: Polity.

Pahl, R. (1984) *Divisions of Labour*, London: Blackwell.

Park, A., Curtice, J., Thomson, K., Bromley, C. and Phillips, M. (2004) *British Social Attitudes: The 21st Report*, London: Sage.

Park, R. (1915) 'The City: Suggestions for the Investigation of Human Behaviour in the City', *American Journal of Sociology*, 20: 577–612.

Paynter, R. (2001) 'The Cult of Whiteness in Western New England', in C. Orser (ed.) *Race and the Archaeology of Identity*, Salt Lake City: University of Utah Press: 125–42.

Peach, C. (1996) 'Does Britain Have Ghettos?', *Transactions of the Institute of British Geographers*, 21 (1): 216–35.

—— (1968) *West Indian Migration to Britain: A Social Geography*, Oxford: Oxford University Press.

Phillips, D. (2006) 'Parallel Lives? Challenging Discourses of British Muslim Self-Segregation', *Environment and Planning D: Society and Space*, 24 (1): 25–40.

Phillips, T. (2005) 'After 7/7: Sleepwalking Back to Segregation', speech delivered to Manchester Council for Community Relations, 22 September: www.humanities.manchester.ac.uk/socialchange/research/social-change/summer-workshops/documents/sleepwalking.pdf.

Phoenix, A. (1996) '"I'm White – So What?" The Construction of Whiteness for Young Londoners', in Lois Weis, Michelle Fine, Linda Powell Pruitt and April Burns (eds) *Off White: Readings on Power, Privilege, and Resistance*, New York: Routledge, 187–97.

Popper, K. (1983) *Realism and the Aims of Science*, London: Hutchinson.

Poulsen, M. (2005) 'The New Geography of Ethnicity in Britain', paper delivered at Royal Geographical Society Annual Conference, 31 August.

Puar, J.K. (1995) 'Resituating Discourses of "Whiteness" and "Asianness" in Northern England: Second Generation Sikh Women and Constructions of Identity', *Socialist Review*, 24: 21–53.

Putnam, R. (2000) *Bowling Alone: The Collapse and Revival of the American Community*, New York: Simon and Schuster.

Reay, D., Hollingworth, S., Williams, K., Crozier, G., Jamieson, F., James, D. and Beedell, P. (2007) '"A Darker Shade of Pale?": Whiteness, the Middle Classes and Multi-Ethnic Inner City Schooling', *Sociology*, 41 (6): 1041–60.

Rex, J. and Moore, R. (1967) *Race, Community and Conflict*, London: Oxford University Press.

Ricoeur, P. (1970) *Freud and Philosophy: An Essay on Interpretation*, New Haven: Yale University Press.

Roediger, D. (1999) *Black on White: Black Writers on What it Means to Be White*, New York: Schocken.

—— (1991) *The Wages of Whiteness: Race and the Making of the American Working Class*, London: Verso.

Rogaly, B. and Taylor, R. (2010) 'They Called Them Communists Then. What Do You Call 'Em Now ... Insurgents?: Narratives of British Military Expatriates in the Context of the New Imperialism', *Journal of Ethnic and Migration Studies*.

Rosser, C. and Harris, C. (1965) *The Family and Social Change: A Study of Family and Kinship in a South Wales Town*, London: Routledge.

Rowe, M. (1998) *The Racialization of Disorder*, Aldershot: Ashgate.

Rustin, M. (1991) 'Psychoanalysis, Racism and Anti-Racism', in *The Good Society and the Inner World*, London: Verso, 57–84.

Saxton, A. (1990) *The Rise and Fall of the White Republic: Class Politics and Mass Culture in Nineteenth Century America*, New York: Verso.

Schmalenbach, H. (1977) *Herman Schmalenbach: On Society and Experience*, Chicago: Chicago University Press.

Seabrook, J. (1973) *City Close-Up*, London: Penguin.

Segrest, M. (1994) *Memoir of a Race Traitor*, Boston: South End Press.

Seshadri-Crooks, K. (2000) *Desiring Whiteness: A Lacanian Analysis of Race*, London: Routledge.

Sherwood, R. (1980) *The Psychodynamics of Race: Vicious and Benign Spirals*, Sussex: Harvester Press.

Simmel, G. (1950 [1905]) 'The Metropolis and Mental Life', in K. Wolff (ed.) *The Sociology of Georg Simmel*, New York: Free Press.

Simpson, L. (2005) 'Measuring Residential Segregation', University of Manchester, Cathie Marsh Centre for Census and Survey Research: www.ccsr.ac.uk/research/documents/segregationpressreleasefurther informationfinal.pdf.

—— (2004) 'Statistics of Racial Segregation: Measures, Evidence and Policy', *Urban Studies*, 41 (3): 661–81.

Simpson, L. and Finney, N. (2009) *Sleepwalking to Segregation? Challenging Myths about Race and Migration*, Bristol: Policy Press.

Skeggs, B. (2005) *Class, Self and Culture*, London: Routledge.

Skeggs, B. and Wood, H. (2008) 'Spectacular Morality: Reality Television and the Re-making of the Working Class', in D. Hesmondhalgh and J. Toynbee (eds) *Media and Social Theory*, London: Routledge, 177–94.

Smith, A.M. (1992) *New Right Discourses on Race and Sexuality*, Cambridge: Cambridge University Press.

Statham, P. (2003) 'Understanding Anti-Asylum Rhetoric: Restrictive Politics or Racist Publics?', in S. Spencer (ed.) *The Politics of Migration: Managing Opportunity, Conflict and Change*, Oxford: Blackwell, 163–77.

Stone, L. and Muir, R. (2007) *Who Are We? Identities in Britain, 2007*, London: IPPR.

Stopford, A. (2004) 'Researching Postcolonial Subjectivities: The Application of Relational (Postclassical) Psychoanalysis Methodology', *Critical Psychology*, 10: 13–35.

Sveinsson, K. (ed.) (2009) *Perspectives: Who Cares About the White Working Class?*, London: Runnymede Trust.

Taguieff, P.-A. (2001) *The Force of Prejudice: On Racism and Its Doubles*, Trans. Hassan Melehy, Minneapolis: University of Minnesota Press.

Tönnies, F. (1988 [1887]) *Community and Society (Gemeinschaft und Gesellschaft)*, New Brunswick, NJ and London: Transaction Publishers.

Townsend, M. and Hinsliff, G. (2005) 'Truth About Calais "Immigrant Menace"', *The Observer*, 17 April: http://observer.guardian.co.uk/uk_news/story/0,,1461711,00.html.

Travis, A. (2005) 'Migrants Forced to Send Cash Abroad', *The Guardian*, 20 July.

Tyler, I. (2008) '"Chav Mum, Chav Scum": Class Disgust in Contemporary Britain', *Feminist Media Studies*, 8 (1): 1–18.

Tyler, K. (2004) 'Reflexivity, Tradition and Racism in a Former Mining Town', *Ethnic and Racial Studies*, 27 (2): 290–302.

—— (2003) 'The Racialized and Classed Constitution of Village Life', *Ethnos*, 68 (3): 391–412.

Urry, J. (2000) 'Sociology of Time and Space', in S. Turner (ed.) *The Blackwell Companion to Social Theory*, London: Blackwell, 416–33.

Walkerdine, V., Lucey, H. and Melody, J. (2001) *Growing Up Girl: Psychosocial Explorations of Gender and Class*, London: Palgrave.

Ward, P. (2004) *Britishness since 1870*, London: Routledge.

Ware, V. (1992) *Beyond the Pale: White Women, Racism and History*, London: Verso.

Waterfield, B. (2005) 'Interview: Franco Frattini, the EU's Justice Balancing Act', *Europolitix.com*, 31 May: www.theparliament.com/latestnews/news-article/newsarticle/interview-franco-frattini-the-eus-justice-balancing-act/.

Watt, N. (2007) 'Cameron in Race Row as Tory Claims that Enoch Was Right', *The Observer*, 4 November: www.guardian.co.uk/politics/2007/nov/04/race.conservatives.

Watt, P. (2007) 'From the Dirty City to the Spoiled Suburb', in B. Campkin and R. Cox (eds) *Dirt: New Geographies of Cleanliness and Contamination*, London: I.B. Tauris, 80–91.

—— (1998) 'Going Out of Town: Youth, "Race", and Place in the South East of England', *Environment and Planning D: Society and Space*, 16: 687–703.

Watt, P. and Stenson, K. (1998) 'The Street: "It's a Bit Dodgy Around There": Safety, Danger, Ethnicity and Young People's Use of Public Space', in T. Skelton and G. Valentine (eds) *Cool Places: Geographies of Youth Cultures*, London: Routledge, 249–66.

Weber, M. (1958 [1905]) *The City*, New York: Free Press.

Webster, C. (2008) 'Marginalized White Ethnicity, Race and Crime', *Theoretical Criminology*, 12 (3): 293–312.

Wells, K. and Watson, S. (2005) 'A Politics of Resentment: Shopkeepers in a London Neighbourhood', *Ethnic and Racial Studies*, 28 (2): 261–77.

Wells-Barnett, I. (1893) *Lynch Law*, excerpt at: www.historyisaweapon.com/defcon1/wellslynchlaw.html.

Wemyss, G. (2008) 'White Memories, White Belonging: Competing Colonial Anniversaries in "Postcolonial" East London', *Sociological Research Online*, 13 (5): www.socresonline.org.uk/13/5/8.html.

Wengraf, T. (2001) *Qualitative Research Interviewing: Biographical Narrative and Semi-Structured Method*, London: Sage.

Wengraf, T. and Chamberlayne, P. (2006) 'Interviewing for Life Histories, Lived Situations and Personal Experience: The Biographical-Narrative-Interpretive Method (BNIM): Short Guide to BNIM Interviewing and Interpretation', available at: tom@tomwengraf.com.

White, L. (2002) 'This Ghetto Is the Home of a Racial Minority in Oldham: Its Residents Are White People', *Sunday Times Magazine*, 13 January: 46–54.

Whyte, W.F. (1943) *Street Corner Society*, Chicago: University of Chicago Press.

Williams, R. (1973) *The Country and the City*, Oxford: Oxford University Press.

Williams, W. (1956) *The Sociology of a Small Village: Gosforth*, London: Routledge.

Wills, J. (2008) 'Making Class Politics Possible: Organizing Contract Cleaners in London', *International Journal of Urban and Regional Research*, 32 (2): 305–23.

Winddance Twine, F. and Gallagher, C. (2008) 'The Future of Whiteness: A Map of the "Third Wave"', *Ethnic and Racial Studies*, 31 (1): 4–24.

X, Malcolm (1969) *The Autobiography of Malcolm X: As Told to Alex Haley*, New York: Random House.

Yancy, G. (2008) *Black Bodies, White Gazes: The Continuing Significance of Race*, Lanham, MD: Rowman & Littlefield.

YouGov (2007) 'Immigration': www.migrationwatchuk.com/Excel/ RESULTSforMW_ImmigrationOMI2908_Nov07.xls.

—— (2004) *Survey on Attitudes to Immigration*, www.migrationwatchuk. org/pressReleases/01-November-2007#164.

—— (2003) *Survey on Immigration and Asylum*, www.yougov.co.uk/ extranets/ygarchives/content/pdf/DBD04101004.pdf.

Young, R. (2008) *The Idea of English Ethnicity*, Oxford: Blackwell.

—— (1997) 'Hybridism and English Ethnicity', in K. Ansell Pearson, B. Parry and J. Squires (eds) *Cultural Readings of Imperialism: Edward Said and the Gravity of History*, London: Lawrence and Wishart, 128–49.

Žižek, S. (1993) *Tarrying with the Negative*, Durham, NC: Duke University Press.

INDEX